Religion and War Resistance in the Plowshares Movement

As the nuclear arms race exploded in the 1980s, a group of U.S. religious pacifists used radical nonviolence to intervene. Armed with hammers, they broke into military facilities to pound on missiles and pour blood on bombers, enacting the prophet Isaiah's vision: "Nations shall beat their swords into plowshares and their spears into pruning hooks." Calling themselves the Plowshares movement, these controversial activists received long prison sentences; nonetheless, their movement grew and expanded to Europe and Australia.

In *Religion and War Resistance in the Plowshares Movement*, Sharon Erickson Nepstad documents the emergence and international diffusion of this unique form of high-risk collective action. Drawing on in-depth interviews, original survey research, and archival data, Nepstad explains why some Plowshares groups have persisted over time while others have floundered or collapsed. Comparing the U.S. movement with less successful Plowshares groups overseas, Nepstad reveals how decisions about leadership, organization, retention, and cultural adaptations influence movements' long-term trajectories.

Sharon Erickson Nepstad is Associate Professor of Sociology at the University of Southern Maine. Her research focuses on social movements, religion, and peace studies. She is the author of *Convictions of the Soul: Religion, Culture, and Agency in the Central America Solidarity Movement* (2004), and she has published numerous articles in *Social Problems, Mobilization, Journal for the Scientific Study of Religion, Critical Sociology, Sociological Inquiry*, and other journals.

Cambridge Studies in Contentious Politics

Editors

Jack A. Goldstone *George Mason University*
Doug McAdam *Stanford University and Center for Advanced Study in the Behavioral Sciences*
Sidney Tarrow *Cornell University*
Charles Tilly *Columbia University*
Elisabeth J. Wood *Yale University*

Ronald Aminzade et al., *Silence and Voice in the Study of Contentious Politics*
Javier Auyero, *Routine Politics and Violence in Argentina: The Gray Zone of State Power*
Clifford Bob, *The Marketing of Rebellion: Insurgents, Media, and International Activism*
Charles Brockett, *Political Movements and Violence in Central America*
Gerald F. Davis, Doug McAdam, W. Richard Scott, and Mayer N. Zald, editors, *Social Movements and Organization Theory*
Jack A. Goldstone, editor, *States, Parties, and Social Movements*
Doug McAdam, Sidney Tarrow, and Charles Tilly, *Dynamics of Contention*
Kevin J. O'Brien and Lianjiang Li, *Rightful Resistance in Rural China*
Silvia Pedraza, *Political Disaffection in Cuba's Revolution and Exodus*
Sidney Tarrow, *The New Transnational Activism*
Charles Tilly, *Contention and Democracy in Europe, 1650–2000*
Charles Tilly, *The Politics of Collective Violence*
Stuart A. Wright, *Patriots, Politics, and the Oklahoma City Bombing*
Deborah Yashar, *Contesting Citizenship in Latin America: The Rise of Indigenous Movements and the Postliberal Challenge*

Religion and War Resistance in the Plowshares Movement

SHARON ERICKSON NEPSTAD
University of Southern Maine

WITHDRAWN

CAMBRIDGE
UNIVERSITY PRESS

FLIP

CAMBRIDGE UNIVERSITY PRESS
Cambridge, New York, Melbourne, Madrid, Cape Town, Singapore, São Paulo

Cambridge University Press
32 Avenue of the Americas, New York, NY 10013-2473, USA

www.cambridge.org
Information on this title: www.cambridge.org/9780521717670

First published 2008

Printed in the United States of America

A catalog record for this publication is available from the British Library.

Library of Congress Cataloging in Publication Data

Nepstad, Sharon Erickson.
Religion and war resistance in the plowshares movement / Sharon Erickson Nepstad.
    p.   cm. – (Cambridge studies in contentious politics)
Includes bibliographical references and index.
ISBN 978-0-521-88892-9 (hardback) – ISBN 978-0-521-71767-0 (pbk.)
1. Plowshares Eight (Group) 2. Nonviolence. 3. Antinuclear movement. 4. Nuclear
disarmament. I. Title. II. Series.
JZ5575.N47 2008
327.1′747–dc22   2007031639

ISBN   978-0-521-88892-9 hardback
ISBN   978-0-521-71767-0 paperback

For my daughters, Linnea and Malaya

Because we want peace with half a heart, half a life and will, the war making continues. Because the making of war is total – but the making of peace, by our cowardice, is partial.

Father Daniel Berrigan

Contents

List of Tables and Figures

Tables

Figures

Preface

I distinctly remember the moment when I started paying closer attention to the Plowshares activists' provocative style of resistance. It was the winter of 1991 and President George H. W. Bush had just initiated a major bombing campaign that launched the Gulf War. Months before, Iraqi dictator Saddam Hussein had invaded Kuwait and President Bush was taking a stand. Although I felt that Hussein's tyranny and his illegal annexation of territory should be addressed by the international community, I was strongly opposed to the war and deeply disturbed by reports of thousands of civilian casualties.

One evening while I was watching the news with my friend Karl Smith, the network covered a story about an anti-war protest that occurred while George and Barbara Bush were worshipping at a church near their vacation home in Kennebunkport, Maine. As the service began, the pastor welcomed the president and his family and then asked the congregation to offer prayer requests. A fifty-one-year-old man sitting near the front said, "I have a concern. Think of the eighteen million people of Iraq; half are children under the age of fifteen. They are children just like the children sitting here. We must think of what it means to be bombed by more than 2,000 planes everyday. We are called to be peacemakers. This is a vicious, immoral attack."[1] He then sat quietly during the sermon, but when the pastor invited everyone to sing the Lord's Prayer, the man spoke up once more. "Before we sing, I have a word," he said. "God abhors this bloodshed. It is a crime

---

[1] Quoted in Balz, Dan. 1991. "Protester Disrupts Service at Church Attended by Bush." *The Washington Post*, February 18, 1991, p. A27.

for the rich to attack the poor."[2] Secret Service officers quickly dragged him out of the church and placed him under arrest.

As we listened to the news coverage of this one-man protest, Karl said, "That's John Schuchardt." He had known Schuchardt personally since they had both been involved in the Plowshares movement. This is a pacifist movement initiated by members of the so-called Catholic Left who garnered national attention during the Vietnam War when they raided Selective Service offices, dousing blood on conscription files and burning draft records. Years later, they once again engaged in property destruction to resist the escalating nuclear arms race, using household hammers to damage nuclear weapons.

Obviously these acts are illegal, but Plowshares participants willingly accept the consequences. In fact, trials are part of their strategy. As activists are charged and brought to court, they put weapons of mass destruction on trial. They use this opportunity to demonstrate how nuclear military policies violate international law and the standards of the Geneva Convention. They also seek to educate the public about nuclear weapons and to make the destructive capacity of these weapons visible. In the U.S. Plowshares movement, activists are almost invariably found guilty, and they have served prison terms ranging from a few months to many years. Yet prison is not perceived as punishment. It is an occasion to continue their witness, to be in solidarity with the most oppressed groups who disproportionately fill the jails, and to strengthen their faith. In the words of activist Jim Douglass:

Jail takes from us the illusion that our lives are our own rather than God's. Jail also brings us into the prayerful situation of sharing a life with the poor, in whom God lives. Jail opens us to the reality of a God who is at one with the oppressed, the present and future victims of Trident [nuclear submarines]. Jail serves the same purpose today for peacemakers as the desert did for early Christian contemplatives – to overcome claims of privilege and to crack open the illusions of self-reliance and ego. I believe that going to jail for peace can deepen a life of prayer in a way few monasteries can.[3]

This attitude is prevalent among Plowshares activists. My friend Karl Smith – who spent years in prison for hammering on a B-52 bomber fitted

---

[2] Balz, Dan. 1991.
[3] As quoted in Dear, John. 1994. *The Sacrament of Civil Disobedience*. Baltimore: Fortkamp Publishing, p. 241.

with Cruise missiles – stated that a common phrase in the movement is "prison is more monastic than punitive."

Methodology

Yet precisely because these activists are in and out of prison, conducting research on them was challenging at times. Before I began my work, I knew that the movement had historically experienced significant repression and that it might not be easy for an outsider to make inquiries, asking people to talk about political "crimes" they committed. In fact, a priest who wrote a book chronicling Catholic Left history from 1961 to 1975 wrote, "The Catholic Left was a very volatile and fluid social phenomenon not at all amenable to routine research methods. In view of its highly illegal activities, one could hardly consult membership lists or expect to have questionnaires returned."[4] Aware of the potential obstacles, I set out to learn as much as I could about the Plowshares movement, recognizing that I would need to take a multi-method approach.

I began by writing to Jonah House, explaining my research interests. Jonah House is an intentional faith-based community of resistance in Baltimore where several Plowshares leaders and many activists live. For more than thirty years it has served as a central base for the movement. I was delighted when the members of Jonah House invited me to visit, where I engaged in participant observation, partaking in their communal life and conducting exploratory interviews. I also attended a gathering of the Atlantic Life Community, a network of Catholic Left anti-war activists (including many Plowshares participants) who meet for weekend retreats several times each year. During this time, I took extensive field notes and had numerous informal conversations with Plowshares activists.

Drawing on the qualitative data I had collected, I designed a mail survey that addressed basic demographic information, religious beliefs and practices, prior history of activism, participation in community, and so forth.[5] I used movement documents to compile a list of individuals who took part in Plowshares actions between September 1980 and June 2001. Then I started the arduous task of locating these people. Since the movement has chosen intentionally to have no formal organization, there is no list

---

[4] Meconis, Charles A. 1979. *With Clumsy Grace: The American Catholic Left, 1961–1975.* New York: Seabury Press, p. x.

[5] See Appendix A for the full questionnaire.

of Plowshares activists, supporters, and their addresses. Moreover, trying to find current contact information for these individuals was complicated by the fact that they live in several different countries and many of them move frequently from prisons to halfway houses to various faith-based communities.

I would not have located many movement participants had it not been for the help of key individuals who gave me critical leads and contacts. Jack Cohen-Joppa provided my first important break. He is a co-editor of *The Nuclear Resister*, a newsletter that provides information on prisoners of conscience. After I explained my project, he graciously sent me many addresses of U.S. Plowshares activists. When I contacted these individuals, I asked them to assist me in locating others in the movement, and many kindly did.

In researching international Plowshares groups, I once again received valuable assistance from several people. I wrote to Lasse Gustavsson, who entrusted me with the addresses of numerous Swedish activists. I also subscribed to the international Plowshares email listserv, through which I came into contact with Susan van der Hijden. Susan is from Amsterdam but participated in a Plowshares action in Great Britain, and was at the time living in the Swedish Plowshares community known as The Fig Tree. She provided me with many Dutch and British contacts. Ciaron O'Reilly was another important resource since his involvement in the movement has taken him across many continents. He is an Australian of Irish heritage who participated in a Plowshares action in the United States. He is one of the founders of the Australian movement, but when I located him, he was working with British and Irish Plowshares groups. Ciaron put me in touch with Plowshares activists in Australia, New Zealand, and Great Britain. Finally, Dr. Wolfgang Sternstein provided me with contact information for numerous German activists.

With the assistance of these people, I was able to locate 112 people out of 161 living Plowshares activists. I sent them my surveys, along with follow-up reminders two months later. This resulted in 54 individuals participating in the project, reflecting a 48 percent response rate, or approximately one-third of the entire movement. Although this rate is not high, the unique circumstances of the project must be taken into consideration. Overall, lower response rates are not unusual in studies of "deviant" or marginal groups. Given the history of repression and government infiltration into the movement, some activists might have justifiably been reluctant to share their experiences with an unknown researcher. In addition, some were serving sentences at the time. Prison authorities examine incoming and outgoing mail, and some facilities prohibit the sending of self-addressed, stamped envelopes to inmates. This probably decreased the response rate somewhat. However, I was surprised at the effort some individuals made to return the surveys to me. One activist in Great Britain sent her survey in three separate mailings since the facility where she was incarcerated did not allow prisoners to send mail that contained more than a few pages. On this side of the Atlantic, an imprisoned American activist gave her responses to a friend during visiting hours, who then mailed the survey to me on her behalf.

While some might question the validity of survey results that draw from only one-third of the movement, I have tried to confirm, supplement, and expand this information with additional data. At the end of the question-naire, I asked if the respondent would be open to participating in an in-depth, follow-up interview. Almost everyone agreed. From those who indicated that they were willing, I selected a sample based on their availability and legal status. I did not interview those who were incarcerated, because of their greater vulnerability and the logistical difficulties of conducting interviews in prisons. But I did include other individuals who did not want to fill out the survey but were amenable to discussing their experiences in an interview format. In all, I conducted thirty-five interviews – twenty-three in the United States and twelve in Europe.[6] These interviews lasted between one and three hours; all were tape-recorded and transcribed.[7]

I have also drawn from documents on the Plowshares movement at the DePaul University archives. These archives include personal correspon-dence between Plowshares leaders, activists, and their families; they con-tain court transcripts, public statements, prison journals, newspaper arti-cles, and movement newsletters. In addition, many Plowshares activists gave me access to their personal files as well as copies of their own writings, documents, and even tape recordings. This multi-method approach pro-duced qualitative and quantitative data, along with historical and contem-porary views. Moreover, it provided an opportunity to verify the accuracy

[6] Of the twelve European interviews, four were conducted in Sweden, four with Dutch activists, three in Great Britain, and one with an Australian Plowshares organizer living in the Irish Republic.
[7] See Appendix B for a list of interviews.

of participants' oral accounts, which was useful since interview respondents were often recalling events that occurred decades ago.

I also benefited greatly from the fact that some of the activists in this study went far beyond the typical role of research subject. As I developed my analysis, I took my ideas back to Plowshares activists for feedback. In fact, several of them read the entire manuscript and sent me extensive written comments. My purpose in doing this was three-fold. First, I had to ensure that I had correctly depicted the history of each movement group. This was particularly important in the Australian and European contexts, where lower levels of mobilization meant that fewer published materials were available on the movements. Second, I hoped to assess the degree to which my analysis made sense to these individuals. In other words, I was looking for what qualitative researchers call "member verification." Third, I felt an obligation to share my findings with those who had openly discussed so much of their lives and, in some cases, delved into the personal and painful reasons why their movements failed.[8]

The feedback from Plowshares activists has undoubtedly enhanced this analysis, and my multi-method approach yielded a rich measure of information about the movement. But there are also some limitations to the data. One is that I intentionally confined my study to those who had committed Plowshares actions, omitting the many individuals who serve in supporting roles by doing media and logistical work. As one of my respondents noted, this essentially removes them from the picture, making the movement look smaller than it actually is. Stellan Vinthagen stated, "If I ... estimate an average of 15 deeply involved supporters within or close to the activists in each action, we get more than 1,000 committed movement participants worldwide (from 77 actions)."[9] My decision to not include supporters was primarily shaped by U.S. Plowshares leaders, who strongly impressed upon me the potential problems that could arise – namely, that the government could use this information to press conspiracy charges against supporters because they would be admitting that they had prior knowledge of these planned "crimes." Not wanting to place anyone in jeopardy, I respected the leaders' request to not contact supporters or family members. Moreover,

---

[8] For further information on this practice of "giving back" to respondents, see Nielsen, Joyce M. 1990. *Feminist Research Methods: Exemplary Readings in the Social Sciences*. Boulder: Westview Press; Reinharz, Shulamit. 1992. *Feminist Methods of Social Research*. New York: Oxford University Press.

[9] Personal correspondence with author, September 1, 2005.

most Plowshares activists would not give me the names of their supporters precisely for these legal reasons, thereby rendering this option impossible, at least in the U.S. context. Another reason for my exclusive focus on Plowshares campaign participants results from the fact that there are important differences between those who take the greatest risks, including prison or potentially death, and those who organize a rally during a Plowshares trial or volunteer to release the group's press statement. As Doug McAdam argues, our analysis of social movement participation will be more accurate when we acknowledge these varying levels of engagement and build our theories accordingly.[10]

My study is further limited by the fact there is a certain degree of self-selection involved. In other words, it is likely that the most committed activists are the ones who willingly responded to my survey and interview requests, and thus they are not a perfect representation of the movement. If this is the case, it is not entirely problematic. Since one of the topics I explore in the book is how activists sustain their commitment to this type of high-risk activism, these are precisely the individuals who can shed light on this topic. Moreover, my sample included activists who are critical of the movement, thereby ensuring that I heard a variety of perspectives, not merely the views of the most ardent Plowshares participants.

I also wish to address my decision to include the names of many Plowshares activists in the book. Traditionally, sociologists have used pseudonyms to protect their respondents' anonymity and privacy. In contrast, journalists maintain that credibility is enhanced when subjects are identified. Mitchell Duneier argues that qualitative researchers ought to consider following journalistic practices because we are held to a higher standard of accountability when actual names are provided, enabling others to follow up or check our work.[11] Recognizing that there are indeed situations where respondents' identities need to be protected, I agree with Duneier that anonymity can sometimes conceal misrepresentations. Moreover, there are other reasons why I chose to identify those Plowshares activists who gave me their consent to do so. For academic purposes, it would simply be impossible to explain how this movement spread

[10] McAdam, Doug. 1986. "Recruitment to High-Risk Activism: The Case of Freedom Summer." *American Journal of Sociology* 92: 64–90.

[11] For a full discussion of these issues, see the appendix of Mitchell Duneier's (1999) book, *Sidewalk*. New York: Farrar, Straus & Giroux.

internationally unless I traced it through specific individuals. In addition, for those who observe or participate in Plowshares actions, key figures and leaders would be easily identifiable, even with pseudonyms, because the movement is small. Finally, naming those who have made significant sacrifices for the cause of peace is, I hope, a way of honoring them.

Further Points of Clarification

Several other issues deserve clarification. First, some readers may question whether Plowshares actions can rightfully be called a *social movement* since the number of people involved is relatively small. Furthermore, Plowshares activists are not the only ones working to abolish war and weapons of mass destruction. They are part of a larger struggle for peace and can be viewed as merely a distinctive network within the broader disarmament movement, but not a movement in itself.

Collective action researchers hold different views about what constitutes a movement. McCarthy and Zald have characterized a social movement as "a set of opinions and beliefs in a population representing preferences for changing some elements of the social structure or reward distribution, or both, of a society."[12] They distinguish this from *social movement organizations* – organizations with a formalized infrastructure (that may include paid staff, clearly defined membership roles, and rules for decision making) that activists often form to achieve their goals. In reality, many movements are compilations of multiple organizations working toward similar aims; for instance, the environmental movement comprises groups such as Greenpeace, the World Wildlife Fund, the Nature Conservancy, and the Sierra Club. Thus McCarthy, Zald, and others have proposed that social movement organizations should be the focus of research because they are the public, visible carriers of these "preferences for change."[13] Others have argued that this focus is too narrow because it excludes groups with no formal, centralized infrastructure. To broaden the scope, della Porta and Diani view movements as "networks of interaction between different actors which may either include formal organizations or not, depending on

[12] McCarthy, John, and Mayer Zald. 1977. "Resource Mobilization and Social Movements: A Partial Theory." *American Journal of Sociology* 82: 1217.
[13] Also see John Lofland's (1996) book *Social Movement Organizations: Guide to Research on Insurgent Realities*. New York: Aldine De Gruyter.

shifting circumstances."[14] Zald recently suggested that we re-conceptualize movements as "ideologically structured action,"[15] while David Snow defines them as "collective challenges to systems or structures of authority" that primarily operate outside of institutionalized channels for expressing dissent.[16] None of these scholars defines a movement by the magnitude of its scope or the number of people involved.

Throughout the book, I refer to Plowshares actions as a movement. I maintain that this nomenclature is appropriate in light of the definitions proposed by della Porta, Diani, Zald, and Snow. Although the movement does not have a formal organization (at least in most countries), Plowshares actions are indeed structured by a unique ideology that has generated a dramatic, radical tactical repertoire distinct from that of other anti-war groups. Moreover, viewing Plowshares activists as merely one part of the disarmament movement would obscure the fact that they are challenging authority structures beyond the state. While most disarmament groups aim their actions toward the government and its military policies, Plowshares activists are also challenging religious leaders who have supported war and weapons of mass destruction – either overtly or by their silence on the topic. They hope to persuade church authorities to reject the Just War tradition and embrace the Gospel of nonviolence. Thus, Plowshares participants have a distinct ideology, strategy, target, and set of objectives that are not necessarily embraced by others in the disarmament movement. The term "movement" can therefore be justifiably applied to Plowshares activists, even though they operate on a much smaller scale and have fewer participants than other peace movement groups.

A second issue deals with the defining parameters of Plowshares actions. Must activists be religious or pour blood to qualify as part of the Plowshares movement? Do activists have to damage (or attempt to damage) nuclear weapons facilities, or can other forms of property be targeted? Is the Plowshares movement a whole philosophy of action or simply a specific set of tactics? These are continuing points of discussion within the movement and, as subsequent chapters will illustrate, Plowshares activists

[14] della Porta, Donatella, and Mario Diani. 1999. *Social Movements: An Introduction.* Oxford: Blackwell, p. 16.

[15] Zald, Mayer N. 2000. "Ideological Structured Action: An Enlarged Agenda for Social Movement Research." *Mobilization* 5: 1–16.

[16] Snow, David A. 2004. "Social Movements as Challenges to Authority: Resistance to an Emerging Conceptual Hegemony." *Research in Social Movements, Conflicts and Change* 25: 11.

overseas have made tactical and ideological adaptations to suit their distinct cultural contexts. For instance, some have retained the practice of spilling blood although others have not, arguing that its symbolism would be misunderstood in more secular societies. In addition, some groups have shifted the focus from weapons of mass destruction to militarism more broadly because certain nations, such as Sweden, do not have nuclear weapons. And not all Plowshares activists are religious – especially in Europe. Given some of these differences, one might ask what qualifies as a Plowshares action. For the most part, I have allowed the activists to answer this question. If they identified themselves as part of the Plowshares movement, and if their campaigns were listed in the movement's self-documented chronology of events, I included them in the study. The only criterion that I stipulated was that the action had to entail actual or attempted destruction of property related to the military or the weapons industry.[17]

A final point of clarification deals with the Catholic nature of the Plowshares movement. The movement emerged in the United States from a long tradition of socially engaged, radical Catholicism. More directly, it was an outgrowth of Catholic Left actions against the Vietnam War. Consequently the Plowshares movement is heavily influenced by Catholic culture, theology, and practice. Yet it is important to note that the movement is not exclusively Catholic. According to my survey, close to two-thirds of U.S. Plowshares activists identified themselves as Roman Catholic. Others come from various Protestant denominations and a handful are Jewish or Buddhist. In the European context, numerous Plowshares activists are not affiliated with any religious tradition. In addition, some of the theology that Plowshares activists cite to justify their style of resistance comes from non-Catholic scholars. Nevertheless, many aspects of the Plowshares movement are still shaped by its Catholic roots, and thus it can be identified as Catholic, in the same way that universities such as Boston College and Georgetown University are, even though their faculty and student body are from diverse faith traditions (or none at all) and they teach and learn many different perspectives, not simply Catholic ones.

Although I characterize the Plowshares movement as Catholic, its influence has spread beyond the confines of institutional Catholicism and organized religion, evoking reactions from people of other backgrounds, including myself. And although I first began paying closer attention to Plowshares

---

[17] While many activists have tried to destroy weapons, some have simply damaged missile launchers or equipment used to make, guide, or transport weaponry.

activists' distinct style of resistance during the first Gulf War, many had been fighting to abolish war long before that point. They also continue their nonviolent struggle today, as the United States is once again involved militarily with Iraq. Many of them say that as long as wars are waged, they will persistently wage peace – whatever the cost. This is an account of why they are committed to this task, the challenges they have faced, and how some have sustained their struggle over the years.

Acknowledgments

Without exaggeration, this book would not have been possible without the assistance of many Plowshares activists who have contributed to my research in numerous ways. I will begin by expressing my gratitude to Karl Smith and Al Zook for providing my first close encounter with the Plowshares movement, roughly a decade before I began collecting the data for this project. Karl and Al gave me insights from their experiences as Plowshares participants and sometimes debated with me at length about the strategy and philosophy of the movement. They were also literally right beside me during my first experiments with civil disobedience. I also wish to thank the members of Jonah House – especially Elizabeth McAlister, Michelle Naar-Obed, and Greg Boertje-Obed – for taking a chance on me when I indicated an interest in doing this study and for inviting me into their home. Thanks, too, to Susan Crane for her assistance in securing the cover photo. My appreciation also extends to Molly Rush, who advised me to contact *The Nuclear Resister* newsletter to obtain contact information for Plowshares participants, and to Jack Cohen-Joppa for giving me the initial leads. I am particularly grateful to Lasse Gustavsson and Ciaron O'Reilly, who gave me contact information for many European and Australian activists; I had little way of finding these individuals without their help. Special thanks to Susan van der Hijden and Scott and Maria Albrecht, who graciously fed and housed me during my research trip to Europe. I am also grateful to Per Herngren and Stellan Vinthagen, who allowed me to dig through their impressively archived files on the Swedish Plowshares movement. Additional thanks to Per for sending his audiotape of Phil Berrigan's memorial service. Most of all, I am indebted to the numerous Plowshares participants who took the time to fill out my survey, who allowed me to conduct interviews with them, and who openly shared so much of their experiences with me. Finally, I was extraordinarily privileged to have several movement activists read the manuscript and give me extensive feedback on matters large and small. Comments from Wolfgang Sternstein, Ciaron O'Reilly, Per Herngren, and Stellan Vinthagen have strengthened my analysis and the accuracy of the book, although any errors are my sole responsibility.

Other individuals provided me with guidance and assistance in the data collection process. Robert Wuthnow and Christian Smith offered useful suggestions as I constructed my survey. Lori Schreier, Kristine Liebner, Kristin Mitchell, Erin Lyttle, and Jen Wise transcribed the interviews, and Daniel Ritter translated some of the Swedish movement's documents. Kathryn DeGraff and her assistants at DePaul University's archives provided me with exceptional service. The costs for collecting and transcribing all this data were covered by grants from Duquesne University and the Philip H. and Betty L. Wimmer Family Foundation.

As I began to analyze and write about my data, I received constructive feedback from many different sources. I thank the members of Princeton's Center for the Study of Religion who challenged me to think about the Plowshares movement in innovative ways. The participants of the Pittsburgh Social Movements forum – especially John Markoff, Kathleen Blee, and Clifford Bob – offered helpful suggestions, particularly on my analysis of leadership and persistence in the U.S. Plowshares movement. I am grateful to Kelly Moore, Rhys Williams, Dan Cress, and Dan Myers, who provided valuable feedback on an earlier draft of the movement's tactical justifications. I thank James Holstein, former editor of *Social Problems*, whose comments on my article, "Persistent Resistance: Commitment and Community in the Plowshares Movement" [Nepstad, Sharon Erickson. 2004. *Social Problems* 51 (1): 43–60 (copyright © 2004 by the Society for the Study of Social Problems)] helped clarify my thinking on activist retention. Many of the ideas and data from that article are presented in Chapter 4, and I am grateful to the SSSP for kindly granting me permission to use this material. Once I had completed the manuscript, it was Sidney Tarrow and Lewis Bateman who expressed interest in the book and guided it through the review and publication process at Cambridge University Press. As one of the editors of the Cambridge Studies in Contentious Politics series, Jack Goldstone read the manuscript several times, encouraging me to refine and sharpen my analysis. I would also like to express my appreciation to Patrick Coy. As a social movements scholar, a former Catholic Worker, and a skilled journal editor, Pat provided insightful comments on the manuscript's

Acknowledgments

content and form. For the generous support of all these individuals, I express my sincere appreciation.

During the years that I composed and revised this manuscript, I also became a mother. This helped me to realize how much I appreciate my own parents, Millard and Virginia Erickson. They are exemplary role models of how to be accomplished educators and writers while simultaneously being attentive and loving parents. I also wish to express my gratitude to my sister, Kathryn-Sonja Erickson Inoferio. Her unwavering faith in me and her steadfast companionship has been a sustaining force over the years. Finally, I thank my daughters, Linnea and Malaya. It was the anticipation of their arrival into the world and into my life that gave me the motivation to keep working on this book. Moreover, my children's Salvadoran and Guatemalan heritage reminds me of the devastation that war has brought to so many nations and peoples and why the Plowshares movement's message of peace needs to be conveyed. It is my hope that Linnea, Malaya, and all children can grow up in a world where humankind rejects war as a method of dealing with conflict. When that day comes, we will be able to dismantle, once and forever, all weapons of mass destruction.

Religion and War Resistance in the Plowshares Movement

Introduction

MOVEMENT CHALLENGES AND TRAJECTORIES

On a crisp Sunday morning in the fall of 2002, Dominican Sisters Ardeth Platte, Carol Gilbert, and Jackie Hudson prepared to celebrate liturgy and put their faith into action. The three nuns, ranging from fifty-four to sixty-seven years old, put on white mop-up suits – the type used by crews that handle toxic waste and hazardous materials. On the back of their suits they had written "Citizens Weapons Inspection Team" and they wore tags on the front identifying themselves as "Disarmament Specialists." They armed themselves with wire cutters, household hammers, and bottles filled with their blood. At about 7:30 that morning – exactly one year after the start of the U.S. war in Afghanistan – the women cut through the gate at a missile silo field near Greeley, Colorado. They walked a bit further, cutting through a second gate that enabled them to reach silo site N-8. With their hammers they struck the tracks that pull the lid off the silo, bringing the missile into firing position. Then they hammered on the silo itself, enacting the prophet Isaiah's vision: "Nations shall beat their swords into plowshares and their spears into pruning hooks; one nation shall not raise the sword against another, nor shall they train for war again" (Isaiah 2:4). Finally, they poured blood on the structure in the pattern of a cross, and concluded with prayer and song. It was nearly an hour before Air Force personnel arrived, surrounding the gray-haired nuns at gunpoint. When the arresting officers asked what they were doing, Sister Gilbert calmly explained that they were fulfilling President George W. Bush's call to dismantle weapons of mass destruction.[1]

---

[1] This is taken from a press release drafted by Jonah House, where Ardeth Platte and Carol Gilbert live. The statement was written from the three nuns' account and then sent out to the Plowshares movement email listserv on October 7, 2002.

President Bush was of course referring to weapons of mass destruction in the Middle East, not those that the United States possesses. But the nuns were trying to draw attention to the fact that while the White House used this issue as the justification for its escalating war against Iraq, the United States itself has massive stockpiles of nuclear weapons. In Colorado alone, forty-nine nuclear missiles had recently been refitted with new W-87 hydrogen warheads – each with 300 kilotons of explosive power, or roughly twenty-five to thirty times the destructive capacity of the bomb dropped on Hiroshima.[2] According to the nuns, not only did this reveal the hypocrisy of the United States, it also exposed the link between militarism and social injustice as billions of dollars are spent on weapons programs that could otherwise be invested in education and social services. As members of religious orders and people of faith, they felt an obligation to act. Invoking international law that prohibits preparation for mass killing, and the Nuremberg principles that call on people to intervene when their government is committing crimes against humanity, these nuns tried to damage the missile silo sufficiently to take it out of commission. They also hoped that their symbolic act would reach the conscience of a nation that condemned the development of weapons of mass destruction elsewhere while vehemently defending its own nuclear arsenal.

Sisters Platte, Gilbert, and Hudson were arrested for their action in Colorado and charged with interference and obstruction of national defense, which carries a maximum sentence of twenty years and a fine of $250,000. They also faced charges of damage to United States property, which could have added another ten years to their prison terms and doubled their fines to $500,000.[3] During their trial, the nuns claimed that they were not guilty because they were acting in compliance with international mandates, but U.S. District Judge Robert Blackburn prohibited the nuns from introducing international law and Nuremberg principles in their defense. Nevertheless, Sister Gilbert did have an opportunity to articulate the moral reasoning behind their action. She stated:

Any nuclear weapon, even by its very existence, is a crime of genocide. In Germany, when they put Jews on the trains and gassed them, it was legal. Nobody was breaking a law. Yet we all wonder how the people of Germany could have allowed Hitler to do this. I believed I had to go there to stop a crime against humanity. I knew this

---

[2] Information from Bill Sulzman of Citizens for Peace in Space. Posted on the Plowshares email listserv on November 7, 2002.

[3] O'Neill, Patrick. 2002. "Dominican Nuns Face Federal Charges," *National Catholic Reporter*, November 8, 2002, pp. 6–7.

little hammer wasn't going to stop the Minuteman missile, but I could say to my God, "This is not in my name."[4]

The nuns were convicted. Ardeth Platte was sentenced to forty-one months in prison, Carol Gilbert received a thirty-three-month sentence, and Jackie Hudson was given thirty months. Before closing the case, Judge Blackburn called the three Dominicans "dangerously irresponsible." Many of their supporters found this statement ironic since the Bush administration was calling for the development of a new generation of smaller missiles that could potentially be used in a limited nuclear battle. In addition, the White House had approved the Robust Nuclear Earth Penetrator – a weapon designed to obliterate weapons stockpiles and deeply buried command bunkers. One of the nuns' supporters reflected: "George W. Bush is quite assuredly tilting the world towards a new nuclear arms race. Who is dangerously irresponsible?"[5]

These three Dominican Sisters were not the first who, based on religious conviction, had plotted to destroy weapons. Nor were they the last. They are part of a group that for decades has used radical nonviolence to intervene in war preparation, drawing on religious symbolism to challenge both the government's production of nuclear weapons and the church's complacency on issues of militarism and war. This group, known as the Plowshares movement, has conducted dozens of similar campaigns in which activists enter weapons production sites or military installations to damage weapons, which they refer to as "acts of disarmament." The typical U.S. Plowshares participant has received a sentence of one to two years for such actions, but some have been given prison terms as long as eighteen years. Yet the substantial costs and risks have not deterred others from joining. Since the movement started in 1980, about 200 people have participated in nearly 80 Plowshares actions.[6]

Many observers consider this movement an abysmal failure. Plowshares activists aim to abolish war and weapons of mass destruction. They also hope to persuade religious authorities to reject the church's traditional Just War position and embrace the nonviolent Gospel message. They have not reached either of these goals, and skeptics argue that they are unlikely to do

[4] Quoted in *Denver Post* writer Diane Carman's column, "Nun's Faith Finds Chink in U.S. Armor." April 6, 2003, p. B-01.

[5] LaForge, John, Nukewatch announcement of the 2003 Nuclear-Free Future Awards, posted on the Plowshares email listserv on October 28, 2003.

[6] For a complete list of Plowshares actions, see Appendix C.

so in the near future. But one of the primary purposes of any social movement is to provoke a response, to challenge people to reconsider status quo assumptions. In this regard, the Plowshares movement has been successful since virtually everyone reacts when they hear about this faith-based movement of felons who destroy government property and pour blood. Some are shocked and outraged, especially when they discover that many participants are priests and nuns. Others consider these actions to be futile and foolish, while some find the movement compelling. Almost everyone is amazed at the price that Plowshares activists are willing to pay and the sacrifices that they make to achieve peace.

This book conveys the story of these activists, whose efforts often go unnoticed by the broader public. It is also an account of the movement's progression over time and the various challenges it has had to address in order to be a continual irritant in the public's conscience and a persistent thorn in the side of the church. Despite numerous challenges, the U.S. Plowshares movement has demonstrated remarkable tenacity and longevity, as activists continue to engage in war resistance even when the consequences are harsh, political conditions are unfavorable, and other peace movements have declined or collapsed. Not only have these activists sustained the movement for decades, they have also facilitated its cross-national expansion. Their international counterparts, however, have not always effectively addressed the developmental tasks that movements face. As a result, some movements have staggered along for years while others have never progressed beyond a handful of sporadic actions. Across different geographic regions, the Plowshares movement has unfolded in distinct ways with divergent results.

The varying trajectories of the Plowshares movement led me to examine three key questions. First, what developmental challenges do activists face and how do their choices shape their movements over time? Second, how have U.S. Plowshares activists sustained their resistance for decades, even when the cost of participation is high and political opportunities have fluctuated? Third, what can be learned by comparing the progression of this movement in the United States, the Netherlands, Germany, Australia, Sweden, and Great Britain?

Social Movement Trajectories

Before exploring the developmental challenges and trajectories of the Plowshares movement in the United States and abroad, it is useful to examine these issues in the collective action literature. Many studies of protest assume a common linear development in which movements erupt, peak, and subside in a predictable wavelike sequence, as depicted in Figure I.1. At every phase in a movement's life cycle, a number of factors and tasks are critical to the ongoing progression of the movement. I briefly summarize each stage and its concomitant issues here.

Movement Emergence

In Stage 1, a combination of factors contributes to the initial expression of protest. Scholars disagree to some extent on the precise elements that are necessary for movement emergence. One group takes a structural approach, arguing that three key variables explain when dissent explodes into collective action. First, the political climate must be favorable in order to enhance protestors' perceived assessment of the likelihood of success. Even when people are convinced that change is desperately needed, they may be reluctant to act unless they believe that it is possible to alter existing conditions. This sense of efficacy comes from the expansion of "political opportunities" or shifts in the broader social environment that increase the power and leverage of challenging groups. This may entail significant demographic transitions, war, political divisions and realignments, changing cultural attitudes, or economic recessions – all of which may undermine the power of a government, leading protesters to conclude that the time is right to mount a campaign of resistance. Second, there has to be a pre-existing organization that will help launch a movement by offering material resources, such as financial support, along with human resources, including leaders and networks for recruiting potential movement participants. These first two factors set the stage for a movement to emerge by providing ripe conditions and sufficient organizational capacity. But a third component is needed to inspire people to act on these favorable circumstances: an insurgent mind-set. People must undergo an ideological shift in which they no longer consider the status quo legitimate, they begin demanding change, and they believe that they have the power to alter the situation.[7] In short, movements emerge when changing social and political conditions create a favorable climate for challengers, when pre-existing groups provide the

---

[7] Piven, Francis Fox, and Richard Cloward. 1977. *Poor People's Movements: Why They Succeed, How They Fail*. New York: Pantheon.

Development of Protest Movements

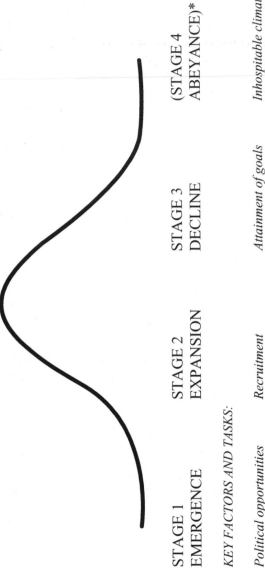

STAGE 1 EMERGENCE	STAGE 2 EXPANSION	STAGE 3 DECLINE	(STAGE 4 ABEYANCE)*
KEY FACTORS AND TASKS:			
Political opportunities	*Recruitment*	*Attainment of goals*	*Inhospitable climate*
Mobilizing organizations	*Mobilization of resources*	*Shifting opportunities*	*Form abeyance structures*
Insurgent consciousness	*Devising strategies*	*Repression*	*Sustain movement culture*
Moral conviction	*Tactical innovation*	*Factionalization*	*Rejuvenate commitment*
	Construct identity	*Trend toward oligarchies*	*Conduct limited actions*
	Framing and media work	*Co-optation*	
	Emotion work		

*Not all movements go into abeyance. Some simply terminate.

Figure I.1 Movement Progression.

necessary resources for mobilization, and when people believe that change is needed and possible.[8]

Other researchers note that people do occasionally protest regardless of whether conditions are favorable. Challenging the underlying assumptions of the structural model, these scholars posit that moral convictions and ideological commitments may override concerns about the efficacy of protest or the lack of an organizational infrastructure. In these circumstances, movements often arise to engage in "politics of moral witness." Barbara Epstein uses this term to describe acts of protest conducted by individuals who feel a moral obligation and personal responsibility to denounce a situation and to call for change. They are often aware that the chance of achieving their goals is small, but feel that action is nonetheless imperative as a form of witness.[9] Thus political opportunities and mobilizing organizations may increase the likelihood of success, but they are not necessarily a prerequisite to movement emergence. What is essential is that potential protesters feel that existing conditions are so reprehensible that something must be done.[10]

Movement Expansion

After initial collective acts of resistance occur, a full-fledged movement does not automatically follow. In order to expand from an outburst of dissent (Stage 1) to a viable social movement that can sustain ongoing acts of protest (Stage 2), organizers must undertake a variety of movement-building tasks. Leaders must establish some type of infrastructure to support a growing movement.[11] They must also devise effective strategies and mobilize the human and material resources required to launch campaigns.[12] They must

[8] This approach is known as the Political Process model. For a full account, see McAdam, Doug. 1982. *Political Process and the Development of Black Insurgency, 1930–1970*. Chicago: University of Chicago Press.

[9] Epstein, Barbara. 1991. *Political Protest and Cultural Revolution: Nonviolent Direct Action in the 1970s and 1980s*. Berkeley: University of California Press.

[10] For further information on cultural approaches to social movements, see Jasper, James M. 1997. *The Art of Moral Protest: Culture, Biography, and Creativity in Social Movements*. Chicago: University of Chicago Press. Also see Nepstad, Sharon Erickson. 2004. *Convictions of the Soul: Religion, Culture, and Agency in the Central America Solidarity Movement*. New York: Oxford University Press.

[11] Gamson, William. 1975. *The Strategy of Social Protest*. Homewood, IL: Dorsey.

[12] McCarthy, John, and Mayer Zald. 1977. "Resource Mobilization and Social Movements: A Partial Theory." *American Journal of Sociology* 82: 1212–1241.

work with the media and frame their issues in a manner that resonates with a wide audience in order to win broader support.[13] They have to recruit members and help individuals overcome obstacles to participation.[14] They must build a sense of community and shared identity among activists[15] and encourage the type of emotions that solidify commitment and sustain motivation.[16] Furthermore, as opponents find ways to effectively counteract the movement, leaders must engage in tactical innovation.[17] If movement organizers are able to achieve these tasks, they may pressure their opponents sufficiently to negotiate and grant concessions.

Movement Decline

Just as a wave crests and subsides, so do many movements. This third stage – movement decline (Stage 3) – can result from a variety of factors. The movement may slow or cease completely because it has successfully obtained its goals or because it has gained sufficient political representation that activists no longer feel they must resort to politics by alternative means.[18] Political

---

[13] For more information about framing techniques to broaden support for movement goals, see the following: Snow, David, E. Burke Rochford Jr., Steven K. Worden, and Robert D. Benford. 1986. "Frame Alignment Processes, Micromobilization, and Movement Participation." *American Sociological Review* 51: 464–481; Snow, David, and Robert D. Benford. 1988. "Ideology, Frame Resonance and Participant Mobilization." *International Social Movement Research* 1: 197–217. Clifford Bob (2005) also offers a compelling comparative examination of framing and media attention in garnering third-party support in his book, *The Marketing of Rebellion: Insurgents, Media, and International Activism*. New York: Cambridge University Press.

[14] For more information on recruitment, see Snow, David, Louis Zurcher, and Sheldon Ekland-Olson. 1980. "Social Networks and Social Movements: A Microstructural Approach to Differential Recruitment." *American Sociological Review* 45: 787–801. For information on recruitment to high-risk movements, see McAdam, Doug. 1986. "Recruitment to High-Risk/Cost Activism: The Case of Freedom Summer." *American Journal of Sociology* 92(1): 64–90. For information on the obstacles to participation, see Klandermans, Bert, and Dirk Oegema. 1987. "Potentials, Networks, Motivations, and Barriers." *American Sociological Review* 52: 519–531.

[15] Taylor, Verta, and Nancy Whittier. 1992. "Collective Identity in Social Movement Communities: Lesbian Feminist Mobilization," pp. 104–129 in Aldon Morris and Carol McClurg Mueller (eds.), *Frontiers in Social Movement Theory*. New Haven, CT: Yale University Press.

[16] Goodwin, Jeff, James Jasper, and Francesca Polletta. 2001. *Passionate Politics: Emotions and Social Movements*. Chicago: University of Chicago Press.

[17] McAdam, Doug. 1983. "Tactical Innovation and the Pace of Insurgency." *American Sociological Review* 48: 735–754.

[18] Meyer, David S. 1993. "Institutionalizing Dissent: The United States Structure of Political Opportunity and the End of the Nuclear Freeze Movement." *Sociological Forum* 8 (2): 157–179.

opportunities may also decrease and the social climate may turn hostile. The same factors that strengthen a movement's power vis-à-vis its opponent – such as internal divisions within authority structures, realigning coalitions, economic downturns, and changing attitudes – can just as quickly shift favor away from protestors. When this occurs, activists may feel that their efforts are less likely to make a difference, reducing their sense of efficacy and consequently their willingness to protest.[19] Repression can also bring a prosperous social movement to a halt. As a movement gains strength, it is often considered a threat to power-holders, who may respond by increasing the costs of protest. This may cause activists to decrease their level of involvement or to drop out of a movement completely.[20] Similarly, countermovements may arise, forcing activists to fight two separate battles – one to obtain their goals and another against those who aim to reverse their gains or discredit the movement.[21]

Internal movement issues can also contribute to diminishing levels of protest. If factions arise and quarrels are not resolved, a movement can fragment, undercutting its power to act collectively. In addition, successful movements often channel more of their energy into building social movement organizations that will handle growing administrative needs. This diverts both human and material resources away from resistance while blunting a movement's militant edge and its willingness to engage in direct action, because it must now be respectable in the eyes of potential donors and constituents.[22] Moreover, once social movement organizations have been established, they may be co-opted by the authority structures they are

---

[19] Tarrow, Sidney. 1994. *Power in Movement: Social Movements, Collective Action and Politics.* Cambridge: Cambridge University Press.

[20] It is important to note that repression does not always subdue protest movements. According to Gene Sharp (1990), repression sometimes backfires by undermining the credibility of a government and eliciting public sympathy for the victims – especially when the victims do not retaliate. Sharp refers to this dynamic as "political jujitsu." Sometimes, however, repression does have its intended effect. For a comprehensive list of the numerous tactics used to stop movements, see Marx, Gary (1979). "External Efforts to Damage or Facilitate Movements: Some Patterns, Explanations, Outcomes, and Complications, pp. 94–125 in Mayer, Zald, and John D. McCarthy (eds.). *The Dynamics of Social Movements: Resource Mobilization, Social Control, and Tactics.* Cambridge, MA: Winthrop.

[21] Lo, Clarence Y. 1982. "Countermovements and Conservative Movements in the Contemporary U.S." *American Review of Sociology* 8: 107–134; Meyer, David S., and Suzanne Staggenborg. 1996. "Movements, Countermovements, and the Structure of Political Opportunity." *American Journal of Sociology* 101 (6): 1628–1660; Mottl, Tahi L. 1980. "The Analysis of Countermovements." *Social Problems* 27(5): 620–634.

[22] Piven, Francis Fox, and Richard Cloward. 1977. *Poor People's Movements: Why They Succeed, How They Fail.* New York: Pantheon.

challenging,[23] or an internal oligarchy of elites may emerge that becomes primarily interested in preserving its own power and privilege rather than promoting the goals of the people they represent.[24] This can undermine adherents' morale and trust, causing them to leave the movement.

Movement Abeyance

After a period of decline, a movement can either cease completely or shift into an "abeyance" stage (Stage 4). Verta Taylor uses this term to describe a phase in which the sociopolitical climate is no longer hospitable to protestors and collective action has dramatically subsided. Although it may appear that the movement has ceased, a small cadre continues to organize, albeit on a more limited scale, and in so doing provides continuity until the next cycle of resistance erupts. During this abeyance stage, movement groups may make little progress toward their goals, and their influence may be nominal. Nevertheless, by keeping the movement alive, they serve several important linking functions between waves of protest. Movements in abeyance sustain activist networks, retain the group's collective identity and goals, and maintain its tactical repertoire. When a new cycle of protest begins, activists can draw upon this knowledge and long-standing tradition rather than reinvent it.[25]

But what enables activists to faithfully and persistently struggle for a cause when their numbers have dwindled, they see little progress, and they encounter greater hostility? Taylor, along with her colleague Leila Rupp, explored this question in their study of the American women's movement from 1945 to 1960.[26] They found that the National Women's Party (NWP) played a critical role in sustaining the movement after the struggle for suffrage, keeping it alive until the second wave of feminism erupted in the 1960s. Although the number of participants was small during this abeyance period, their commitment to the cause remained steady, mainly because

---

[23] Coy, Patrick, and Timothy Hedeen. 2005. "A Stage Model of Social Movement Co-optation: Community Mediation in the United States." *The Sociological Quarterly* 46(3): 405–435; Meyer, David S. 1993. "Institutionalizing Dissent: The United States Structure of Political Opportunity and the End of the Nuclear Freeze Movement." *Sociological Forum* 8(2): 157–179.

[24] Michels, Robert. 1966 [1962]. *Political Parties*. New York: Free Press.

[25] Taylor, Verta. 1989. "Social Movement Continuity: The Women's Movement in Abeyance." *American Sociological Review* 54: 761–775.

[26] Rupp, Leila, and Verta Taylor. 1990. *Survival in the Doldrums: The American Women's Rights Movement, 1945 to the 1960s*. Columbus: Ohio State University Press.

of the rich cultural life that the NWP cultivated. The National Women's Party sponsored numerous activities, mostly held at Belmont House in Washington, DC, which served as the movement's headquarters. The party regularly celebrated Susan B. Anthony's birthday and the anniversary of women's suffrage and it hosted receptions to honor politicians who supported the Equal Rights Amendment. Belmont House also functioned as a "free space"[27] where feminist beliefs and values were reinforced and emotional bonds were forged. Several women lived at the house, others stayed for short periods while conducting lobbying work, and many women visited on a regular basis. This provided a context for friendships to evolve and deepen over time, which in turn strengthened members' commitment and devotion. The NWP community became a wellspring that rejuvenated feminist activists in weary times, thereby keeping the women's movement from dying out completely.

Richard Wood also emphasizes the importance of a vibrant movement culture in sustaining activism over time – not only during doldrum periods, which Taylor and Rupp examined, but also in the heat of the struggle. In his study of faith-based and race-based organizing in Northern California, Wood argues that one of the key challenges that groups face is organizational stability and maintaining continuity of individual involvement. Organizations that develop intensely shared cultural elements – such as meaningful symbols, rituals, and narratives – are more likely to elicit solidarity and strong commitment from their members. As a result, these groups are more likely to endure. Wood notes, "Vague acceptance of shared symbols or meanings can help a group cohere during calm times. But in the more raucous waters of political engagement, with the constant threat of fragmentation through conflict or dissipation through loss of commitment, more deeply held cultural elements become important for holding a group together."[28]

Alternative Trajectories

Many movements do follow this trajectory of emergence, expansion, decline, and either termination or abeyance. But does the wave metaphor

---

[27] Evans, Sarah M., and Harry C. Boyte. 1992. *Free Spaces*. Chicago: University of Chicago Press.

[28] Wood, Richard L. 2002. *Faith in Action: Religion, Race, and Democratic Organizing in America*. Chicago: University of Chicago Press.

Figure I.2   Movements with Intermittent Activity.

Figure I.3   Movements with Limited Expansion.

Figure I.4   Sustained or Persistent Movements.

accurately capture all movements? Comparative historical studies demonstrate that societies experience periods of heightened activity, such as the 1960s, when struggles spur on other acts of resistance, culminating in a general "cycle of protest."[29] Yet while this wavelike dynamic may capture the level of contention or quiescence in a given society during a particular historical era, not all individual movements experience a dramatic rise, peak, and descent. Some may display intermittent activity at unpredictable times, as shown in Figure I.2. Others may start out with strong potential but, for various reasons, expand only to a limited degree, as shown in Figure I.3. And a few rare movements may actually survive and continue – despite changing sociopolitical conditions, repression, and internal tensions – without ever shifting into the abeyance stage. These persistent movements, shown in Figure I.4, may be better characterized by the metaphor of a river that flows continuously but the speed and volume of the water varies depending on the season and the level of rain.

---

[29] Tarrow, Sidney. 1994. *Power in Movement: Social Movements, Collective Action and Politics.* Cambridge: Cambridge University Press; Tilly, Charles. 1993. *European Revolutions, 1492–1992.* Oxford: Blackwell.

Introduction: Movement Challenges and Trajectories

Movement paths can unfold in numerous ways, but this is rarely acknowledged by collective action researchers, who seldom study movements that fail to fully mobilize. Consequently we know little about why some movements emerge but falter, while others expand and then terminate or shift into abeyance. Moreover, we do not know why and how some movements, such as the U.S. Plowshares movement, continue against great odds. The assumption of a linear, wavelike progression is so ingrained that there has been little comparison of movements with different trajectories that would enable us to understand theoretically the influences that shape their development. By comparing the Plowshares movement in the United States, Australia, and Europe, I will demonstrate that their varying trajectories were influenced in part by the way they handled a number of micro-level issues that typically arise in a movement's progression. These include the challenges of establishing legitimacy, determining the movement's structure and leadership, and finding ways to retain members.

Those who take a structural view – that is, those who think that movements are mostly influenced by factors such as political openness, availability of resources, levels of repression, and so forth – may feel that I place too much emphasis on these micro-foundational tasks. Moreover, most structuralists stress that micro-level choices are circumscribed by the macro conditions in which activists operate. For instance, in his study of insurgent movements in Uganda, Mozambique, and Peru, Jeremy Weinstein argues that the structural factor of resource availability shaped rebel leaders' recruitment techniques. Insurgent groups with an abundance of economic resources used financial incentives to encourage people to join their movements. Those that lacked funds were forced to win and retain participants on the basis of ethnic, religious, or ideological appeals. The varying motives of recruits in turn affected their movements' internal organization and strategies. Ideologically motivated insurgents were more likely to defer to the movement's hierarchy, follow orders, and comply with leaders' appeals for restraint; consequently, the movement could maintain a centralized organization and violence against civilians was minimal. In contrast, the financially motivated rebel recruits were less disciplined, often destroying property and attacking indiscriminately. Thus, Weinstein concludes, "Decisions about recruitment, organization, and violence [i.e. tactics] cease to be driven by the actions of individuals and become, instead, choices made under binding constraints imposed by the resources that a group has at its disposal and the membership it has attracted to participate. Leadership, skill, and ideology all take a backseat to broader, macro-level factors that structure the universe of possibilities individual rebels confront."[30]

Although I acknowledge that such structural factors are important, I contend that – at least in the Plowshares movement – they do not have the greatest explanatory power in accounting for the movement's divergent trajectories in various regions.[31] Several points lead me to this conclusion. First, Plowshares groups in countries that experienced relatively advantageous conditions and expanding political opportunities – critical factors according to structuralists – actually had a harder time establishing themselves and moving into the expansion stage than those operating under unfavorable circumstances. During the 1980s, for example, the European population was more sympathetic to the goals of disarmament movements than the U.S. public was. A 1985 poll reported that only 4 percent of U.S. citizens believed that their government should begin dismantling their nuclear stockpile, regardless of whether the Soviet Union did so, while 15 percent of the Dutch population and 23 percent of Germans held this view.[32] Furthermore, the European political climate was conducive to such anti-nuclear weapons movements because there was widespread opposition to NATO's decision to deploy nearly 600 Pershing missiles in Central Europe. In the Netherlands, 3.75 million people – more than a quarter of the population – signed a petition to stop this deployment,[33] while Germans increasingly questioned military policies as they realized that their country was likely to be the battleground in a nuclear exchange between East and West.[34]

---

[30] Weinstein, Jeremy. 2006. *Inside Rebellion: The Politics of Insurgent Violence*. New York: Cambridge University Press.

[31] This is consistent with the findings of Lee Ann Banaszak's (1996) study of the women's suffrage movement in the United States and Switzerland. She discovered that material resources and macro forces (such as the presence of political opportunities, characteristics of the political system, and alliances with other political groups) had little effect on these movements' trajectories and accomplishments. Rather, the strategic choices of each group determined whether women won the right to vote. For further information, see Banaszak, Lee Ann. 1996. *Why Movements Succeed or Fail: Opportunity, Culture, and the Struggle for Woman Suffrage*. Princeton, NJ: Princeton University Press.

[32] DeBoer, Connie. 1985. "The Polls, the European Peace Movement and the Deployment of Nuclear Missiles." *Public Opinion Quarterly* 49(1): 119–132.

[33] Klandermans, Bert, and Dirk Oegema. 1987. "Potentials, Networks, Motivations, and Barriers: Steps Towards Participation in Social Movements." *American Sociological Review* 52: 519–531.

[34] Boutwell, Jeffrey. 1983. "Politics and the Peace Movement in West Germany." *International Security* 7(4): 72–92; Mandelbaum, Michael. 1983. *The Nuclear Future*. Ithaca: Cornell University Press.

European government structures were also advantageous for peace activists. Because parliamentary systems are comprised of multiple parties, there are more possible points of division, which in turn can increase the movements' leverage and power vis-à-vis the state. Moreover, European movements against nuclear weapons had a greater chance of establishing political allies. This occurred in the Federal Republic of Germany, where progressive political groups flourished during this period.[35] The largest and most influential leftist group, the Green Party, took up the cause of nuclear disarmament. Similarly, Labor and Social Democratic parties in Great Britain, the Netherlands, and Scandinavia represented the goals of the peace movement, thereby granting activists access to institutionalized channels of opposition.[36] This led one analyst to conclude that "because it is part of left-wing politics in Europe, the anti-nuclear weapons movement is likely to prove more enduring there than in the United States."[37]

In contrast, the Plowshares movement in the United States began and expanded during a conservative political era. This was exemplified in the policies and popularity of President Ronald Reagan, who was elected in part because of his commitment to strengthen American military capacities.[38] Moreover, the U.S. government is, for all intents and purposes, comprised of only two parties, since independent political parties rarely have any significant influence or representation. And although some members of the U.S. Congress did support a proposal to freeze the development of certain weapons programs,[39] many politicians were reluctant to support disarmament if it meant cutbacks in military expenditures and job losses.[40] As Sam Marullo noted, "Major corporations depend on defense contract profits to stay in business, and local officials depend on the influx of money and jobs into their communities. Members of Congress benefit as well from the jobs

---

[35] Boutwell, Jeffrey. 1983. "Politics and the Peace Movement in West Germany." *International Security* 7(4): 72–92; Mueller, Harald, and Thomas Risse-Kappen. 1987. "Origins of Estrangement: The Peace Movement and the Changed Image of America in West Germany." *International Security* 12(1): 52–88.

[36] Boutwell, Jeffrey. 1983. "Politics and the Peace Movement in West Germany." *International Security* 7(4): 72–92.

[37] Mandelbaum, Michael. 1984. "The Anti-nuclear Weapons Movements." *PS* 17(1): 24–32. Quotation from p. 31.

[38] Meyer, David. 1993. "Protest Cycles and Political Process: American Peace Movements in the Nuclear Age." *Political Research Quarterly* 46(3): 451–479.

[39] Meyer, David. 1990. *A Winter of Discontent: The Nuclear Freeze and American Politics.* New York: Praeger.

[40] Melman, Seymour. 1985. *The Permanent War Economy.* New York: Simon and Schuster.

created in their home districts; they are loath to cut such contracts or close military bases."[41] Hence Plowshares activists in the United States faced a less hospitable sociopolitical climate than their counterparts in Europe.[42]

Yet the issue of conducive conditions and expanding opportunities is to some extent irrelevant because Plowshares activists' decisions to act are largely unaffected by the political climate and their chances of obtaining their goals. Although the movement began in the 1980s when there was extensive debate about the arms race, Plowshares actions continued throughout the 1990s even though concern about nuclear weapons dissipated as the Cold War ended. While many peace movement organizations subsided or collapsed completely during this time,[43] the U.S. Plowshares movement persisted. Moreover, as the three Dominican Sisters' campaign illustrates, Plowshares actions are still occurring in the twenty-first century even though the risks associated with these tactics have become more serious since the terrorist attacks of September 11, 2001. Activists feel that they must continue their resistance, regardless of the cost or the likelihood of success, as long as war and weapons of mass destruction exist. This is not a movement driven primarily by political instrumentality but rather by moral conscience, whereby "one rejects what the moral law rejects, without calculating one's chances of getting away with it or of achieving a change in public policy.... The rejection of the present evil is valid for its [own] sake."[44]

Another reason why I am reluctant to use structural explanations of movement trajectories is because structuralists assert that other external

---

[41] Marullo, Sam. 1992. "Political, Institutional, and Bureaucratic Fuel for the Arms Race." *Sociological Forum* 7(1): 29–54.

[42] David Meyer (1993, "Institutionalizing Dissent") argues that this inhospitable climate actually aided movement growth because conventional political channels were not open. Once groups such as the Nuclear Freeze movement gained greater political representation, the movement actually declined because they were no longer organizing mass protest rallies and public demonstrations to gain media attention; instead, most of their energy was directed toward lobbying and Congressional endorsements for their proposals. Although I believe that both explanations are viable, they are not directly pertinent because the Plowshares movement is primarily an expressive movement that is not driven by political instrumentality but rather by the need to engage in acts of moral witness. For further elaboration of this point, see my 2004 article, "Dissenters and Disciples: Tactical Choice and Consequences in the Plowshares Movement." *Research in Social Movements, Conflict, and Change* 25: 139–160.

[43] Edwards, Bob, and Sam Marullo. 1995. "Organizational Mortality in Declining Social Movements: The Demise of Peace Movement Organizations in the End of the Cold War Era." *American Sociological Review* 60: 908–927.

[44] Yoder, John Howard. 1992. *Nevertheless: Varieties of Religious Pacifism*. Scottsdale, PA: Herald Press, pp. 57, 59.

contingencies, such as repression, have a significant influence on movement development.[45] Structuralists maintain that repression can stop incipient movements or hasten an established movement's demise by increasing the costs of protest, causing activists to drop out of the movement and deterring others from joining.[46] In my research, lower levels of repression are not correlated with movement expansion or persistence since Plowshares groups that faced fewer sanctions actually had greater difficulties establishing and sustaining their movements. For example, Plowshares activists in the U.S. receive longer prison sentences than those in Europe and Australia. As Table I.1 shows, the mean and median sentences vary considerably across the movements. In the U.S. case, the mean (i.e., statistical average) is skewed by two activists who received particularly long sentences of 18 years. Therefore the median – the number that equally divides these cases in half – is a more accurate depiction of the typical sentence. The median indicates that half of all U.S. Plowshares activists received sentences of 18 months or less and half received sentences of greater than 18 months. Thus U.S. activists spent 15 more months in prison than their European counterparts and nearly 16 months more than Australian activists. Despite these harsher punishments, the U.S. Plowshares movement has had greater success in evoking and maintaining protest than Plowshares activists in other regions. While repression has shaped the movement in ways that will be discussed later, it has not determined its trajectory. Rather, activists' reaction to these sanctions is critical in determining whether their movement will collapse or persist.

In short, activists may not control the structural conditions in which they operate, but they do have a choice in how they will respond to these conditions. If the political climate is not favorable and the likelihood of repression is high, they can decide to wait until circumstances improve. Yet they may also choose to carry out their campaigns even though the impact of their actions might be minimal and the sanctions severe. Similarly, movement

---

[45] This is the general conclusion that Debra Minkoff asserts in her study of women's and racial minority organizations during 1955 to 1985. For further information, see Minkoff, Debra. 1999. "Bending with the Wind: Strategic Change and Adaptation by Women's and Racial Minority Organizations." *American Journal of Sociology* 104 (6): 1666–1703.

[46] McAdam, Doug. 1982. *Political Process and the Development of Black Insurgency, 1930–1970.* Chicago: University of Chicago Press; Tarrow, Sidney. 1993. "Cycles of Collective Action: Between Moments of Madness and the Repertoire of Contention." *Social Science History* 17(2): 281–308; Tilly, Charles. 1978. *From Mobilization to Revolution.* Reading, MA: Addison-Wesley.

Table I.1. *Comparison of Plowshares Activists' Prison Sentences by Region (percentages)*

Sentence	United States (%)	Europe (%)	Australia (%)
5 months or less	11.5	72.7	75
6–11 months	3.8	0	0
12–23 months	42.4	27.3	25
2–3 years	11.5	0	0
3–4 years	3.8	0	0
4–8 years	19.3	0	0
8+ years	7.7	0	0
Total	100	100	100
Mean	52.2 months	4.3 months	5.3 months
Median	18.0 months	3.0 months	2.2 months

leaders can design their organizations to be relatively immune to the effects of fluctuating resources, such as those that Weinstein describes. For example, many Plowshares activists choose to live in intentional communities committed to voluntary poverty so that they are free from material concerns that would inhibit their activism. Thus the movement has no budget, operates with virtually no funds, and deliberately recruits only those who share their ideological and religious convictions. Although I am not dismissing the relevance of macro-level factors, the emphasis in this book is on activists' micro-level responses to structural conditions.

Developmental Challenges

Broad societal forces *influence* movement trajectories but they do not *determine* them. Macro-structural factors can make organizers' tasks more or less difficult, tipping the balance in their favor or stacking the odds against them. Yet movements sometimes falter or fail under the best of circumstances because of activists' inability to manage developmental challenges such as generating legitimacy and establishing some type of movement infrastructure. Conversely, some movements continue without going into abeyance, even when conditions are abysmal, the political climate is hostile, and repression is strong. This type of persistence occurs, as we shall see, when the movement has successfully resolved earlier developmental challenges and creatively responds to adverse circumstances by implementing measures to retain and sustain activists over the long run. I now offer a closer look at a few of the developmental challenges that protestors face as they seek to expand and maintain their levels of resistance.

Establishing Legitimacy

Once a movement emerges, it cannot shift into the expansion stage unless it establishes some degree of legitimacy. If it fails to achieve this, activists may simply be viewed as a handful of isolated, disgruntled individuals – the so-called lunatic fringe – rather than a collective force addressing issues that merit serious consideration. Bert Useem and Mayer Zald argue that legitimacy can be achieved in two ways. First, a movement can obtain *legitimacy of numbers* by demonstrating that it does not represent a few marginal voices but rather reflects a broader constituency that supports sociopolitical change. Second, "a movement achieves *legitimacy of means* by convincing the public that it is an appropriate vehicle to achieve its constituents' goals. A movement not only must justify its goals, but also justify its *modus operandi* as a social movement."[47] Given the serious risks and costs associated with the Plowshares movement, it has never been able to attract large numbers of participants, although the broader disarmament movement did gain legitimacy of numbers as hundreds of thousands joined in low-risk demonstrations in Europe and the United States.[48] The more challenging task for the Plowshares movement was convincing people that their tactics were a suitable method for challenging military policies. Given its controversial use of blood and property destruction, legitimacy of means was not easy to obtain.

Determining Movement Structure and Leadership

In addition to establishing legitimacy, burgeoning movements must also form some type of infrastructure to support ongoing acts of protest. This raises a number of questions. Should a movement establish a formal organization or remain a loosely coordinated network of activists? Should there

---

[47] Useem, Bert, and Mayer N. Zald. 1980. "From Pressure Group to Social Movement: Organizational Dilemmas of the Effort to Promote Nuclear Power." *Social Problems* 30(2): 149.

[48] Meyer, David. 1993. "Protest Cycles and Political Process: American Peace Movements in the Nuclear Age." *Political Research Quarterly* 46(3): 451–479; Rochon, Thomas R. 1988. *Mobilizing for Peace: The Antinuclear Movements in Western Europe*. Princeton: Princeton University Press.

be a single center of power or should it be distributed among autonomous local groups? Each option has distinct advantages and disadvantages. On the one hand, the establishment of a movement organization with centralized power often has a dampening effect on direct action,[49] but it provides coordination and stability that can facilitate movement survival.[50] On the other hand, decentralized networks may increase participation and commitment by involving more people in the process of planning and implementing campaigns. But the movement's impact may not be as great, especially on the national level because actions are not synchronized, thus undercutting the perception of widespread mass dissent.

Regardless of whether activists choose to create a formal organization or function as an informal network of grassroots groups, they must establish a workable form of leadership. Failure to create some decision-making capability means that the group will have difficulty acting as a collective force and thus struggle to move into the expansion stage. Movements have constructed different forms of leadership, but each has its own pitfalls that can potentially derail a nascent movement. In some instances, leadership falls to charismatic individuals who command a following through the magnetism of their personalities.[51] Although charismatic figures may be particularly effective at recruiting and motivating members, they may also become easy targets for repression. And if a movement is dependent on a single charismatic leader who then dies or is incarcerated, the movement may begin to falter since no one is prepared to assume that role.[52]

Other movements have designed their leadership structure to reflect their commitment to egalitarianism. In some cases, hierarchical relations or centralized decision-making are rejected in favor of rotating leadership. Yet this also has potential problems. Leaders may only hold this position

[49] Jenkins, Craig, and Craig M. Eckert. 1986. "Channeling Black Insurgency: Elite Patronage and Professional Development of the Black Movement." *American Sociological Review* 51: 812–829; Piven, Francis Fox, and Richard A. Cloward. 1977. *Poor People's Movements: How They Succeed, Why They Fail.* New York: Pantheon.

[50] Gamson, William. 1975. *The Strategy of Social Protest.* Homewood, IL: Dorsey; Staggenborg, Suzanne. 1988. "Stability and Innovation in the Women's Movement: A Comparison of Two Movement Organizations." *Social Problems* 36: 75–92; Wehr, Paul. 1986. "Nuclear Pacifism as Collective Action." *Journal of Peace Research* 22: 103–113.

[51] Weber, Max. 1946. "The Sociology of Charisma as Authority," pp. 245–252 in Hans Gerth and C. Wright Mills (eds.), *From Max Weber.* New York: Oxford University Press.

[52] Nepstad, Sharon Erickson, and Clifford Bob. 2006. "When Do Leaders Matter? Hypotheses on Leadership Dynamics in Social Movements." *Mobilization* 11(1): 1–22; Bob, Clifford, and Sharon Erickson Nepstad. 2007. "Kill a Leader, Murder a Movement? The Impact of Assassination on Social Movements." *American Behavioral Scientist* 50 (10): 1370–1394.

long enough to develop a base of knowledge, a set of skills, and key relationships, which are then lost when the next leader assumes power. Although some of these resources may be transferred, time and energy are diverted from protest campaigns as the new leader learns the ropes. Another solution has been to distribute power to multiple leaders simultaneously, often designating certain tasks (for example, recruitment, fund-raising, media spokesperson, and so on) to specific individuals. But this can generate its own challenges if factions arise or a vituperative dynamic operates among the leaders. More time may be spent arguing over the movement's direction or attempting to build consensus than actually protesting.

Numerous movements have adopted a democratic leadership system in which all participants take part in problem-solving and strategy development.[53] This has numerous advantages. Shared ownership in decision-making can strengthen members' commitment to the movement and help activists acquire skills in negotiating agendas and developing campaigns. It can also enhance creativity and tactical innovation by multiplying the amount of input received. It may also promote greater acceptance of differences among activists, as people deliberate alternative ways to achieve shared goals. However, democratic or consensus-based decision-making takes a great deal of time and energy, which can be detrimental for movements that need to act quickly. Moreover, when activists hold diverging interests or values, discussions can digress into endless debate that deepens internal divisions and interpersonal conflict.[54]

Regardless of the type of leadership that is selected, it is critical that movement participants accept the chosen form of decision-making and perceive their leaders as having authority. If this does not occur, internal dissention will undercut the movement and obstruct its ability to grow.

Member Retention

If a movement has gained sufficient legitimacy and successfully established some type of infrastructure and leadership, then it has the capacity to expand. Organizers must then devise effective strategies, construct a

---

[53] Klandermans, Bert. 1989. "Introduction: Leadership in Decision Making." *International Social Movement Research* 2: 215–224.

[54] For further elaboration of these issues, see the following: Mansbridge, Jane. 1983. *Beyond Adversary Democracy*. Chicago: University of Chicago Press; Polletta, Francesca. 2004. *Freedom Is an Endless Meeting: Democracy in American Social Movements*. Chicago: University of Chicago Press.

collective identity for the group, mobilize resources, and recruit and moti-
vate members. If they successfully accomplish these tasks, the movement
will probably grow. Yet in order to sustain protest and avoid movement
demise, organizers must not only recruit participants but also find ways to
retain them over time.

While we know a great deal about the recruitment process, there is little information about how individuals remain engaged over the long haul.
This is surprising since many movements do in fact lose a proportion of
their participants before they achieve their goals.[55] Although organizers can
continue to recruit members to replace those who drop out, this requires
a great investment of time and energy – not only to bring people into the
movement but also to socialize them into the culture of protest, facilitat-
ing the internalization of movement ideology and an activist identity. As
any business knows, high turnover rates undermine productive capacity
because new workers need time to develop skills and more personnel must
be devoted to training these recruits, which channels human resources away
from the production process. The same holds true in the business of resistance. Even if organizers manage to replace dropouts with new recruits at
a fairly steady pace, they expend significant time and effort on this task
instead of challenging their opponents. Member retention, therefore, is a
critical developmental task for any movement since its vitality and longevity
depend on it.

Given the importance of this task, it is remarkable that only a handful of
studies offer insight into the factors associated with activist retention. Several studies reveal that the intensity of participants' commitment matters.[56]
As Weinstein's research indicates, not all activists join a movement with
similar motivations or comparable levels of dedication. Ideologically motivated, high-commitment activists are more likely to remain engaged over
time, despite movement setbacks and serious risks, whereas those activists
who seek short-term gains are typically the first to abandon the struggle.
Consequently, the proportion of high- and low-commitment participants
can shape a movement's trajectory.[57]

---

[55] Klandermans, Bert. 1997. *The Social Psychology of Protest*. Cambridge, MA: Blackwell Publishers.

[56] Klandermans, Bert. 1997.

[57] Weinstein makes a distinction between high-commitment "investors" (who are willing
to fight and accept great risks in return for the promise of future rewards) and low-
commitment rebel "consumers" who seek immediate gains through their participation

But dedication to a cause is not fixed or constant. It can dissipate or wane, even among the most devoted activists. Since research indicates that strong commitment is correlated with trust in movement leadership, intensity of moral convictions, and the extent of a member's emotional ties to other activists,[58] movement organizers must continually reinforce dedication by reaffirming the legitimacy of their goals, tactics, and leaders, and by deepening interpersonal relationships among participants. Such efforts are necessary if leaders wish to keep their cadres intact.

Reinforcing commitment is only one piece of the retention equation. Leaders must also help individuals overcome the barriers to long-term activism and counter the factors that contribute to members' decision to quit. Especially when it comes to the type of high-risk activism that the Plowshares movement advocates, the determination to persistently resist may require more than personal fortitude and resolve. In his study of participants in the 1964 Freedom Summer campaign, Doug McAdam found that strong ties to other activists and to movement organizations provided a degree of support and accountability that helped participants overcome their fears and carry through with their commitment to civil rights work in Mississippi, despite the very real threat of violent reprisals.[59] Yet Freedom Summer was only a three-month campaign. When we examine longer term, high-risk movements, we find that leaders need to institutionalize practices that help people address the issues that can derail ongoing activism.[60] If leaders do not do so, the heavy costs of participation may result in the depletion of activist ranks and cause the movement to subside.

Cross-National Movements and Cultural Adaptation

While all movements need to establish legitimacy, an infrastruture, and retention practices, those that spread cross-nationally face additional challenges as well. Cross-national movements are those that originate in one

---

in insurgent movements. For further information, see Weinstein, Jeremy M. 2006. *Inside Rebellion: The Politics of Insurgent Violence*. New York: Cambridge University Press.

[58] Barkan, Steven E., Steven F. Cohn, and William H. Whitaker. 1993. "Commitment Across the Miles: Ideological and Microstructural Sources of Membership Support in a National Antihunger Organization." *Social Problems* 40: 362–373; Barkan, Steven E., Steven F. Cohen, and William Whitaker. 1995. "Beyond Recruitment: Predictors of Differential Participation in a National Antihunger Organization." *Sociological Forum* 10: 113–134.

[59] McAdam, Doug. 1988. *Freedom Summer*. New York: Oxford University Press.

[60] Nepstad, Sharon Erickson. 2004. "Persistent Resistance: Commitment and Community in the Plowshares Movement." *Social Problems* 51(1): 47.

country but diffuse to another, as actors abroad adopt the tactics, ideas, and goals of a foreign-born movement.[61] But establishing this movement within their own country requires organizers to modify it to fit their own unique context, which constitutes a fourth developmental challenge: cultural adaptation.[62]

As the Plowshares movement expanded to Europe and Australia, activists in those regions had to adapt the movement in several key ways. First, in many cases they had to recast the religious basis of Plowshares tactics, identity, and ideology to resonate with societies that are significantly more secular than the United States. Second, they found that they could not simply adopt the type of leadership and infrastructure that had evolved in the United States, in part because their participants were motivated by an eclectic set of beliefs and values, unlike the relatively homogeneous religious activists who constitute the American Plowshares movement. Since a movement's culture and ideology often shape the form of leadership that they choose, a simple replication of the U.S. leadership model would not work. Third, European Plowshares activists recognized that they were challenging governments that in some instances were very different from the United States government. This was especially true for those in the Netherlands, Germany, and Sweden – where the state is more accommodating to radical groups and progressive causes – and thus their strategies had to be redefined to suit these distinctive authority structures.

Depending on the way they handled these four development challenges, the international Plowshares movement branches have unfolded in different ways. The German, Dutch, and Australian Plowshares movements failed to accomplish these four developmental tasks and thus never progressed beyond a few sporadic actions, as shown in Figure I.2. In the Swedish case, activists spent a great deal of time and energy trying to establish a workable infrastructure and leadership system. Their efforts were complicated because their membership was heterogeneous, making it difficult to come

---

[61] For further elaboration of these cross-national diffusion processes see McAdam, Doug and Dieter Rucht. 1993. "The Cross-National Diffusion of Movement Ideas." *The Annals of the American Academy of Political and Social Science* 529: 56–74; Snow, David, and Robert D. Benford. 1995. "Alternative Types of Cross-National Diffusion in the Social Movement Arena," pp. 23–39 in Donatella della Porta, Hanspeter Kriesi, and Dieter Rucht (eds.), *Social Movements in a Globalizing World*. London: Macmillan.

[62] For further information about cultural adaptations in cross-national social movements, refer to Chabot, Sean. 2000. "Transnational Diffusion and the African-American Re-invention of the Gandhian Repertoire." *Mobilization* 5: 201–216; Fox, Richard. 1989. *Gandhian Utopia: Experiments with Culture*. Boston: Beacon Press.

to agreements and generating considerable internal conflicts. The Swedish trajectory most closely reflects Figure I.3 – movements that fail to expand. One segment of the British Plowshares movement did successfully overcome these developmental challenges. However, the cultural adaptations that it implemented were so far-reaching that the British movement hardly resembles the originating American movement. This in turn has caused some disagreement between those British activists who want to remain true to the founding vision and spirit of the U.S. Catholic Left and those who are interested in creating a political force that could have a real effect on military policy.

I explore each of these cases in greater depth in subsequent chapters. In Part I, I examine the U.S. Plowshares movement, beginning with an overview of its history and how its leadership and infrastructure evolved. Next I discuss how this movement established *legitimacy of means* by developing an alternative interpretation of Scripture that justifies their controversial tactics and by appealing to international law. Then I provide an account of the ways that U.S. Plowshares leaders have retained activists and sustained the movement in inhospitable conditions without shifting into the abeyance phase. I complete Part I by offering some insight into the developmental challenge the U.S. movement now faces since one of its charismatic leaders has died. In Part II, I turn to the Plowshares movements in Europe and Australia, exploring the particular challenges and factors that shaped each group's trajectory. I conclude with a discussion of these findings and their implications for the study of protest and collective action.

PART I

The U.S. Plowshares Movement

1

Historical Development of the U.S. Plowshares Movement

The Brandywine Peace Community began a vigil at the General Electric (GE) Plant in King of Prussia, Pennsylvania, in the late 1970s. One of Brandywine's members, Bob Smith, initiated the vigil when he learned that GE was making first-strike nuclear weapons at this facility near Philadelphia. Publicly, the Pentagon espoused a policy of Mutually Assured Destruction (MAD). This strategy dictated that the United States must keep pace with or ahead of the Soviet Union's expanding military capacities to maintain a threat of reciprocal annihilation that would deter a Soviet attack. In reality, the United States had shifted from deterrence toward a first-strike strategy whereby a new generation of extremely powerful nuclear weapons could decimate an enemy's military bases, destroying its ability to retaliate.[1]

This new policy produced dramatic innovations in weapons technology. To be effective, the first-strike strategy requires the obliteration of all enemy military targets: command posts, strategic air bases, nuclear storage depots, communication centers, and so forth. But driven by the arms race, the Soviets had massively expanded their military facilities. To efficiently demolish this growing number of targets, the Pentagon initiated the development of multiple individually targeted reentry vehicles (MIRVs). As Robert Aldridge noted, "MIRVs changed the concept of one missile destroying one target to one missile being able to destroy many targets. Many MIRVs can be put on one missile so that more targets can be destroyed without increasing the number of missiles."[2] To illustrate, the older Polaris nuclear

---

[1] Dunn, David H. 1997. *The Politics of Threat: Minuteman Vulnerability in American National Security Policy.* New York: St. Martin's Press.

[2] Aldridge, Robert C. 1983. *First Strike! The Pentagon's Strategy for Nuclear War.* Boston: South End Press, p. 29.

submarines were loaded with 16 missiles and each missile had one warhead, making it capable of destroying 16 targets. By the 1980s, the first-strike Trident nuclear submarines were loaded with 24 missiles and each missile had 14 independently targeted warheads. Hence one Trident submarine could attack 336 different targets; each target would be hit by a bomb that possessed two to three times the explosive power of the bombs dropped on Hiroshima and Nagasaki.[3]

GE was under contract to produce the powerful, ultra-accurate warheads known as the Mark 12A, which were placed on land-based MIRVs called Minuteman and MX missiles. As Brandywine members held their vigil outside the King of Prussia GE plant, they watched while hundreds of workers went into the facility, engaged in what activists call the "business of genocide." They shared this information with others they had met at Pentagon protests, including members of Jonah House – a radical faith community committed to war resistance. Soon, several Jonah House people regularly attended the GE vigils. One of those people was John Schuchardt, who noticed that security was quite minimal around plant No. 9, where the Mark 12A was being developed. As he observed workers entering through a back door, Schuchardt started to think it would be fairly easy to get into the facility. He recalled:

[We knew] these weapons were not defensive; they are criminal and genocidal. I thought, if we believe this, then what is our responsibility? Here we are vigiling but is it possible that a group of us could go in and bring this production line to a halt? These warheads have all these electronic components that would be very vulnerable to a hammer blow.... So I said to Bob, "Can we live with ourselves if we just stand here and vigil?" He and I discussed it and decided it was fraught with all kinds of considerations. I assumed this type of property destruction would involve millions of dollars and I knew the demons would scream. And how would it be accepted by the peace movement? Would it be supported? So we made a list of about ten people that we thought were respected leaders of the peace movement, and we divided it up between us and held confidential conversations.... All the people we talked to said it would cause a jolt, that there would be some who wouldn't understand, and that has been the case.[4]

Schuchardt was obviously aware that this proposed action would stir controversy. But as an experienced defense lawyer, he knew that a legal trial

[3] Aldridge, Robert C. 1983. *First Strike! The Pentagon's Strategy for Nuclear War*. Boston: South End Press, p. 49.

[4] Interview with John Schuchardt, conducted by the author, July 22, 2003.

would provide the opportunity to explain why the activists felt compelled to intervene. So he and several others explored the idea. For nine months, they strategized and prayed together; eventually, eight people chose to act. The eight then set out to resolve such practical issues as gaining access to the King of Prussia facility. They decided that their best opportunity to enter was when hundreds of workers were filing past security gates to start the morning shift. To blend in with the employees, the activists manufactured false identification cards. They also had a nurse draw their blood, which they would carry into the plant in baby bottles. Everyone ensured that their responsibilities and families would be cared for while they were in jail. Finally, the group wrote a press release. While they were drafting the statement, someone turned to the biblical book of Isaiah. They suddenly realized they were enacting Isaiah's vision. Schuchardt stated, "When I was talking about this with Bob [Smith], it was a practical question of how we could render this electronic equipment harmless. We thought we could take in some hammers. I wasn't putting two and two together until the Isaiah passage when we realized, yes, this really will be hammering swords into plowshares."[5]

On September 9, 1980, the months of planning came to fruition. The eight – including Father Daniel Berrigan, Philip Berrigan, Dean Hammer, Father Carl Kabat, Elmer Maas, Sister Anne Montgomery, Molly Rush, and John Schuchardt – arrived at the plant. Montgomery and Kabat spoke with the guard while the other six slipped into the facility. When the guard notified security that several individuals had entered without authorization, the two explained that there was nothing to be concerned about since this was a nonviolent witness. They would be entirely cooperative with GE's staff, they stated, as soon as the group had disarmed as many weapons as they possibly could. Meanwhile, the other activists quickly found the room where the warheads were stored. Molly Rush described the experience:

We had all these alternative plans in the event that we didn't make it. If we got stopped at the back door, we'd kneel and pray. If we got stopped at the security desk or if something was locked and we couldn't get in – we had all these alternative plans. But somehow it felt holy that we actually got into that room because we didn't know where things were inside that building. We just kept walking until we walked into the test area and there were these golden-colored warheads on a table.[6]

---

[5] Interview with John Schuchardt, conducted by the author, July 22, 2003.
[6] Interview with Molly Rush, conducted by the author, March 26, 2001.

Similarly, Daniel Berrigan observed:

> The building is huge: we had no idea exactly where the cones could be found. Of one thing we were sure. If we were to reach the highly classified area of shipping and delivery and were to do there what we purposed, Someone must intervene, give us a lead.... Our Informant is otherwise known in the New Testament as Advocate, Friend, Spirit. We had been at prayer for days. And the deed was done. We eight looked at one another, exhausted, bedazzled with the ease of it all. We had been led in about two minutes, and with no interference to speak of, to the heart of the labyrinth.[7]

Once they located the missile re-entry vehicles, they hammered upon them and poured blood over various security documents. Then they kneeled in a circle, held hands, and prayed.

Shortly thereafter, GE's security staff apprehended the activists and called the police. Once they were arrested, the group released its statement to the press. It read:

> We commit civil disobedience at General Electric because this genocidal entity is the fifth leading producer of weaponry in the U.S. To maintain this position, GE drains $3 million a day from the public treasury, an enormous larceny against the poor. We also wish to challenge the lethal lie spun by GE through its motto, "We bring good things to life." As manufacturers of the Mark 12A reentry vehicle, GE actually prepares to bring good things to death. Through the Mark 12A, the threat of first-strike nuclear war grows more imminent. Thus GE advances the possible destruction of millions of innocent lives.... In confronting GE, we choose to obey God's law of life, rather than a corporate summons to death. Our beating of swords into plowshares is a way to enflesh this biblical call. In our action, we draw on a deep-rooted faith in Christ, who changed the course of history through his willingness to suffer rather than to kill. We are filled with hope for our world and for our children as we join in this act of resistance.[8]

The activists soon learned that they were charged with more than a dozen different felonies and misdemeanors. Schuchardt recalled:

> The reaction from the authorities was vicious and furious. Even as an experienced criminal defense lawyer, I had never guessed that they could multiply and fabricate thirteen separate charges. I was really shocked at the [charges of] aggravated assault, simple assault, terroristic threats, on and on and on. They just opened the

---

[7] Berrigan, Daniel. 1987. "Swords into Plowshares," pp. 54–65 in Arthur J. Laffin and Anne Montgomery (eds.), *Swords into Plowshares: Nonviolent Direct Action for Disarmament*. San Francisco: Harper & Row. Quotation from pp. 56–57.

[8] Berrigan, Daniel. 1987. "Swords into Plowshares," pp. 54–65 in Arthur J. Laffin and Anne Montgomery (eds.), *Swords into Plowshares: Nonviolent Direct Action for Disarmament*. San Francisco: Harper & Row. Quotation from pp. 55, 65.

Pennsylvania statutes...and fired at us with five shotguns, double-barreled. Then the federal authorities said that they would be prosecuting us as well. We had anticipated that we were facing 30 years. We didn't know that we were facing potentially 75 years with all these fabricated charges.[9]

Most of the charges were eventually dropped, but the group was convicted of burglary, conspiracy, and criminal mischief.[10] They received sentences ranging from eighteen months ten years.[11] These long sentences were certainly designed to deter others from similar actions. But the sanctions against the "Plowshares Eight" did not have their intended effect. Within months, another action took place, and a movement was under way that continues into the twenty-first century.

History of the U.S. Peace Movement

Before exploring how the GE Plowshares action launched a full-fledged movement, it is useful to place this unique type of faith-based activism into the broader historical context of anti-war movements in the United States.

The Historic Peace Churches

Christian opposition to war has a long history. Several centuries before Plowshares activists took their hammers into GE's King of Prussia plant, the so-called Historic Peace Churches – the Mennonites, Church of the Brethren, and the Religious Society of Friends (Quakers) – proclaimed that pacifism was integral to their faith. These groups did not participate in military service because they believe it contradicts Christ's commandment to love one's enemies. In the face of persecution, many peace church members

---

[9] Interview with John Schuchardt, conducted by the author, July 22, 2003.

[10] Laffin, Arthur J. and Anne Montgomery. 1987. *Swords into Plowshares: Nonviolent Direct Action for Disarmament.* San Francisco: Harper & Row, pp. 33–34.

[11] The Plowshares Eight appealed their convictions. While awaiting the decision for an appeal, most refused to accept bail. Daniel Berrigan was released after five days, due to a health concern, while Elmer Maas was in jail for seventeen and a half months. Nearly ten years later, they were resentenced by a new magistrate, Judge James Buckingham. Buckingham was considerably more sympathetic, allowing the eight to bring in expert testimony and to introduce international law. The prosecutor made no sentencing recommendation, and General Electric – facing its own legal problems for defrauding the government on a military contract – did not request restitution for the damaged missiles. The eight were sentenced to time served and placed on parole. For more information, see "Plowshares Eight Spared Further Jail" published in *The Washington Post*, April 12, 1990, p. A18.

fled to the United States, where most Mennonites and Brethren took a position of non-resistance. That is, they refused to participate personally in combat but did not directly challenge the state's decision to wage war. Thus, during the Revolutionary and Civil Wars, many paid "exemptions" that allowed them to hire substitutes for their required military service.[12] The Religious Society of Friends, however, reflects a different type of pacifism. Rather than isolating themselves from violence, Quakers actively struggle to abolish war. Many have refused to support the military in any way, including military exemption payments and non-combat services. As a result, they have been fined and imprisoned and some have fled to Canada.[13]

In the twentieth century, many U.S. Mennonites and Brethren shifted closer to the Quaker form of religious pacifism because compulsory draft policies no longer permitted exemption payments. However, the conscription law of 1917 did allow religious pacifists to serve in non-combat positions, and by 1918 the government also offered conscientious objectors the option of working in military-regulated agricultural jobs. Despite this, 450 men rejected these alternatives during World War I, even though the average prison term for such an act was twenty to twenty-five years and some men were even sentenced to death.[14]

Other Pacifist Organizations

About the same time that U.S. Historic Peace Churches were struggling with new conscription laws, three international pacifist organizations emerged. One of the first was the International Fellowship of Reconciliation (IFOR). IFOR developed out of an ecumenical meeting in 1914 in Switzerland, organized by Christians who sought a way to prevent the impending advent of World War I. The war actually broke out before their conference concluded, and two participants, a British Quaker and a German Lutheran, made a commitment to work for peace and reconciliation, even though their nations were at war with each other.[15]

---

[12] Lynd, Staughton, and Alice Lynd. 1995. *Nonviolence in America*. Maryknoll, NY: Orbis, p. xxiv.

[13] Cooney, Robert, and Helen Michalowski. 1987. *The Power of the People: Active Nonviolence in the United States*. Philadelphia: New Society Publishers.

[14] All of the life sentences imposed on conscientious objectors were eventually repealed. For further information, see: Cooney, Robert, and Helen Michalowski. 1987. *The Power of the People: Active Nonviolence in the United States*. Philadelphia: New Society Publishers, p. 45.

[15] Wittner, Lawrence S. 1993. *One World or None: A History of the World Nuclear Disarmament Movement Through 1953*. Stanford: Stanford University Press.

34

The secular counterpart to the Fellowship of Reconciliation is the War Resisters League (WRL). Founded in 1923, the WRL aims to organize all those who agree with their statement of purpose: "War is a crime against humanity. We are therefore determined not to support any kind of war and to strive for the removal of all causes of war."[16] While many people of faith joined the FOR, socialists, anarchists, and secular humanists were drawn to the WRL.

The third pacifist organization is the Women's International League for Peace and Freedom (WILPF). In 1915, the International Congress of Women held a gathering in The Hague, Netherlands, to discuss the destruction wrought by World War I. Those in attendance decided to organize a committee that would send delegations to neutral and warring countries, calling on them to mediate an end to the conflict. A second meeting was held in 1919, when participants voted to make the organization permanent. At its peak, WILPF had about 50,000 members in forty countries.[17]

Nuclear Disarmament Organizations

World War I galvanized pacifist opposition, but IFOR, WRL, and WILPF all suffered membership losses during World War II because many felt that armed struggle was the only viable way to end Hitler's tyranny. However, these organizations were revitalized when the onset of the Cold War generated fresh opposition to nuclear weapons and a renewed call for disarmament. One group that joined the call was the National Committee for a Sane Nuclear Policy, commonly known as SANE. Organizers launched SANE into national prominence in November 1957 when they placed an ad in the *New York Times* that called for an immediate moratorium on nuclear testing.[18] The ad, signed by forty-eight prominent figures, evoked a strong response, and within a year SANE had 25,000 members in 130 chapters throughout the country.[19]

---

[16] Wittner, Lawrence S. 1993. *One World or None: A History of the World Nuclear Disarmament Movement Through 1953.* Stanford: Stanford University Press, p. 40.

[17] Wittner, Lawrence S. 1993. *One World or None: A History of the World Nuclear Disarmament Movement Through 1953.* Stanford: Stanford University Press, p. 41.

[18] For a full account of the ad, see the *New York Times*, November 15, 1957, "Seven Years for a Sane Nuclear Policy," p. A1.

[19] McCrea, Frances B., and Gerald E. Markle. 1989. *Minutes to Midnight: Nuclear Weapons Protest in America.* Newbury Park, CA: Sage Publications.

Whereas SANE used conventional methods of protest and concentrated on educating the public about nuclear weapons, others saw the need for direct resistance. Thus, Quaker activist Lawrence Scott formed an organization called Nonviolent Action Against Nuclear Weapons (eventually renamed the Committee for Nonviolent Action, or CNVA) that brought thirty-five pacifists to the Nevada nuclear test site in 1957. Eleven of the protesters trespassed onto the site and were promptly arrested.[20] One of them was Albert Bigelow, who announced a few months later that he planned to sail into the U.S. Pacific Ocean testing zone. Bigelow explained the motivation behind this campaign:

I am going because, as Shakespeare said, "Action is eloquence." Without some such direct action, ordinary citizens lack the power any longer to be seen or heard by their government. I am going because it is time to *do something* about peace, not just *talk* about peace. . . . I am going because it is cowardly and degrading for me to stand by any longer, to consent, and thus to collaborate in atrocities. . . . When you see something horrible happening, your instinct is to do something about it. You can freeze in fearful apathy or you can even talk yourself into saying that it isn't horrible. I can't do that. I have to act. This is too horrible. We know it. Let's all act.[21]

In May of 1958, Bigelow and his crew set sail. When they arrived in Hawaii, they were told that a federal court had issued an injunction against their action. The crew decided that they would continue their voyage regardless of the consequences, and they headed for the U.S. nuclear test site in Eniwetok. They were soon intercepted by the Coast Guard, which arrested the men on charges of contempt. After they were brought to trial, convicted, and placed on probation, the crew set sail once more, managing to leave U.S. territorial waters before being apprehended. They were sentenced to sixty days in prison, but their action attracted international news coverage that inspired others to complete the campaign. On July 1, 1958, several individuals sailed into the U.S. nuclear test site, temporarily bringing the testing to a halt.[22]

[20] Cooney, Robert, and Helen Michalowski. 1987. *The Power of the People: Active Nonviolence in the United States.* Philadelphia: New Society Publishers.
[21] Bigelow, Albert. 1995 [1958]. "Why I Am Sailing into the Pacific Bomb-Test Area," pp. 178–183 in Staughton Lynd and Alice Lynd (eds.), *Nonviolence in America.* Maryknoll, NY: Orbis. Quotation from pp. 182–183.
[22] This account was drawn from the following sources: Cooney, Robert, and Helen Michalowski. 1987. *The Power of the People: Active Nonviolence in the United States.* Philadelphia: New Society Publishers; and Wittner, Lawrence S. 1997. *Resisting the Bomb:*

These events fueled the growth of the nuclear disarmament movement in the 1950s, with CNVA's emphasis on direct action complementing SANE's more conventional approach. But the momentum slowed significantly in the 1960s as activists' attention shifted toward the civil rights movement and the Vietnam War. In addition, the ratification of the 1963 test ban treaty led many to believe that the United States was willing to negotiate with the Soviet Union to establish safer nuclear policies. This perception was strengthened by subsequent agreements such as the Nuclear Non-Proliferation Treaty of 1968 and the Strategic Arms Limitation Treaty (SALT) in 1972.[23] Despite the fact that nuclear weapons still posed a serious threat, many disarmament groups declined or collapsed during this period, while others – notably the Historic Peace Churches and the older pacifist organizations – drifted into abeyance.[24]

The disarmament movement was far from over, however. In the late 1970s, it was revived by the growing concern about nuclear power. This issue generated national attention in 1977 when a group called the Clamshell Alliance mobilized 1,400 people to nonviolently occupy the Seabrook nuclear power plant construction site in New Hampshire. The action incited new enthusiasm, and the Clamshell Alliance's organizational form and strategy served as a prototype for other groups throughout the country. Within a few years, nearly 1,000 grassroots groups were using this type of direct action to stop nuclear power.[25]

Shortly after the Seabrook action, disarmament and anti-nuclear power activists joined forces, forming a coalition organization called Mobilization for Survival (MfS). When the 1979 Three Mile Island accident occurred at a nuclear power plant in Pennsylvania, MfS ranks expanded and organizers felt the need for a more focused strategy.[26] They therefore asked Randall Forsberg to propose a course of action for the movement. Drawing on various arms control proposals, Forsberg developed a "Call to Halt the Arms Race" that emphasized a "mutual freeze on the testing, production, and

---

A History of the World Nuclear Disarmament Movement, 1954–1970. Stanford, CA: Stanford University Press.

[23] Boyer, Paul. 1984. "From Activism to Apathy: The American People and Nuclear Weapons, 1963–1980." *The Journal of American History* 70 (4): 821–844.

[24] Wittner, Lawrence S. 1984. *Rebels Against War: The American Peace Movement, 1933–1983.* Philadelphia: Temple University Press.

[25] McCrea, Frances B., and Gerald E. Markle. 1989. *Minutes to Midnight: Nuclear Weapons Protest in America.* Newbury Park, CA: Sage Publications.

[26] McCrea, Frances B., and Gerald E. Markle. 1989. *Minutes to Midnight: Nuclear Weapons Protest in America.* Newbury Park, CA: Sage Publications, p. 92.

deployment of nuclear weapons and of missiles and new aircraft designed primarily to deliver nuclear weapons."[27] Support for Forsberg's initiative grew quickly after Ronald Reagan became president in 1981 and demanded the expansion of U.S. nuclear arsenals. As Reagan's policies intensified the arms race, local groups intensified their level of protest, hoping to win Congressional endorsement for the proposed nuclear freeze. By the early 1980s, the disarmament movement was flourishing once again.

The growing momentum of the peace movement evoked responses from numerous Christian groups. The National Council of Churches endorsed the Nuclear Freeze, and its president proclaimed that "Jesus Christ stands in direct opposition to everything nuclear weapons represent."[28] The Freeze proposal was also supported by many mainline Protestant churches and even a few conservative groups, such as the Southern Baptists, who somewhat reluctantly joined Billy Graham in critiquing the nuclear arms race.[29] Most American Catholics backed these disarmament initiatives as well. Although historically supportive of U.S. military policies, Catholic attitudes began to shift during the Vietnam War. By the early 1980s, almost sixty bishops joined the Catholic peace organization *Pax Christi*.[30] An official statement came in 1983 when the National Conference of Catholic Bishops issued a pastoral letter entitled *The Challenge of Peace*. This document – which the bishops endorsed by a vote of 238 to 9 – called for a comprehensive test ban treaty and the eventual elimination of nuclear weapons.[31] When the bishops released their pastoral letter, many members of U.S. religious communities were already supportive of this position, as polls indicated that 78 percent of Catholics, 57 percent of Protestants, and 82 percent of Jews endorsed the Nuclear Freeze proposal.[32]

---

[27] As quoted in Rochon, Thomas R., and David S. Meyer. 1997. *Coalitions and Political Movements: The Lessons of the Nuclear Freeze*. Boulder: Lynne Reinner Publishers, p. 5.

[28] As quoted on page 179 of Lawrence Wittner's (2003) book, *Toward Nuclear Abolition: A History of the World Nuclear Disarmament Movement, 1971 to the Present*. Stanford: Stanford University Press.

[29] Wittner, Lawrence S. 2003. *Toward Nuclear Abolition: A History of the World Nuclear Disarmament Movement, 1971 to the Present*. Stanford: Stanford University Press.

[30] Castelli, Jim. 1984. *The Bishops and the Bomb: Waging Peace in the Nuclear Age*. Garden City, NY: Doubleday; Musto, Robert G. 1986. *The Catholic Peace Tradition*. Maryknoll, NY: Orbis Books.

[31] Wittner, Lawrence S. 2003. *Toward Nuclear Abolition: A History of the World Nuclear Disarmament Movement, 1971 to the Present*. Stanford: Stanford University Press, p. 180.

[32] Wittner, Lawrence S. 2003. *Toward Nuclear Abolition: A History of the World Nuclear Disarmament Movement, 1971 to the Present*. Stanford: Stanford University Press, p. 181.

Table 1.1. *Influences on U.S. Plowshares Activists (percentages)*

Persons	Degree of influence				
	Strong (%)	Moderate (%)	Weak (%)	None (%)	Total
Dorothy Day	83.3	6.7	6.7	3.3	100
Gandhi	80.6	9.7	9.7	0	100
Martin Luther King, Jr.	74.2	19.4	6.4	0	100
Thomas Merton	41.4	41.4	17.2	0	100
Pope John XXIII	20.0	36.7	23.3	20	100
Pope John Paul II	0	7.4	37.0	55.6	100
Augustine	0	7.1	35.7	57.2	100

Catholic Influences on the Plowshares Movement

As this historical overview shows, the Plowshares movement is not the only faith-based peace initiative, nor was it the first to use nonviolent direct action against nuclear weapons. But it is distinct from these other peace groups because of its emphasis on dramatic moral witness, its call for resistance rather than protest, and its ability to endure over time. To understand why the Plowshares movement departed from traditional peace and disarmament organizations, we must examine the Catholic activists and thinkers who influenced it.

Dorothy Day and the Catholic Worker Movement

As the founder of the Catholic Worker movement, Dorothy Day has been called the mother of American Catholic pacifism,[33] and her influence on Plowshares activists is indelible. Philip Berrigan, a central leader in the Plowshares movement, stated that "More than any other institution or individual, the Catholic Worker movement influenced [my brother] Dan and me, especially with its tradition of nonviolent direct action."[34] Clearly, many others in the U.S. Plowshares movement share this sentiment, as 83.3 percent of survey respondents state that Dorothy Day had a very strong influence on them, as shown in Table 1.1.

---

[33] McNeal, Patricia. 1992. *Harder than War: Catholic Peacemaking in Twentieth-Century America.* New Brunswick: Rutgers University Press.

[34] Berrigan, Philip. 1996. *Fighting the Lamb's War: Skirmishes with the American Empire.* Monroe, ME: Common Courage Press, p. 96.

But Dorothy Day was far from a typical Catholic. Prior to her religious conversion in 1927, Day was deeply engaged in progressive causes including socialism, anarchism, and women's suffrage. Despite her involvement in the suffrage movement, she actually felt that voting had little value since the country needed a comprehensive revolution.[35] She believed that direct action of the masses was the only way that substantive change would ever occur. As a result, she never voted.[36] Instead, she immersed herself in political groups committed to the radical transformation of society, but these groups typically viewed the church as a status quo-enforcing institution. Consequently, Day was not a likely candidate for conversion. However, a number of personal events fueled her growing interest in religion. As a young woman, she became pregnant, but her lover threatened to leave her if she carried the child to term. Day agreed to an abortion, but the relationship ended nonetheless. Shortly afterward, she wed a man twenty years her senior and moved to Europe. The marriage ended as the couple quickly discovered that they were not compatible. After returning to the United States, Day met Forster Batterham, an atheist and anarchist with whom she lived in a common-law marriage. Batterham was adamantly opposed to the institution of the family and frequently reminded Day that their relationship was not a marriage but rather a comradeship.[37] But when Day became pregnant and gave birth to a daughter, her spiritual yearnings grew. In her autobiography she wrote:

No human creature could receive or contain so vast a flood of love and joy as I felt after the birth of my child. With this came the need to worship, to adore. I had heard many say that they wanted to worship God in their own way and did not need a church in which to praise Him.... But my very experience as a radical, my whole make-up, led me to want to associate myself with others, with the masses, in praising and adoring God.[38]

Eventually Day decided to join the Catholic Church, even though it led to the painful demise of her relationship with Batterham, who could not tolerate her religiosity.[39]

[35] Day, Dorothy. 1952. *The Long Loneliness*. San Francisco: Harper & Row.

[36] Klejment, Anne. 1996. "The Radical Origins of Catholic Pacifism: Dorothy Day and the Lyrical Left During World War I," pp. 15–32 in Anne Klejment and Nancy L. Roberts (eds.), *American Catholic Pacifism: The Influence of Dorothy Day and the Catholic Worker Movement*. Westport, CT: Praeger.

[37] Day, Dorothy. 1952. *The Long Loneliness*. San Francisco: Harper & Row.

[38] Day, Dorothy. 1952. *The Long Loneliness*. San Francisco: Harper & Row, p. 135.

[39] Roberts, Nancy L. 1984. *Dorothy Day and the Catholic Worker*. Albany: State University of New York Press.

Day initially struggled to integrate her political convictions and her faith. When she met fellow Catholic Peter Maurin, who shared her views, they began producing a newspaper in 1933 called *The Catholic Worker* (imitating the communist periodical, *The Daily Worker*). The paper addressed labor issues, poverty, militarism, and U.S. foreign policy through the perspective of Catholic social teachings. Shortly thereafter, the Catholic Worker movement also established communal farms and "houses of hospitality" that provide food and shelter to the poor. Soon, daily works of mercy in service to the homeless became the defining characteristic of the movement.

Although it is dedicated to serving the destitute, the Catholic Worker movement does not advocate charity but rather social justice. It holds that it is not enough to feed the poor and shelter the homeless; the cause of these social ills must also be addressed.[40] Movement members are thus committed to solidarity with the poor, voluntary poverty, Christian communitarianism, and pacifism. The Catholic Worker movement also embraces a form of anarchism that entails greater personal responsibility for others and less reliance upon the government. Acknowledging the dangers of nationalism, they declare that their sole allegiance is to God.[41] Philip Berrigan explained this anarchist perspective:

> We are to hold the state accountable . . . and call it to justice to the point where it evaporates from view and you no longer need it. We may only need the state to help pick up the garbage, fix the potholes, deliver the mail and do those innocuous chores. If we had our druthers, it would go out of existence. We would have a community of sisters and brothers living in justice and peace with one another.[42]

Under Dorothy Day's leardership, the Catholic Worker movement expanded. Although she possessed many skills that facilitated the movement's growth, Day's greatest contribution was the ability to transform conviction into action. One of her most celebrated campaigns took place in 1955 when New York City held defense drills to prepare the population for a nuclear attack, as mandated by the Civil Defense Act. Anyone

---

[40] Chatfield, Charles. 1996. "The Catholic Worker in the United States Peace Tradition," pp. 1–13 in Anne Klejment and Nancy L. Roberts (eds.), *American Catholic Pacifism: The Influence of Dorothy Day and the Catholic Worker Movement*. Westport, CT: Praeger; Murray, Harry. 1990. *Do Not Neglect Hospitality: The Catholic Worker and the Homeless*. Philadelphia: Temple University Press.

[41] McNeal, Patricia. 1992. *Harder Than War: Catholic Peacemaking in Twentieth-Century America*. New Brunswick: Rutgers University Press.

[42] As quoted in John Dear's "The Life of Resistance: A Conversation with Phil Berrigan." Available online at www.fatherjohndear.org.

who did not participate risked a one-year prison sentence and a $500 fine. But when the drills began – with sirens signaling people to head to their designated fall-out shelters – Day and several Catholic Workers refused to cooperate, gathering in City Hall Park in protest. They were arrested, but the scene was re-enacted the following year, when Day and six Catholic Workers were joined by twenty-three others, mostly members of the War Resisters League and the Fellowship of Reconciliation. With each passing year, the number of protesters grew. Yet Day was heavily criticized for her actions, which landed her in jail on more than one occasion. For instance, some argued that these acts of non-cooperation were primarily symbolic, having little influence on policy. Day responded:

It is a gesture, perhaps, but a necessary one. Silence means consent, and we cannot consent to the militarization of the country without protest. Since we believe that air raid drills are part of a calculated plan to inspire fear of the enemy, instead of the love which Jesus Christ told us we should feel, we must protest these drills. It is an opportunity to show we mean what we write when we repeat over and over that we are put here on this earth to love God and our neighbor.[43]

By 1961, nearly 2,000 people of various affiliations joined the Catholic Worker crowd in the park.[44] New York newspapers proclaimed the civil defense drills an exercise in futility, and city officials eventually ended the practice.[45]

Thomas Merton

Dorothy Day legitimized direct action and civil disobedience as an appropriate Catholic response to expanding militarism. While Day became the model of peace activism for many progressive Catholics, Thomas Merton became their spiritual guide. Born in France in 1915, Merton was orphaned at a young age. His mother, an American, died when he was just six years old, and his father, a New Zealander, passed away before Merton's sixteenth birthday. As he entered adulthood, Merton studied at Cambridge University in England, where he drank heavily and caroused frequently. After fathering a child out of wedlock, he decided to spend time in New

---

[43] Quoted in Forest, Jim. 1997. *Love is the Measure: A Biography of Dorothy Day*. Maryknoll, NY: Orbis Books, p. 99.
[44] McNeal, Patricia. 1992. *Harder Than War: Catholic Peacemaking in Twentieth-Century America*. New Brunswick: Rutgers University Press, p. 91.
[45] Forest, Jim. 1997. *Love is the Measure: A Biography of Dorothy Day*. Maryknoll, NY: Orbis Books.

York with his maternal grandparents. They encouraged him to stay in the United States, where he enrolled at Columbia University. During this time, Merton grew deeply concerned as fascism took root in Spain and Hitler's power grew in Germany. Yet his political convictions were not derived from a faith commitment because religion had not been a central part of his life. This changed, however, when he studied the work of English poet and Jesuit priest Gerard Manley Hopkins. As he read about Hopkins' conversion to Catholicism, he felt a desire for faith stirring within him. "Something began to push me, to prompt me," he wrote. "It was a movement that spoke like a voice. 'What are you waiting for?' it said.... 'Why do you still hesitate? You know what you ought to do. Why don't you do it?'"[46] Merton tried to ignore this inner voice, but eventually went to the local parish and asked how he could convert. Shortly thereafter he was baptized into the Catholic faith.[47]

Merton soon explored the possibility of entering the priesthood, and he eventually joined the Trappists – a contemplative order known for its penitential way of life. At the Trappist monastery, Merton wrote poetry and books on spiritual practice. In the early 1960s, his writings increasingly addressed poverty, nuclear weapons, racism, and war; many of these articles were published in *The Catholic Worker*. Although he was occasionally silenced by his superiors, some of whom considered *The Catholic Worker* a communist-controlled publication, he took heart as Pope John XXIII released the encyclical *Pacem in Terris* (Peace on Earth). In this document, the pope stated that war was no longer a viable option for resolving international disputes and he condemned all threats to life, including nuclear weapons. As a monk, and later a religious hermit, Merton was prohibited from taking an active role in the burgeoning Catholic peace movement. Yet his writings, which emphasized the spiritual roots of peacemaking, were widely read by progressive Catholics. And as the Cold War intensified and the arms race expanded, Merton's call for a strong Christian response grew clearer. In one issue of *The Catholic Worker*, he put forth the following plea.

What are we to do? The duty of the Christian in this crisis is to strive with all his power and intelligence, with his faith, his hope in Christ, and love for God and man, to do the one task which God has imposed upon us in the world today. That task is

---

[46] Forest, Jim. 1991. *Living with Wisdom: A Life of Thomas Merton*. Maryknoll, NY: Orbis Books, p. 53.

[47] Forest, Jim. 1991. *Living with Wisdom: A Life of Thomas Merton*. Maryknoll, NY: Orbis Books, p. 54.

to work for the total abolition of war. There can be no question that unless war is abolished the world will remain constantly in a state of madness and desperation in which, because of the immense destructive power of modern weapons, the danger of catastrophe will be imminent and probable at every moment everywhere. Unless we set ourselves immediately to this task, both as individuals and in our political and religious groups, we tend by our very passivity and fatalism to cooperate with the destructive forces that are leading inexorably to war.... Christians must become active in every possible way, mobilizing all their resources for the fight against war.[48]

In this "fight against war," Merton called peace activists to detach themselves from the results of their efforts. Rather than calculating the likelihood of success or failure, he emphasized that no good action was ever a waste, even if it did not yield the desired outcome:

Do not depend on the hope of results. When you are doing ... an apostolic work, you may have to face the fact that your work will be apparently worthless and even achieve no result at all, if not perhaps results opposite to what you expect. As you get used to this idea, you start more and more to concentrate not on the results but on the value, the rightness, the truth of the work itself.... As for the big results, they are not in your hands or mine, but they can suddenly happen, and we can share in them.... The great thing, after all, is to live, not to pour out your life in the service of a myth: and we turn the best things into myths. If we can get free from the domination of causes and just serve Christ's truth, you will be able to do more and will be less crushed by the inevitable disappointments.... The real hope ... is not in something we think we can do, but in God who is making something good out of it in some way we cannot see. If we can do His will, we will be helping in this process. But we will not necessarily know all about it beforehand.[49]

Catholic Resistance to the Vietnam War

Merton's and Day's influence on a younger generation of Catholics became evident during the Vietnam War. Day had keen foresight on this issue, writing as early as 1954 that the U.S. military was going to play an increasingly influential role in Vietnam as French rule declined.[50] As this became a reality, many progressive Catholics responded. In fact, the first protest against

[48] *The Catholic Worker* (New York), October 1961.

[49] Quoted from "Letter to Jim Forest, February 21, 1966" (1985), pp. 294–297 in William H. Shannon (ed.), *The Hidden Ground of Love: The Letters of Thomas Merton on Religious Experience and Social Concerns.* New York: Farrar, Straus & Giroux.

[50] Klejment, Anne, and Nancy L. Roberts 1996. "The Catholic Worker and the Vietnam War." pp. 153–169 in Anne Klejment and Nancy L. Roberts (eds.), *American Catholic Pacifism: The Influence of Dorothy Day and the Catholic Worker Movement.* Westport, CT: Praeger.

U.S.–Vietnamese relations was instigated in 1963 by two young Catholic Workers, Tom Cornell and Chris Kearns. Outraged over South Vietnam's repression of Buddhist monks, the two picketed the home of the South Vietnamese representative to the United Nations. They carried a sign stating, "We demand an end to U.S. military support of Diem's regime."[51] In little more than a week, nearly 200 people had joined the picket, which was covered by ABC news.[52] Two years later, Dorothy Day set the stage for further Catholic Worker involvement in the anti-war movement by signing a public declaration of resistance to the U.S. war in Vietnam. Known as the "complicity statement," this document called on people to refuse to (1) serve in the armed forces; (2) produce military equipment; or (3) cooperate with the government's war plans in any way.[53] Numerous Catholics signed the declaration even though the Universal Military Training and Service Act deemed it illegal to advise draftees to refuse military service.[54]

Meanwhile, some Catholic radicals were considering alternatives to polite forms of protest. The first step toward more provocative expressions of dissent occurred when Cornell and Kearns burned their draft cards. When *Life* magazine published a photograph of Kearns dropping a draft card into a burning cauldron, several members of Congress introduced the Rivers Amendment, which set stiff penalties for anyone following suit. The first person to violate the new law was another young Catholic Worker, David Miller. In October 1965, in the largest anti-war rally to date, Miller stood in front of a crowd in New York City and set his draft card on fire. He served nearly two years in prison for his public defiance of the Rivers Amendment. Shortly after Miller's action, five more men burned their draft cards – three of them Catholic Workers. Eventually, 3,500 draft cards were publicly destroyed through various means, essentially rendering the Rivers Amendment unenforceable.[55]

---

[51] Meconis, Charles A. 1979. *With Clumsy Grace: The American Catholic Left, 1961–1975*. New York: Seabury Press, p. 7
[52] Zaroulis, Nancy, and Gerald Sullivan. 1984. *Who Spoke Up? American Protest against the War in Vietnam, 1963–1975*. Garden City, NY: Doubleday, pp. 12–13.
[53] Klejment, Anne, and Nancy L. Roberts. 1996. "The Catholic Worker and the Vietnam War," pp. 153–169 in Anne Klejment and Nancy L. Roberts (eds.), *American Catholic Pacifism: The Influence of Dorothy Day and the Catholic Worker Movement*. Westport, CT: Praeger, p. 160.
[54] Colaianni, James. 1968. *The Catholic Left: The Crisis of Radicalism within the Church*. Philadelphia: Chilton Book Company.
[55] McNeal, Patricia. 1992. *Harder Than War: Catholic Peacemaking in Twentieth-Century America*. New Brunswick: Rutgers University Press.

The draft card burnings inspired other Catholics to create new tactics. One of these individuals was Philip Berrigan, a Josephite priest, who called for a shift from protest to resistance. He felt that merely expressing opposition to the Vietnam war was not enough to stop it and that the faith-based peace movement needed to actually subvert Pentagon practices. After contemplating various courses of action, Berrigan and Catholic Worker Tom Lewis decided to directly obstruct the military's conscription system. Lewis recounted:

We, Phil Berrigan and myself, had already been in the military. As far as our burning draft cards, it didn't make any sense because we really weren't liable. It was a gesture, with no personal risk. . . . So I was searching along with Phil for a really creative, positive response to what was happening . . . I had great respect for people who were considering immolating themselves – yet there had to be some kind of alternative to that. Then, of course, Dorothy Day and her philosophy about filling the jails to put a lot of pressure on the system. . . . Maybe that was the place to be; at this point in history maybe the *only* human response to that was to be in jail. Because it *was mad!* . . . So it was the consideration of really being in jail which led to the other thing: What do you do to get locked up? We decided to do something really strong and the connection with draft cards was very important. . . . So we came up with that as a real possibility – the idea of doing *something* with the draft records. Doing something, we decided, was pouring blood on them, keeping the symbolism, the Christian symbolism of blood, as something of bloodletting and also something of reconciliation.[56]

Eventually two others, Reverend James Mengel and David Eberhardt, enacted the plan with Lewis and Berrigan. In October 1967, the four raided the draft board located at the Customs House in Baltimore, Maryland. When they entered the building, they discovered fortuitously that the security guard had left his post, so they entered the draft board offices with ease. When they arrived at the reception desk, Philip Berrigan, wearing his clerical collar, asked if he could check the records of his parishioners. The secretary refused. Berrigan described what happened next:

Three of us broke through this little gate and entered the draft board proper, yanking open draft files and pouring our blood over them. This lasted about a minute, because the secretaries were furious, grabbed us from behind, and locked their arms around our waists. We didn't resist or try to break loose. We sat down and waited to be arrested. Jim Mengel, having made a last-minute decision not to pour blood, handed out copies of the New Testament. The enraged clerks threw

[56] Lewis as quoted in Meconis, Charles A. 1979. *With Clumsy Grace: The American Catholic Left, 1961–1975.* New York: Seabury Press, pp. 19–20.

them back in his face. Afterward, we were accused of frightening the secretaries, but I don't remember them showing fear. They were enraged, and when they testified against us they were still angry. We had invaded the state's sanctuary, poured our blood over...its sacred files. We had damaged property, a crime far greater than destroying human life.[57]

The four men were prosecuted and found guilty. While they were out on bail awaiting sentencing, Philip Berrigan began plotting another raid. This time he invited his brother, Jesuit Daniel Berrigan, to join him. In May of 1968, the two brother priests, along with seven others, walked into the draft board office in Catonsville, Maryland. They grabbed about 600 files, took them out to the facility's parking lot, and doused them with napalm – the jellied gasoline that had burned so many Vietnamese children. They released a statement to the press that read: "We destroy these draft records not only because they exploit our young men but also because they represent misplaced power concentrated in the ruling class of America.... We confront the Catholic Church, other Christian bodies, and the synagogues of America with their silence and cowardice in the face of our country's crimes."[58]

This second raid gained considerable media coverage, and in contrast to the Baltimore action, the presiding judge allowed the accused to explain why they had committed this act. After offering their testimony, Daniel Berrigan summarized the group's sentiments in a poem:

> Our apologies good friends
> for the fracture of good order
> the burning of paper instead of children
> the angering of orderlies in the front parlor of the charnel house
> we could not so help us God do otherwise
> for we are sick at heart
> our hearts give us no rest for thinking of the Land of
> > burning
> > children.[59]

When the trial came to a close, the judge instructed the jury to ignore the testimony of the nine. He stated that their motive was not relevant and the jury should simply determine whether the group had committed the

---

[57] Berrigan, Philip. 1996. *Fighting the Lamb's War: Skirmishes with the American Empire*. Monroe, ME: Common Courage Press, p. 89.

[58] Lewis, Daniel. 2002. "Philip Berrigan, Former Priest and Peace Advocate in the Vietnam War Era, Dies at 79." *The New York Times*, December 8, 2002, p. A36.

[59] As quoted in Berrigan, Philip. 1996. *Fighting the Lamb's War: Skirmishes with the American Empire*. Monroe, ME: Common Courage Press, p. 105.

crimes of which they were accused. After two hours of deliberation, the jury returned a verdict of guilty on three charges – interference with the Selective Service Act of 1967, destruction of Selective Service records, and destruction of U.S. government property. All nine were sentenced to three years in prison.[60]

The draft board raids marked a departure from traditional tactics of the faith-based peace movement. This strategic innovation was applauded by some, such as Tom Cornell, who hoped this would take the anti-war movement into a bold new direction. Cornell wrote:

The burning of the Catonsville files signals a shift in tactics, from nonviolent protest to resistance to revolution.... The Catonsville Action may prove to be a powerful model for the next phase of nonviolent revolution in America.... The action was small, carefully planned by people who knew and trusted each other, and easily controlled. It was designed so that no one would be in danger of physical harm nor otherwise violated. It was aimed at things, at property that is violating young men and causing immense grief, suffering and death around the world, property that has no right to exist, but which current folklore invest with a certain mystical inviolability. The participants in the action made no effort to conceal their identities. They know what penalties they face and do not shrink from paying the price.... Some of our friends were shocked by the Catonsville Action, primarily, I suspect, because of the terrible price that is likely to be exacted. Do they think that revolutions come for the asking, or that its victims are always anonymous? Even a nonviolent revolution, or rather, especially a nonviolent revolution will demand blood, our blood, not theirs, and that's the difference.[61]

Numerous activists followed the path that the Berrigans and their colleagues blazed. The exact number of draft board raids that occurred between 1967 and 1971 is unknown, but estimates range from 53 to more than 250.[62]

Others in the peace movement were cautious about this new impulse, concerned that property destruction exceeded the limits of nonviolence and set a dangerous precedent. Shortly after the Catonsville action, Thomas Merton wrote:

The napalming of draft records by the Baltimore [sic] Nine is a special and significant case because it seems to indicate a borderline situation: as if the Peace Movement

---

[60] Berrigan, Philip. 1996. *Fighting the Lamb's War: Skirmishes with the American Empire*. Monroe, ME: Common Courage Press, p. 108.

[61] As quoted in Cornell, Tom. 1990 [1968]. "Nonviolent Napalm in Catonsville," pp. 203–208 in Angie O'Gorman (ed.), *The Universe Bends Toward Justice*. Philadelphia: New Society Publishers, pp. 206–208.

[62] McNeal, Patricia. 1992. *Harder Than War: Catholic Peacemaking in Twentieth Century America*. New Brunswick: Rutger University Press, p. 197.

too were standing at the very edge of violence.... The Peace Movement may be escalating beyond peaceful protest. In which case it may also be escalating into self-contradiction.

What were the Berrigans and others trying to do? It seems to me that this was an attempt at prophetic nonviolent provocation. It bordered on violence and was violent to the extent that it meant pushing some good ladies around and destroying some government property. The evident desperation of the Baltimore Nine has, however, frightened more than it has edified. The country is in a very edgy psychological state. Americans feel terribly threatened.... In such a case, the use of nonviolence has to be extremely careful and clear.[63]

The "Catonsville Nine" responded by stating that their action was nonviolent because it protected life by destroying government-issued licenses to kill. Furthermore, they argued that "Some property has no right to exist. Hitler's gas ovens, Stalin's concentration camps, atomic-biological-chemical weaponry, files of conscription and slum properties are examples."[64]

There was ambivalence about these tactics among Catholic Workers as well.[65] Dorothy Day initially gave her approval, calling the raids a "very strong and imaginative witness" that fell within the parameters of nonviolence. She soon changed her opinion, however, concerned about the potential for unintended violence, especially by young radicals who were less disciplined. She was also deeply concerned about the prison terms that inevitably followed the raids because she saw that young draft card burners were ill-prepared for the emotional and mental toll caused by incarceration.[66] Jim Forest, who raided a draft board in Milwaukee, stated: "In the end, she [Day] didn't agree with what we had done, but she treasured us and supported us, wrote about us, published our things in the newspaper.... But

---

[63] Merton as quoted in Meconis, Charles A. 1979. *With Clumsy Grace: The American Catholic Left, 1961–1975.* New York: Seabury Press, pp. 36–37.

[64] As quoted in Cornell, Tom. 1990 [1968]. "Nonviolent Napalm in Catonsville," pp. 203–208 in Angie O'Gorman (ed.), *The Universe Bends Toward Justice.* Philadelphia: New Society Publishers, pp. 205–206.

[65] For a detailed account of Dorothy Day's evolving attitude toward the draft board raids, see Anne Klejment's "War Resistance and Property Destruction: The Catonsville Nine Draft Board Raid and Catholic Worker Pacifism," pp. 272–309 in Patrick G. Coy (ed.), *A Revolution of the Heart: Essays on the Catholic Worker.* Philadelphia: Temple University Press.

[66] Klejment, Anne, and Nancy L. Roberts. 1996. "The Catholic Worker and the Vietnam War," pp. 153–169 in Anne Klejment and Nancy L. Roberts (eds.), *American Catholic Pacifism: The Influence of Dorothy Day and the Catholic Worker Movement.* Westport, CT: Praeger.

she also made it clear that this was not her idea of the best way to bring about the change that we wanted."[67]

The draft board raid controversy expanded further when the Catonsville Nine were ordered to turn themselves into federal authorities. Marking another calculated break from traditional nonviolence, four of the nine refused,[68] instead going underground. Daniel Berrigan described the process that led to this decision:

There was a sense that we were facing both a great opportunity and a great danger. On the one hand, it was a strict canon of nonviolence that one took the consequences of illegal activity and paid up. On the other, there was the war. When would it end, what had we accomplished, if anything, toward its ending? We had to admit it. Our action in Catonsville, and all the draft board actions since then, had failed even to mitigate the war. And the question arose: must we submit to the punishing arm of the same powers that were pursuing the war?

It was a harsh dilemma, an utterly new field of moral decision. The alternative to turning ourselves in was also narrow. It meant that we must disappear underground, become fugitives, involve others in a network of conspiracy, risk further charges and longer sentences. None of us had ever lived in the underground: its demands, its loneliness, its cutoff from friendship and work. These were daunting realities, even in prospect. There was also the question of public understanding, and our responsibility. Consistency and moral coherence were much on our minds. We surmised we had helped the Catholic community to make the war a matter of debate, then of unease, even of scorn. We had helped raise questions never before argued in the church.... These were solid achievements; their undoing would be a tragedy for all concerned. We knew it, and the knowledge hurt. But if there was hurt, there was also a strange and fierce elation. A choice before us: to delay the unwarrantedly high price exacted for an act of conscience! And more: a chance to underscore once more, in a highly imaginative way, our opposition to war. My own decision was fairly easy; but I feared for Philip, who already faced a long sentence, six years. Further interference with the gears of law would bring on a storm of retaliation. But I knew at heart that he would not submit: the truth was the only burden he chose to carry.[69]

---

[67] As quoted in Klejment, Anne, and Nancy L. Roberts. 1996. "The Catholic Worker and the Vietnam War," pp. 153–169 in Anne Klejment and Nancy L. Roberts (eds.), *American Catholic Pacifism: The Influence of Dorothy Day and the Catholic Worker Movement*. Westport, CT: Praeger.

[68] At this point, there were only eight surviving members of the Catonsville Action. David Darst, a member of the Christian Brothers community, had been killed in an automobile accident in Minnesota.

[69] Berrigan, Daniel. 1987. *To Dwell in Peace: An Autobiography*. San Francisco: Harper and Row, pp. 238–239.

After living underground for a short time, Philip Berrigan decided to make a public appearance and then turn himself in. He found a priest in New York City, Father Harry Browne, who made the arrangements with the Federal Bureau of Investigation (FBI). The FBI agreed to allow Browne to hold a "paraliturgical surfacing service,"[70] at which Berrigan would make a statement and then submit to arrest. But Berrigan never had the chance to make his speech. Before the service, the FBI surrounded the church, broke into the priest's apartment with guns drawn, and handcuffed him.

Daniel Berrigan made similar plans to surrender after an anti-war event on Cornell University's campus. FBI agents were in the crowd that night, waiting for the moment to seize him. But, much to Dan Berrigan's surprise, that is not what happened. Instead, after a theater group used giant puppets to re-enact the Last Supper and Father Berrigan finished his speech, the lights came down on the stage. Someone asked Berrigan if he wanted to disappear once more. He said yes. Then, he explained, "In the disarray and noise and darkness, I was given hasty instructions. Something large and encompassing went over my head; a pole was thrust into my hand; I was instructed sotto voce to grasp an unknown hand, and follow, follow. Thus concealed under the immense papier-mâché [puppet], I made my escape."[71] He managed to dodge the FBI for a few more months, making periodic public appearances to denounce the war, until he was eventually arrested at a friend's home in Rhode Island.

As the Catonsville activists began serving their sentences, many felt that the public would forget them. But they were in the national headlines again when FBI Director J. Edgar Hoover pressed charges against a number of Catholic Left activists. Hoover accused them of plotting to kidnap presidential advisor Henry Kissinger. These charges were derived from letters furtively sent between Philip Berrigan and Elizabeth McAlister, who discussed the possibility of making a citizens' arrest of Kissinger for war crimes. Berrigan was also charged with conspiring to destroy utilities under government buildings. He commented:

We had looked at the utilities under government buildings, in order to investigate how we might shut off the heat. . . . We would shut off the heat and then, as workers left their buildings, hand out leaflets denouncing the war in Vietnam. We weren't

[70] Meconis, Charles. 1979. *With Clumsy Grace: The American Catholic Left, 1961–1975*. New York: Seabury Press, p. 68.
[71] Berrigan, Daniel. 1987. *To Dwell in Peace: An Autobiography*. San Francisco: Harper & Row, p. 244.

going to risk anyone's life, and we never talked about blowing up heating ducts. That was the government's version, which had nothing to do with reality . . . but the FBI was looking for me and I couldn't pull this action off. No one else wanted to, and that ended our conspiracy.[72]

Despite the fact that the government had no solid evidence, seven people were charged and brought to trial in Harrisburg, Pennsylvania, in 1972.[73]

This was a sobering time for the movement. Not only did the "Harrisburg Seven" face potential life sentences, but suspicion grew as activists wondered how the FBI had obtained its information. Moreover, many people were shocked when the trial revealed that two of the accused – Father Philip Berrigan and Sister Elizabeth McAlister – had an intimate relationship. In 1969, the two had secretly taken wedding vows. They did not make their marriage public because, as Berrigan explained, "Elizabeth didn't want to leave her community . . . I was facing six years in prison . . . Liz would then be alone, without financial and moral support from her religious order. We agreed that a public announcement would not be a good thing, and she remained with her order until we announced our marriage three years later."[74] Many activists felt betrayed by their secrecy; others were angry, feeling that the whole affair might discredit the movement. Some were perplexed since Berrigan had been a vocal proponent of celibacy as part of a revolutionary lifestyle. He had criticized those within the Catholic Left who had married because he felt that marriage would make people less willing to take risks to end the war.[75]

The Harrisburg trial had the potential to bring the Catholic Left movement to a halt because it tied up activists' time and energy and fostered internal tensions. By the time the prosecution had finished its case and the jury deliberated, the future of the movement seemed to be at stake. When the verdict came in, the courtroom was packed with Catholic Left activists and supporters. To nearly everyone's surprise, the jurors acquitted the defendants on all counts, causing the crowd to cheer wildly as

[72] Berrigan, Philip. 1996. *Fighting the Lamb's War: Skirmishes with the American Empire.* Monroe, ME: Common Courage Press, p. 126.

[73] Polner, Murray, and Jim O'Grady. 1997. *Disarmed and Dangerous: The Radical Lives and Times of Daniel and Philip Berrigan.* New York: Basic Books.

[74] Berrigan, Philip. 1996. *Fighting the Lamb's War: Skirmishes with the American Empire.* Monroe, ME: Common Courage Press, p. 154.

[75] Berrigan, Philip. 1971. *Prison Journals of a Priest Revolutionary.* New York: Ballantine Books, p. 210.

the defendants broke into a chorus of "Amazing Grace." Although some defendants still had to finish their prison terms for draft board raid convictions, there was nevertheless a sense of victory and hope that Catholic war resistance would continue.[76]

Establishing Movement Leadership and Structure

The Catholic Left's struggle against the Vietnam War fostered a new style of resistance. It also laid the groundwork that the Plowshares movement would build upon as it emerged and faced the developmental challenges of creating a movement infrastructure and establishing leadership. The issue of leadership was easily addressed since the draft board raids thrust Philip and Daniel Berrigan into the national limelight. As the media focused on these two, they proved to be passionate, eloquent spokespersons for the Catholic Left. An award-winning poet, Daniel Berrigan added an artistic flair to the movement's message. Philip Berrigan was the tactical innovator who had a remarkable ability to inspire people to acts of courage and sacrifice. One activist commented, "Phil was a giant. He was unwavering and clear . . . and he was able to challenge people to take personal responsibility . . . to take great risks with their own lives for the purpose of doing what needs to be done. He was a military commander in that way."[77] The fact that both Berrigans were priests undoubtedly increased their moral authority as well. Yet much of their credibility was derived from the fact that they were not simply talking heads; they had courageously placed themselves on the front line of this nonviolent revolution and had paid the price for doing so. The admiration they evoked quickly transformed these brothers into charismatic leaders who guided the burgeoning Plowshares movement in the 1980s.

Plowshares activists also inherited a basic movement infrastructure that had evolved among Catholic peace activists. The movement's organizational form is essentially an extension of Catholic Worker communitarianism in which members pool their resources and live together in "houses of hospitality."[78] Dorothy Day and Peter Maurin established the

---

[76] Meconis, Charles A. 1979. *With Clumsy Grace: The American Catholic Left, 1961–1975*. New York: Seabury Press, p. 130.

[77] Interview with anonymous Plowshares activist, conducted by author, August 22, 2003.

[78] O'Gorman, Angie, and Patrick G. Coy. 1988. "Houses of Hospitality: A Pilgrimage into Nonviolence," pp. 239–271 in Patrick G. Coy (ed.), *A Revolution of the Heart: Essays on the Catholic Worker*. Philadelphia: Temple University Press.

first Catholic Worker house in New York City, but they called others to form houses of hospitality in locations throughout the United States and abroad.[79] People responded, and today (2008) there are 185 Catholic Worker communities worldwide.[80] Each community independently determines its goals and activities through a consensus process, but the communities are linked together in a loose network that communicates through newsletters, retreats, and visits. In short, the movement had developed a decentralized organizational structure in which decision-making occured at the grassroots level. This was coupled, however, with deference to Dorothy Day's leadership and authority. As Anne Klejment notes, "In theory, each Catholic Worker member was free to follow conscience while the community defined its practices and goals. Yet the Worker was hardly a democratic movement. While Day did not oversee all details of the movement, she sometimes chose to exert leadership vigorously . . ."[81]

This combination of charismatic authority and a decentralized organizational form has worked well for the Catholic Worker movement, which is now seventy-five years old. This structure has also enabled Catholic Workers to avoid some of the issues that typically cause movement demise. For instance, the movement's anarchist orientation has kept it from being co-opted by the government or moving toward conventional forms of political participation. Moreover, the commitment to voluntary poverty means that participants do not devote great amounts of staff time to fund-raising, because their overhead costs are low. Yet many activists believe that the emphasis on community is the main reason why the Catholic Worker movement has persisted, even during World War II when it faced great hostility for its pacifist stance.

Learning from the Catholic Worker example, Plowshares leaders decided to root their movement in faith-based intentional communities. Experiences in the anti-Vietnam War movement further underscored their decision. Philip Berrigan, for instance, became convinced of the necessity of community while he was serving time in a federal prison for draft board

---

[79] Murray, Harry. 1990. *Do Not Neglect Hospitality: The Catholic Worker and the Homeless.* Philadelphia: Temple University Press.

[80] This number reflects the movement's own estimate (see www.catholicworker.org).

[81] Klejment, Anne. 1988. "War Resistance and Property Destruction: The Catonsville Nine Draft Board Raid and Catholic Worker Pacifism," pp. 272–309 in Patrick G. Coy (ed.), *A Revolution of the Heart: Essays on the Catholic Worker*. Philadelphia: Temple University Press. Quote from page 294.

raids. He and other anti-war prisoners met four or five times a week for prayer, Bible study, political discussion, and action.[82] He argued that it was this fellowship that sustained him:

During my years behind bars, I had seen young men succumb to despair. Arriving with high ideals, they broke under the strain of prison life.... Others withdrew into sullen shells, devoured by anger and loneliness. They had taken a principled stand, but without the support of a loving community they couldn't withstand the brutality of prison.... Resisters cannot persist and survive without community. Sooner or later, they will be frustrated and crushed.[83]

Thus, while the Berrigans built community inside prison, Elizabeth McAlister and other activists were forming intentional communities on the outside. After the Harrisburg trial, about a dozen people held a series of meetings in New York to discuss the future of the Catholic Left movement. McAlister had written a document that suggested five possible options they might pursue: "(1) organizing more actions of civil disobedience, (2) organizing for the McGovern candidacy, (3) linking up with national peace organizations, (4) speaking and writing, and (5) making an effort to build a nonviolent movement through developing resistance communities."[84] They chose to concentrate primarily on the last option.

In 1973, Catholic Left activists rented a row house in one of Baltimore's poorest neighborhoods. Philip Berrigan, who had recently been released from prison, Elizabeth McAlister, and several others moved in, naming their community Jonah House. Following the Catholic Worker tradition, Jonah House places a strong emphasis on voluntary poverty, recognizing that it is the U.S. population's obsession with possessions and property that has led to the stockpiling of weapons to protect them. Thus members hold all resources in common, working as independent painting contractors when necessary to earn funds for basic living expenses. Although Jonah House is strongly influenced by the Catholic Worker, it distinguishes itself by defining its central vocation as war resistance. While Jonah House members do works of mercy, such as gathering food to distribute to the needy,

---

[82] Berrigan, Philip, and Elizabeth McAlister. 1989. *The Time's Discipline: The Beatitudes and Nuclear Resistance*. Baltimore: Fortkamp Publishing.

[83] Berrigan, Philip. 1996. *Fighting the Lamb's War: Skirmishes with the American Empire*. Monroe, ME: Common Courage Press, pp. 166–167.

[84] Meconis, Charles A. 1979. *With Clumsy Grace: The American Catholic Left, 1961–1975*. New York: Seabury Press, p. 132.

their primary goal is abolishing war. Plowshares activist John Heid offers a metaphor that justifies this division of labor:

We use the analogy of a truck out of control. The driver is not in the seat, the emergency brake is off, and the truck is going down a hill, rolling over people. There are dead and wounded behind the truck. The dead need to be buried, a work of mercy. The wounded need to be tended to, a work of mercy. But the truck keeps rolling over people. Who is going to get in the truck and hit the brake? ... So we need people behind the truck to tend to the wounded and bury the dead and we need people to maybe even get in front of the truck or try to jump inside. I think that's the balance of what the Catholic Worker and the Plowshares movement are trying to do – to recognize that we've got this war apparatus, this violent apparatus, and the brake is off and the driver is out and we have a responsibility to respond to that as best as we can.[85]

In addition to its direct action against militarism, Jonah House began building connections with other faith-based communities committed to social justice. They forged relationships with the progressive evangelical group *Sojourners* and the interfaith Community for Creative Nonviolence (CCNV), both in Washington DC, Koinonia Partners in Georgia, and the Pacific Life and Ground Zero Communities in Washington State, to name just a few such communities. As a way to tangibly support one another and keep these networks intact, Jonah House began sponsoring "Faith and Resistance retreats" for reflection, discussion, and action.

Organizers soon decided to hold these retreats several times a year – during the Holy Week of Easter, on the anniversary of the Hiroshima and Nagasaki attacks, and on the Catholic commemoration of the Massacre of the Innocents, shortly after Christmas. They are held in Washington D.C. to enable participants to engage in "witness actions" at the White House and the Pentagon. As the Faith and Resistance retreats became established events, participants dubbed themselves the Atlantic Life Community because activists come mostly from the mid-Atlantic region of the East Coast. Through these retreats, Jonah House created a movement infrastructure that parallels the Catholic Worker network except that these faith communities place the highest priority on war resistance.[86]

In the first few years, Jonah House and the Atlantic Life Community acted against the U.S. war in Indochina by digging graves on the White

---

[85] Interview with John Heid, conducted by the author, July 24, 2003.

[86] Klejment, Anne. 1988. "War Resistance and Property Destruction: The Catonsville Nine Draft Board Raid and Catholic Worker Pacifism," pp. 272–309 in Patrick G. Coy (ed.), *A Revolution of the Heart: Essays on the Catholic Worker*. Philadelphia: Temple University Press.

House lawn and pouring blood at the Pentagon. But when the Vietnam War ended, they contemplated ways to apply their provocative tactics to the nuclear arms race. As political analysts discussed the possibility of "limited nuclear wars," Jonah House residents decided to take a stand against the government's policies and the church's silence. They found their opportunity for action when John Schuchardt shared his thoughts about breaking into the General Electric plant. Eventually Philip and Daniel Berrigan agreed to participate, and others were recruited from the Catholic Left network. Schuchardt recalled, "How did it come to these eight people? It was all word of mouth, personal ties, face-to-face conversations. It was [possible] because of the trust in the community and the pre-existing relationships that had already been built among us."[87]

It was thus out of this infrastructure that the idea of the Plowshares Eight action was conceived, gestated, and birthed. At first, it was only intended to be a one-time campaign. But just three months later, Peter DeMott – Vietnam veteran, former seminarian, Catholic Worker, and Jonah House resident – carried out the second Plowshares action. Although most Plowshares campaigns are carefully planned for many months, DeMott acted spontaneously. He had gone to the General Dynamics Electric Boat shipyard in Groton, Connecticut, for the christening of the USS *Baltimore* – a fast-attack submarine. The public was invited to the event, and several activists went to protest the escalating militarism that this submarine symbolized. While they were in the shipyard, DeMott noticed that a Trident submarine was under construction at another dock. He recalled:

[There was] this huge Trident submarine under construction. It wasn't in the water, it was on the dock itself, surrounded by this snow fence – nothing very substantial. I also noticed that there was a van that belonged to the Electric Boat shipyard, General Dynamics, parked there and it had the keys in the ignition. I thought, wouldn't it be neat to use this vehicle to make a statement against the Trident submarine and against nuclear weaponry. I just saw it sitting there and I thought – why not? So I got in the van, rolled up the windows, and locked the doors. Then I backed it over to the rudder area. I don't know if you have any idea how big they are. They are about 600 feet long, two football fields long, four stories high. It's just enormous.... I backed the van over the fence and then when I got a few feet away from the rudder, I backed it very forcefully into the rudder. Then I shifted gears and pulled forward five or ten feet and then floored it again.... I did that four or five times.

Immediately, of course, when people heard the first crash and thud, they looked around and said, "What the heck is going on?" Right away the security people came

<hr />

[87] Interview with John Schuchardt, conducted by the author, July 22, 2003.

running but I had rolled up the windows and locked the doors so I just kept about my business. Eventually, someone found a two-by-four and smashed the window, reached in, and grabbed me. I didn't resist. I just went peacefully with them and they took me to the security offices and began to interrogate me.... I hadn't planned it. When I got up that morning, I hadn't any idea that I would do it. I just happened to be in the right place at the right time and saw this golden opportunity to make a statement against the madness of nuclear weapons, and I took that opportunity.[88]

After DeMott's action, it did not take long before other campaigns occurred. In July of 1982, nine people returned to the Electric Boat shipyard in Connecticut. Four members of the group canoed out to the Trident submarine USS *Florida* and boarded it. They hammered on missile hatches, poured blood, and renamed the sub "USS *Auschwitz*" using spray paint. Simultaneously the other five entered the facility's storage yard, where they poured blood and hammered on Trident sonar spheres. Several months later, seven people conducted similar actions on the Trident USS *Georgia*.[89] In the next four years, nearly a dozen Plowshares campaigns took place. Schuchardt stated, "When we were in prison, Peter DeMott rammed the submarine. Then there were a few more ... and after a few years somebody used the word *movement*, which was a surprise [to us]."[90] Although the costs associated with this type of activism are high, the movement expanded over the next decades to include about eighty actions in seven different countries.[91]

---

[88] Interview with Peter DeMott, conducted by the author, July 23, 2003.

[89] These accounts are drawn from Laffin, Arthur. 1987. "A Chronology of the Plowshares Disarmament Actions: September 1980–September 1986," pp. 32–45 in Arthur Laffin and Anne Montgomery (eds.), *Swords Into Plowshares: Nonviolent Direct Action for Disarmament*. San Francisco: Harper & Row.

[90] Interview with John Schuchardt, conducted by the author, July 22, 2003.

[91] For a full listing of the Plowshares actions to date, see Appendix C in this book. Also refer to Arthur Laffin's (2003) book, *Swords Into Plowshares: A Chronology of Plowshares Disarmament Actions, 1980–2003*. Marion, SD: Rose Hill Books.

2

Tactical Legitimation and the Theology of Resistance

The General Electric action in King of Prussia became the inaugural event that launched the Plowshares movement. That action would never have grown into a full-fledged movement, however, if its tactics were considered an illegitimate means of resistance. Yet, as the draft board raid controversy illustrated, property destruction was not a tactic that automatically received approval from religious activists or the broader peace movement. On the contrary, there were many negative reactions, as Philip Berrigan indicated in his "Letter from a Baltimore Jail," written shortly after the Catonsville raid. Berrigan wrote:

> Some of you have been sorely perplexed with me; some of you have been angry, others despairing. One parishioner writes of quarreling with people who thought me mad. After all, isn't it impudent and sick for a grown man (and a priest) to slosh blood...on draft files; to terrorize harmless secretaries doing their job; to act without ecclesiastical permission and to disgrace the collar and its sublime office? ...You had trouble with blood as a symbol – uncivilized, messy, bizarre....You had trouble with destruction of property, with civil disobedience, with priests getting involved, and getting involved this much. Let's face it: perhaps half of you had trouble with us acting at all.[1]

The parallel to the well-known "Letter from a Birmingham Jail" was intentional since the purpose of Berrigan's correspondence was the same as Dr. King's – namely, justifying his method of resistance. King's approach to civil rights activism marked a notable shift from the traditional litigation strategies of the National Association for the Advancement of Colored People (NAACP). Some criticized him for taking the movement from the

---

[1] Berrigan, Philip. 1971. *Prison Journals of a Priest Revolutionary*. New York: Ballantine Books, pp. 15–16.

courtroom to the streets, while others publicly condemned his decision to use civil disobedience. King's letter is filled with paraphrases of these critiques: "You may well ask, 'Why direct action? Why sit-ins, marches, etc.?'...You express a great deal of anxiety over our willingness to break laws...[Some] constantly say 'I agree with you in the goal you seek, but I can't agree with your methods of direct action.'"[2] King's eloquent letter silenced his critics and unequivocally justified the movement's tactics. Establishing *legitimacy of means* is one of the developmental challenges that leaders must address if they hope to build a movement on initial expressions of dissent.[3] Therefore, just as King validated direct action and civil disobedience as acceptable methods of protest in the civil rights movement, the Catholic Left began developing a rationale for its tactical style.

To obtain legitimacy of means, Plowshares activists had to justify property destruction and address the question of tactical effectiveness. Critics argued that Catholic Left methods had no substantive influence on U.S. military policies. In a 1971 *New York Times* article, Andrew Greeley, a sociologist and priest, argued:

The truth is that Catholic "radicals" don't make any difference at all. They have no popular support, they can deliver no bloc of votes, they are totally incapable of affecting any social change, they will have no impact on larger society – save for consuming considerable amounts of media space. On the contrary, all the available data suggest that Berrigan-style protests are counterproductive for the causes they support.[4]

Others believed that the long prison terms associated with Catholic Left tactics would restrict participation in other disarmament campaigns. Even some members of the Catholic Peace Fellowship argued that organizing a large-scale peace movement would have greater impact than encouraging Catholic activists to become professional prisoners.[5] Furthermore, many felt that the public would soon forget these acts of prophetic provocation, minimizing the movement's ability to reach the nation's moral conscience.

---

[2] King, Martin Luther, Jr., 1964. *Why We Can't Wait*. New York: Mentor Books, pp. 79, 82, 84.

[3] Useem, Bert, and Mayer N. Zald. 1982. "From Pressure Group to Social Movement: Organizational Dilemmas of the Effort to Promote Nuclear Power." *Social Problems* 30 (2): 144–156.

[4] Greeley, Andrew. 1971. "L'Affaire Berrigan." *The New York Times*, February 19, 1971, p. A37.

[5] Polner, Murray, and Jim O'Grady. 1997. *Disarmed and Dangerous: The Radical Lives and Times of Daniel and Philip Berrigan*. New York: Basic Books, p. 349.

Tactical Legitimation and the Theology of Resistance

Without tactical validation, the Plowshares Eight would have been dismissed as a group of eccentric zealots and the General Electric action would have remained an isolated incident. In this chapter, I explore how Plowshares activists and supporters established legitimacy of means, inspiring others to follow their example, thereby shifting the movement into the expansion stage.

Explaining Symbolic Action

Although Martin Luther King, Jr.'s use of civil disobedience was considered radical in his era, it subsequently became a standard form of protest in many movements. For a sizeable number of Catholics in the peace movement, this method was both acceptable and familiar, as Dorothy Day had previously refused to cooperate with the air raid drills and some young Catholic Workers had violated the law by burning their draft cards or refusing military induction. Yet Plowshares tactics are not typical acts of civil disobedience. One of the Plowshares movement's first tasks, therefore, was to explain why symbolic acts of disobedience are necessary in the nuclear age. Sister Anne Montgomery stated:

Civil disobedience is, traditionally, the breaking of a civil law to obey a higher law, sometimes with the hope of changing the unjust civil law. For example, the lunch counter sit-ins in the 1950s[6] challenged the validity of segregation laws in the South. But we should speak of such actions as divine obedience, rather than as civil disobedience. The term "disobedience" is not appropriate because any law that does not protect and enhance human life is no real law. In particular, both divine and international law tell us that weapons of mass destruction are a crime against humanity and it is the duty of the ordinary citizen to actively oppose them....

It is almost impossible today to find a direct action like the lunch counter sit-ins of the 1950s that directly touches those in power; for example, it is hard to break a law legitimizing a weapon except in a symbolic way. For this reason, symbolic direct action has become increasingly important. We can take symbolic direct action by blocking the doors of the factories that produce arms or the trains that transport them. We can dismantle one or two nuclear weapons as a symbol of our deeper responsibility to disarm the violence created by such weapons. Symbols have a condensed, almost physical power and are especially important in an age when the

---

[6] The first restaurant sit-ins to challenge racial discrimination occurred in Chicago in 1943, led by members of the Congress of Racial Equality (CORE). Additional sit-ins occurred in St. Louis in 1949, Baltimore in 1953, and scores of other locations in the South throughout the 1950s. The tactic became more widespread after students in Nashville launched lunch counter sit-ins in 1960.

inundation of words makes us nonlisteners. Symbols touch us on a deep, subconscious level and release memories and fears, aspirations and energies.[7]

Symbols can indeed be powerful, but they are also subject to multiple interpretations, and activists' intended meaning may not be clear to observers. Thus activists had to explain Plowshares symbols, especially the use of blood. On a basic level, blood is a visual reminder of what these weapons are designed for, and is used to break through the rationalizations that justify weapons of mass destruction. Plowshares activist Mary Sprunger-Froese explained:

War has been sanitized... because we mostly do it through our technology and satellite surveillance. Back when people [fought] hand to hand, you would see the blood and gore and you would see the consequences. Now we're so far removed and we watch war coverage on TV like it's a miniseries. That's so desensitizing, deadening. So when we use blood, it has a very powerful effect.... The blood is very real, very arresting, shocking, and in your face. It says, "This is what we're talking about – human life. All this technology is made to destroy it, to spill human blood."[8]

Greg Boertje-Obed, Plowshares activist and ex-army officer, adds:

It's making visible what these weapons are about because many people have a problem with killing but in the military now you just push a button and the killing is distant, removed. That makes it much easier. We've found that the military people are offended when you pour blood on their weapons because they don't like to think of it as a bloody machine.... So it's very necessary to try to break through that with a symbol that is shocking. It may not affect people in a positive way but there is the chance that later on, in another moment, people can be affected by it. I met a U.S. marshal who was a fundamentalist Christian and he was especially turned off by the blood. He said that we were wasting the blood and it was a sin. It could have been given to somebody and used to save a life; he was just stuck on it. He could not see that the military weapons are a sin and that nuclear weapons are a crime.[9]

In addition to exposing the violence that nuclear weapons are capable of, blood calls Christians to remember the example of Christ, who gave his own life rather than shedding the blood of others. Through his sacrifice, new life emerges. One woman commented, "War is bloody but blood also

---

[7] Montgomery, Anne. 1987. "Divine Obedience," pp. 25–31 in Arthur Laffin and Anne Montgomery (eds.), *Swords Into Plowshares: Nonviolent Direct Action for Disarmament*. San Francisco: Harper & Row, p. 29.

[8] Interview with Mary Sprunger-Froese, conducted by the author, May 29, 2003.

[9] Interview with Greg Boertje-Obed, conducted by the author, October 21, 2000.

signifies life, redemption, and the conversion we seek as people of faith."[10] Boertje-Obed adds that Plowshares activists use their own blood during these actions as an indication of their willingness to sacrifice in order to bring about a social conversion. He stated:

From a faith perspective, we often try to explain [the use of blood] from the example of Jesus giving his blood. In the Eucharist, he gave his life. Symbolically, when we drink the cup, we are supposed to be giving our lives also. So we believe Jesus was nonviolent and taught that you are to give your life rather than take life. When we pour blood, we are saying that we are giving our lives and we will not shed anyone's blood.[11]

The movement also has had to clarify the symbolism of property destruction. This clarification began shortly after the tactic was initially introduced during the draft board raids. The Catonsville defendants stated that property rights should not take precedence over human rights and that property designed to annihilate life has no right to exist in the first place. Activist Kathleen Rumpf found this argument compelling:

The hammering, I think, is equally difficult for people [to accept] as the blood is. What helped me understand it was listening to Dan's [Berrigan] testimony on the stand during his Plowshares trial. He described these weapons as gas ovens without walls. I thought about Nazi Germany, the Holocaust, and how evil it all was. I knew from doing our legal work that international law says that we are responsible for the crimes of our government just as the Germans were responsible for the crimes of their government. And I thought, what if the people in Germany had gone to the ovens and taken them apart before they were ever used? Isn't that what I was trying to do? These weapons are ovens that will incinerate all of us if they are used; they are ovens without walls. That made it so crystal clear for me.[12]

Another movement participant contends that these tactics symbolize the need to transform weapons. He stated:

We are often asked the question about whether property destruction is nonviolent and there are a number of ways of answering it. One is to analyze the term "property." Are nuclear weapons property? We say no; they are anti-property. They're about destroying what is human, what is proper, what is good, what is decent.... The proper thing to do is to disable them, to disarm them, to unmake them, to convert

---

[10] Interview with Kathleen Rumpf, conducted by the author, May 29, 2003.
[11] Interview with Greg Boertje-Obed, conducted by the author, October 21, 2000.
[12] Interview with Kathleen Rumpf, conducted by the author, May 29, 2003.

them into something that *is* property. We try to say this warship should be used to bring food to starving nations. We're trying to unmake their killing nature. We're not damaging property; we're improving a weapon that is designed to kill innocent people, civilians, children and therefore [this tactic] can in no way be considered violent because you are rendering a violent piece of machinery nonviolent. It's nonviolent because you have made it inoperable, incapable of hurting others.[13]

Biblical Civil Disobedience and the Prophetic Tradition

Understanding the symbolism of Plowshares actions does not automatically lead to tactical acceptance. To achieve acceptance, the Catholic Left had to persuade people of faith that these methods of resistance are consistent with biblical teachings and that this course of action has merit even if it does not yield immediate results. Thus, Plowshares activists turned to scripture to establish legitimacy of means.

Plowshares activists argue that there is a long-standing history within the Judeo-Christian tradition of refusing to cooperate or comply with government mandates. Theologian Ched Myers posits that two types of nonviolent resistance are evident in the Bible.[14] First, there is *defensive disobedience* that entails non-cooperation with laws and policies that inflict violence, promote idolatry, or oppress people. One of the oldest examples of defensive disobedience is the biblical account of Moses' birth. As recorded in the book of Exodus, Pharaoh ordered the midwives to kill all Hebrew infant males, but they refused, claiming that Jewish women were so strong that they gave birth before help arrived (Exodus 1:8–2:10). Another example is found in the Old Testament book of Daniel, where Daniel refused to eat food served in the king's court because it violated Jewish dietary restrictions. Similarly, three of his contemporaries – Shadrach, Meshach, and Abednego – did not comply with the king's order to worship a golden statue; as a result, they were sentenced to death and thrown into a furnace. To everyone's astonishment, they were later found "walking around in the flames, singing to God...and the flames in no way touched them or caused them pain or harm" (Daniel 3:24, 50). Later, Daniel again clashes with the king, who declared himself god and decreed that all prayers must be addressed to him. When Daniel defied this order, he was arrested and thrown into a den

---

[13] Interview with Greg Boertje-Obed, conducted by the author, October 21, 2000.

[14] Myers, Ched. 1987. "By What Authority?: The Bible and Civil Disobedience," pp. 237–248 in Jim Wallis (ed.), *The Rise of Christian Conscience*. San Francisco: Harper & Row.

of lions. However, as the story goes, the lions did not harm him because God was pleased with Daniel's faithfulness, granting him protection from the king's wrath.[15] All of these biblical stories indicate that it is acceptable to break laws when those laws violate one's moral conscience.

The second form of biblical nonviolent resistance is what Myers calls *offensive civil disobedience*. This involves public dissent and prophetic action "intending to, through confrontation and engagement, expose moral, legal or political contradictions in existing policy."[16] The Old Testament is filled with accounts of prophets who challenged oppressive rulers. In each case, their message was similar: "Cease to do evil. Learn to do good. Search for justice. Help the oppressed" (Isaiah 1:16–17). These prophets not only denounced injustices; they also envisioned a day when "God will wield authority over the nations and adjudicate between peoples; they will hammer their swords into plowshares, their spears into sickles. Nation shall not lift sword against nation; and there will be no more training for war" (Isaiah 2:4–5).

The Plowshares movement views itself as part of this prophetic tradition. Its members believe they have a duty to proclaim God's word, even if the population ignores their message. Success, therefore, is not measured primarily by the degree of social change or the extent to which one's goals are achieved. Rather, success is following God's will. One activist stated, "Our goal, our purpose, our approach is not primarily to have an effect. It is first of all to be faithful. When you follow the gospel, it's not in order to be a success. It's an attempt to be faithful to God, to God's will for today, to be the voice of conscience."[17] Consistent with the ideas of Thomas Merton, Plowshares activists feel that apostolic works may not always yield quick results, but as people of faith they trust that they are planting seeds that God will bring to fruition in time. Philip Berrigan observed, "You do a thing because, in your conscience, it's the right thing to do and it's a just and decent thing to do.... And God, out of this action, perhaps touches some lives. That's all I can say about success. It has to do with fidelity."[18]

---

[15] For the full account, see Daniel 6:22–23.

[16] Myers, Ched. 1987. "By What Authority?: The Bible and Civil Disobedience," pp. 237–248 in Jim Wallis (ed.), *The Rise of Christian Conscience*. San Francisco: Harper & Row. Quotation on pp. 237–238.

[17] Interview with Greg Boertje-Obed, conducted by the author, October 21, 2000.

[18] Berrigan, Philip. 1997. "How to Spend Time in Jail, A Useful Guide." *Church World: Maine's Catholic Weekly*. Volume 68, No. 9, August 7. Quotation on p. 4.

Tactical Legitimation and the Theology of Resistance

Many people of faith agree that Christians have a duty to proclaim God's message and denounce immoral government practices. Yet most feel that this can be done without resorting to property destruction and other disruptive methods. Here I briefly summarize some of the key points that Plowshares activists made as they sought to establish legitimacy of means by demonstrating that their tactics were consistent with scriptural examples and teachings.

The Idolatry of Nuclearism

After the United States dropped an atomic bomb on Hiroshima, Dorothy Day noted that "the Lordship of Christ has been replaced by the Lordship of the bomb"[19] – a sentiment that was underscored by Oppenheimer's decision to name the first nuclear test "The Trinity." According to Plowshares activists, Americans have become thoroughly enamored with the power of these weapons. This has led to a state of "nuclearism" in which the U.S. population has become psychologically and politically dependent on its nuclear capacity.[20] The Catholic Left believes that this mentality has transformed nuclear weapons into gods of metal, because people have placed their ultimate faith in the power of these missiles, violating God's commandments, "Thou shall have no other gods before me," and "Do not bow down to any idol and worship it."[21] As Arthur Laffin notes, "To pledge our ultimate allegiance to the state and to place our security in idols of death betrays our faith in God and constitutes ultimate blasphemy."[22]

Plowshares activists maintain that the Bible provides examples of how people of faith should respond to such idolatry. One man cites Moses' reaction to a golden calf that the people of Israel created and worshipped during their journey to the Promised Land. He suggested that if Moses' actions pleased God, so do own their efforts to smash the contemporary gods of metal:

---

[19] As quoted in Berrigan, Philip, and Elizabeth McAlister. 1989. *The Time's Discipline: The Beatitudes and Nuclear Resistance*. Baltimore: Fortkamp Publishers, p. 83.

[20] Lifton, Robert, and Richard Falk. 1982. *Indefensible Weapons: The Political and Psychological Case against Nuclear Weapons*. New York: Basic Books.

[21] Deuteronomy 5:7, 9.

[22] Laffin, Arthur, and Anne Montgomery. 1987. "The Nuclear Challenge," pp. 3–24 in Arthur Laffin and Anne Montgomery (eds.), *Swords Into Plowshares: Nonviolent Direct Action for Disarmament*. San Francisco: Harper & Row, p. 12.

Nuclear weapons are the idols of today. People put their faith in an inanimate object and that's idolatry and it's also blasphemy because you're saying that this weapon takes the place of God. There are examples in the Bible of people turning over idols. In so doing, you are returning the objects to their proper use instead of being used for false worship. One example is when the Israelites made a golden calf and Moses came and destroyed it, turned it into fine flakes. Was that violent? We wouldn't see that as violent and most Christians today don't think that what Moses did was a terrible deed. It's the same idea.[23]

Just as Moses called the Israelites to repentance, Plowshares activists hope their actions will make others aware of the idolatrous nature of nuclear weapons. Molly Rush described how hammering on the missile re-entry vehicles at General Electric made her conscious of the psychological and spiritual hold these warheads had:

For me, the breakthrough came when I hit that gold [warhead] and a little chip of it came up and hit me under the chin. It was an incredible breakthrough. Up until that time, I realized that they were like gods of metal . . . but it was the physical piece that broke through to my own awareness. I understood that I was somehow captured by these things as much as anyone else. I thought they were invulnerable, beyond human action. I had bought into this idolatry, too, even though I was trying to do something against them. They seemed so out of human comprehension or action. I was astounded that the weapons I imagined to be invulnerable to our little household hammers showed the marks from our blows.[24]

These Plowshares actions, therefore, are not only designed to destroy idols, but also to reach the conscience of idol worshippers.

Gospel Nonviolence

A second element of the movement's prophetic message is aimed directly at the church, calling it to reject the Just War tradition and embrace the nonviolence that Christ lived and preached. The movement's understanding of biblical nonviolence is rooted in the Sermon on the Mount in which Christ teaches,

You have heard that it was said, "An eye for an eye and a tooth for a tooth." But I say to you, do not resist one who is evil. But if anyone strikes you on the right cheek, turn to him the other also; and if anyone would sue you and take your coat, let him have your cloak as well; and if anyone forces you to go one mile, go with him two miles. . . . You have heard that it was said, "Love your neighbor and hate

---

[23] Interview with Greg Boertje-Obed, conducted by the author, October 21, 2000.
[24] Interview with Molly Rush, conducted by the author, March 26, 2001.

your enemy." But I tell you: Love your enemies and pray for those who persecute you. (Matthew 5:38–41, 43–44)

Plowshares activists challenge traditional interpretations of this passage that suggest Jesus was encouraging passivity. They maintain that scripture must be read in light of the historical and cultural context of Jesus's era. In other words, a "sociology of the Bible" or "political hermeneutics" is needed to accurately understand Jesus's message.[25]

Catholic Left activists agree with the views of theologian Walter Wink, who notes that most interpretations of the Gospel fail to take the social, political, and historical dynamics of first-century Palestine into account, and thus they offer erroneous conclusions. Moreover, Wink argues that biblical translators have often allowed their own context to shape their interpretations. For instance, the first English version of the Bible was commissioned by King James, whose translators interpreted the Greek term *antistenai* as "Do not resist evil." Wink writes,

When the court translators working in the hire of King James chose to translate *antistenai* as "Resist not evil," they were doing something more than rendering Greek into English. They were translating nonviolent resistance into docility. Jesus did not tell his oppressed hearers not to resist evil ... His entire ministry is utterly at odds with such a preposterous idea. The Greek word is made up of two parts: *anti*, a word still used in English for 'against,' and *histemi*, a verb which in its noun form (*stasis*) means violent rebellion, armed revolt, sharp dissention.... The term generally refers to a potentially lethal disturbance or armed revolution. A proper translation of Jesus' teaching would then be, 'Do not strike back at evil (or one who has done you evil) in kind.... Do not retaliate against violence with violence.'[26]

As a political ruler, King James had a vested interest in encouraging submission and passivity, but the translation he commissioned actually contradicts the authentic message of Jesus.

Wink supports his alternative interpretation by examining the three examples that Jesus offers directly after this passage. Jesus tells his audience, "If anyone strikes you on the right cheek, turn to him the other also." Drawing on sociocultural information about first-century Palestine, Wink states the left hand was reserved for unclean tasks; using it for other purposes was strictly forbidden. Thus the right hand would have been used

---

[25] Myers, Ched. 1988. *Binding the Strong Man: A Political Reading of Mark's Story of Jesus.* Maryknoll, NY: Orbis Books, p. xxv.

[26] Wink, Walter. 1987. *Violence and Nonviolence in South Africa: Jesus' Third Way*. Philadelphia: New Society Publishers, p. 13.

to strike another individual. However, the only way to hit someone on the right cheek with one's right hand is with a backhanded slap. Backhanding was a common method of denigrating those of inferior status. Romans backhanded Jews, masters backhanded slaves, and parents backhanded children. Wink notes that "What we are dealing with here is unmistakably an insult, not a fistfight. The intention clearly is not to injure but to humiliate, to put someone in his or her 'place.'"[27] It is clear, then, that Jesus is addressing subordinated individuals who are at the bottom of the social hierarchy. Why, then, does he advise them to turn the other cheek? According to Wink:

Because this action robs the oppressor of the power to humiliate. The person who turns the other cheek is saying, in effect, "Try again. Your first blow failed to achieve the intended effect. I deny you the power to humiliate me." ... Such a response would create enormous difficulties for the striker. Purely logistically, how do you now hit the other cheek? You cannot backhand it with your right hand. If you hit with your fist, you make yourself an equal, acknowledging the other as a peer. But the whole point of the back of the hand is to reinforce the caste system and its institutionalized inequality. ... You have been forced, against your will, to regard that person as an equal human being. You have been stripped of your power to dehumanize the other.[28]

The second scriptural example – "If anyone would sue you and take your coat, let him have your cloak as well" – also requires background information about conditions in Palestine during Jesus's lifetime. Wink notes that indebtedness was a widespread problem in that society, due partially to Roman imperialism. The Romans placed heavy taxes on the rich in order to maintain their empire. As a result, the upper class pursued non-liquid investments, such as land, to secure their wealth. However, land was perceived as an ancestral inheritance that ought to be reserved for future generations, and thus it was seldom sold, even when people were desperately poor. To increase their access to land, the wealthy raised interest rates on loans. When debtors were unable to repay their loans, lenders had the right to confiscate their land. Thus from this passage we know that Jesus is speaking to those who are so far in debt that they have already been stripped of their land, leaving only the clothes on their back as collateral. If they are unable to make restitution and are brought to court to forfeit their coat,

[27] Wink, Walter. 1987. *Violence and Nonviolence in South Africa: Jesus' Third Way*. Philadelphia: New Society Publishers, p. 15.

[28] Wink, Walter. 1987. *Violence and Nonviolence in South Africa: Jesus' Third Way*. Philadelphia: New Society Publishers, p. 16.

one of their few remaining possessions, why does Jesus advise them to hand over their shirt as well? Is he encouraging resignation to this exploitative system? Wink offers another explanation.

Why does Jesus counsel them to give over their inner garment as well? This would mean stripping off all their clothing and marching out of court stark naked! .... There stands the creditor, beet-red with embarrassment, your outer garment in one hand, your underwear in the other. You have suddenly turned the tables on him. You had no hope of winning the trial; the law was entirely in his favor. But you have refused to be humiliated, and at the same time you have registered a stunning protest against a system that spawns such debt.... Nakedness was taboo in Judaism, and shame fell not on the naked party, but on the person viewing or causing one's nakedness (Genesis 9:20–27).... The entire system by which debtors are oppressed has been publicly unmasked. The creditor is revealed to be not a "respectable" money lender but a party in the reduction of an entire social class to landlessness and destitution. This unmasking is not simply punitive, however; it offers the creditor a chance to see, perhaps for the first time in his life, what his practices cause, and to repent.[29]

Finally, we come to the third example, in which Jesus admonishes his audience "that if anyone forces you to go one mile, go with him two miles." During Jesus's lifetime, Palestine was under Roman occupation. Roman law specified the amount of forced labor that the military could impose, allowing troops to order civilians to carry soldiers' packs for one mile. Carrying anything beyond this distance was punishable by law, since Roman rulers wanted to limit the degree of resentment in the population. This forced-labor policy was designed to keep troops mobile while simultaneously reminding the local population of their subjugated status. In this context, isn't Jesus's teaching tantamount to aiding and abetting an imperial force? Paralleling the first two examples, Wink argues that Jesus is encouraging his listeners to assert their dignity even under these exploitative circumstances. Although they may not be able to change the law, they do have a choice in how they will respond. Jesus is encouraging them to take the initiative, reclaiming their own power even under oppressive conditions. If such an action does not change the attitude of the oppressor or subvert imperial Roman rule, a nonviolent confrontation will nevertheless empower the oppressed.[30]

[29] Wink, Walter. 1987. *Violence and Nonviolence in South Africa: Jesus' Third Way*. Philadelphia: New Society Publishers, pp. 18–19.
[30] Wink, Walter. 1987. *Violence and Nonviolence in South Africa: Jesus' Third Way*. Philadelphia: New Society Publishers, pp. 20–22.

While Wink's analysis is persuasive to religious pacifists, non-pacifist theologians have cited different biblical passages that, in their opinion, cast doubt upon the claim that Jesus preached nonviolence. For instance, some biblical scholars have pointed to Jesus's proclamation: "Do not think that I have come to bring peace on earth; I have come not to bring peace but a sword" (Matthew 10:34). Ultimately for Plowshares activists, however, all debates on violence come down to the example of Jesus. They argue that he chose the path of the suffering servant, readily accepting death rather than imposing it on others. Daniel Berrigan summed it up by stating, "In whatever modest or clumsy way, we are called to honor the preference of Christ for suffering rather than inflicting suffering, for dying rather than killing.... There are two ways: the way of the cross, and the way of putting others on the cross."[31] Father John Dear, a Jesuit and Plowshares activist, concurs:

Nonviolence is no longer a pious option or a political tactic. It is the key to understanding Jesus. The only things we know for sure about Jesus are that he did not kill and he opposed violence of any kind. He rejected violence of both oppressor and oppressed. He taught a third way – active nonviolent resistance to evil. He urged his followers to love God, to love one's self, to love one's neighbors, and most radical of all, to love even one's enemies.[32]

Jesus Committed Civil Disobedience

As Plowshares activists provocatively call the church to embrace nonviolence and denounce war, they have no qualms about violating social norms or breaking the law in the process. This is because they believe that Christ himself disregarded cultural pretenses and committed civil disobedience. When he first called his disciples, he defied the Jewish social system by inviting an ostracized tax collector to join him. Furthermore, he rejected Pharisaical rules of ritual purity by eating with notorious sinners, and he made himself "unclean" when he touched a leper (Mark 2:13–3:6). Jesus and his disciples also defied Sabbath laws by picking grain and healing the sick, causing the religious authorities of the day to question, "Why do they do what is not lawful on the Sabbath?" Jesus responded, "The Sabbath was made for humans, not humans for the Sabbath" (Mark 2:27). This example

---

[31] Margaret McKenna as quoted in Dear, John. 1996. *Apostle of Peace: Essays in Honor of Daniel Berrigan*. Maryknoll, NY: Orbis Books, pp. 13, 69.

[32] Dear, John. 2001. *Living Peace: A Spirituality of Contemplation and Action*. New York: Doubleday, p. 85.

diminishes activists' apprehensions about committing civil disobedience. Dominican Sister Jackie Hudson reflected, "I became aware of the Jesus who put life above the law. I became aware of the Jesus who was willing to suffer to lessen the suffering of others. In essence, the Jesus who picked grain and cured the sick on the Sabbath gave me the permission I needed . . . to challenge rather than acquiesce to authority figures.[33]

Jesus Was Confrontational and Disruptive

Although some Catholics sympathize with the Plowshares activists' views, and even agree that civil disobedience is sometimes necessary, many criticize their tactics as too confrontational. In response to this critique, movement participants point to the story of Jesus cleansing the Temple in Jerusalem and overturning the tables of money collectors. He targeted the Temple, they argue, because it was a place where the poor were exploited in the name of God. Worshippers were encouraged, virtually required, to purchase an expensive sacrificial lamb or dove so that their prayer would be pure and acceptable to God. If someone could not afford this, bankers were on hand to loan money at exorbitant interest rates.[34] Moreover, all practicing Jews were subject to a religious tax, which was paid at the Temple. This transformed the site from a place of worship into a bank that collected Temple tax payments, tracked debts, and financed credit. The ruling class had turned a "house of prayer into a den of thieves" (Mark 11:17). Outraged by this oppression, Jesus drove the moneychangers and their animals out and shut the Temple down.

Plowshares activists and supporters note that Jesus did not simply advocate lower taxes for the poor or interest-rate reform; he challenged the entire system and disrupted business as usual.[35] The story legitimizes the symbolic but confrontational nature of the movement's tactics by revealing the intensity with which Jesus resisted an evil and exploitative institution.[36] Bill Kellerman noted:

---

[33] Response from Jackie Hudson's survey, collected by the author in June 2001.

[34] Kellerman, Bill. 1987. "The Cleansing of the Temple: Jesus and Symbolic Action," pp. 245–261 in Jim Wallis (ed.), *The Rise of Christian Conscience*. San Francisco: Harper & Row.

[35] Kellerman, Bill. 1987. "The Cleansing of the Temple: Jesus and Symbolic Action," pp. 245–261 in Jim Wallis (ed.), *The Rise of Christian Conscience*. San Francisco: Harper & Row. Also see Myers, Ched. 1988. *Binding the Strong Man: A Political Reading of Mark's Story of Jesus*. Maryknoll, NY: Orbis Books.

[36] Douglass, James. 1968. *The Nonviolent Cross: A Theology of Revolution and Peace*. Toronto: The Macmillan Company.

Tactical Legitimation and the Theology of Resistance

Jesus' primary political method was dramatic symbolic action.... The Temple was truly the economic mainstay of a city whose primary business was religious tourism. Passover was the commercial equivalent of the Christmas rush. At Passover time, Jerusalem's population of 30,000 could be doubled or even quadrupled. That's a lot of rooms at the inn. As many as 18,000 lambs would be slaughtered as sacrifices. We're talking about powerful economic interests. The Temple had received special permission from Rome to collect its own tax.... The Temple functioned as a bank; it was not only a source of loans for those without proper credit but also the depository for records of indebtedness. High taxes and runaway interest rates had forced many small farmers into sharecropping and indentured slavery, making the Temple instrumental in an oppressive system....

When, therefore, Jesus goes to the front porch of the Temple, where the money changers have set up shop, he's not simply annoyed with the inflated price of doves. He has chosen the public place that is the most visible symbol of complicity between the occupying forces and the religious authorities. The Temple represents the intersection of the Roman money market and the local economy, the spiritual idolatry of status quo power.... Jesus is not engaged in civil disobedience in the classic sense of breaking an unjust law in order to change it. He had often been taken to task for violating the Mosaic law, particularly around the Sabbath, but here he is not interested in improving the letter of the law, either Roman or Jewish, one jot or tittle. He is simply doing a strong action of visible truth in a place protected by law and authority.[37]

Plowshares leaders maintain that their disruptive tactics challenge the government, the military, and the church in a manner that parallels Jesus's Temple action. They are careful to note, however, that while Jesus's manner was confrontational, it was completely nonviolent as he did not physically harm or mistreat anyone. They want to dispel the belief that violence is sometimes biblically justified, as some religious authorities submit, based on this Temple-cleansing story. Father John Dear states, "Jesus is active and provocative but not harmful. Unfortunately, readers of the Gospel down through the centuries have interpreted this central story as an act of violence, and have justified every form of murder, including the mass murder of war, in the name of Jesus.[38]

In short, to establish that their provocative and disruptive methods constitute a legitimate means of resistance, Plowshares participants argue that they are simply acting in accordance with the example that Jesus set. Such

---

[37] Kellerman, Bill. 1987. "The Cleansing of the Temple: Jesus and Symbolic Action," pp. 245–261 in Jim Wallis (ed.), *The Rise of Christian Conscience*. San Francisco: Harper & Row. Quotation on pp. 258–259.

[38] Dear, John. 2001. *Living Peace: A Spirituality of Contemplation and Action.*" New York: Doubleday, p. 63.

tactical justification is clearly heard in the following statement by Bill Kellerman:

Some of the questions that arise whenever symbolic action and civil disobedience are contemplated could be directed toward Jesus and his action. These questions include: why does Jesus have to be so confrontational? Won't he turn people off? Does Jesus really want to communicate? Isn't this violence against property? Couldn't Jesus just stand outside the Temple and get his point across just as well? Why doesn't Jesus work within the system, go through Pilate or the Sanhedrin? Or even become high priest? Wouldn't he have greater impact from a position of public power? Why does Jesus risk his life and freedom? Think how much more he could do staying in Galilee quietly preaching and healing. After all, you can't do ministry while sitting in jail or hanging on a cross. These questions are put with some irony, but if they are real questions for ourselves, then let's not hesitate to ask them of Jesus as well.[39]

The Cross Symbolizes Resistance to the State

In the Temple story, Jesus provocatively challenged institutionalized religion. But U.S. Plowshares activists emphasize that Jesus also resisted the government. They note that Roman imperial authorities put him on trial for charges of "stirring up the people for revolt, forbidding payment of tribute to Caesar, and calling himself a king" (Luke 23:2). The accusation of refusing to pay tribute to Caesar reflected a fundamental tension of that era. Living under Roman rule, Jewish authorities had forged a deal that allowed Judaism to co-exist alongside the Roman civic religion as long as it remained politically innocuous. As part of the agreement, however, all Jews had to pay a religious tax. This tax grew increasingly controversial as it came to symbolize the Roman Empire's control of religious practices and freedoms. Therefore, when authorities questioned Jesus' stance on this issue, his response – "Render to Caesar the things that are Caesar's and to God the things that are God's" – was tantamount to proclaiming his foremost allegiance to God.[40]

Charging Jesus with the crime of "calling himself a king" indicates that the Romans considered him a political subversive – not merely a religious heretic, as many assume. Proclaiming oneself king was considered seditious,

---

[39] Kellerman, Bill. 1987. "The Cleansing of the Temple: Jesus and Symbolic Action," pp. 256–261 in Jim Wallis (ed.), *The Rise of Christian Conscience*, San Francisco: Harper & Row. Quotation on p. 261.

[40] Stringfellow, William, and Anthony Towne. 1971. *Suspect Tenderness: The Ethics of the Berrigan Witness*. New York: Holt, Rinehart and Winston.

and another political dissident, a Zealot leader, was prosecuted for this as well.[41] The Zealots were a rebel movement trying to overthrow the Roman Empire and establish a Jewish theocracy. At least one of Jesus's disciples, "Simon the Zealot," was part of this group (Luke 6:15 and Acts 1:13), and others may have been as well, perhaps making Jesus guilty by association.[42] Moreover, the sentence that Jesus received, death by crucifixion, was a Roman form of capital punishment reserved for political prisoners.[43] Oscar Cullman notes, "If Jesus had been convicted of blasphemy by the Jews, and if Pilate had merely to ratify this verdict, Jesus would have been stoned to death,"[44] which was the Jewish method of execution. Finally, Roman procurator Pontius Pilate had enacted a practice of releasing one prisoner who was selected by the local population. Pilate allowed the crowd to choose between Jesus and the Zealot Barabbas, who is described as one of "the rebels in prison, who had committed murder in the insurrection" (Mark 15:7). When Pilate placed Jesus alongside Barabbas, it indicates that the two were being condemned for the same type of crime. Ched Myers concludes that "Jesus and Barabbas each represent fundamentally different kinds of revolutionary practice, violent and nonviolent, both of which have led to a common fate: prison and impending execution."[45]

With this background on Jesus's crucifixion, Plowshares activists argue that the authentic meaning of the cross has been lost over the centuries. Rather than advocating the traditional view that the cross reflects God's sacrifice for the redemption of humanity's sins, they maintain that it represents Jesus's willingness to challenge government injustices, defy its authority, and refuse to compromise religious convictions to comply with the law. It symbolizes confrontation with an exploitative institution and Jesus's willingness to accept death in the struggle for justice. One person offered a contemporary version of Jesus' command to pick up the cross and follow him. He noted, "[A] modern translation of Jesus' call would be: 'If you would be my disciples, face your electric chair and follow me.' I have a strange picture of electric chairs replacing crosses over altars and on church walls. Such

---

[41] Cullman, Oscar. 1963. *The State and the New Testament*. London: SCM Press.

[42] For a more complete discussion of the number of disciples who may have been Zealots, see Douglass, James. 1968. *The Nonviolent Cross: A Theology of Revolution and Peace*. Toronto: The Macmillan Company.

[43] Myers, Ched. 1987. "By What Authority?: The Bible and Civil Disobedience," pp. 237–246 in Jim Wallis (ed.), *The Rise of Christian Conscience*. San Francisco: Harper & Row, p. 243.

[44] Cullman, Oscar. 1963. *The State and the New Testament*. London: SCM Press, p. 37.

[45] Myers, Ched. 1988. *Binding the Strong Man: A Political Reading of Mark's Story of Jesus*. Maryknoll, NY: Orbis Books, p. 380.

a tack would surely bring the cross home from pious sentimentalism and abstraction."[46]

To follow Jesus, one must be prepared to continue this resistance to the state. As Philip Berrigan put it, "A Christian life is much more than written or spoken words. It is bearing the cross, a metaphor for nonviolent confrontation with a criminal superstate."[47] Similarly, Greg Boertje-Obed stated: "This is what it means to follow Jesus. Jesus said, 'Take up your cross, deny yourself, follow me.' We interpret taking up the cross to mean risking punishment by the state because, at that time, the cross was the Roman means of execution. So following Jesus means risking our lives and being punished by the state, the empire – the Roman Empire at that time and the U.S. Empire today."[48]

Apostles Were Repeat Offenders

Biblical accounts of the early Christian church further underscore activists' claim that defying the government is part of their faith tradition. They note that many of the early apostles were repeatedly incarcerated. Daniel Berrigan calls specific attention to passages in the New Testament book of Acts in which an angel is sent to rescue the apostles from jail, only to free them to commit their crimes again. This, he says, is the "angel of recidivism."[49] Another Plowshares activist describes the apostles' unrepentant spirit:

The stories about this angel [of recidivism] are found primarily in the Acts of the Apostles, chapters 5 and 12. First, Peter meets with the believers in Jerusalem. People bring their sick there hoping that Peter's shadow will fall on them. The High Priest and his supporters, the Sadducees, become jealous of the apostles and have them arrested and thrown into the public jail. But an angel of the Lord opened the door of the prison during the night, brought them out, and said to them, "Go stand in the Temple court and give the people the message of life." Accordingly, they entered the Temple at dawn and resumed their teaching. This kind of behavior is what landed them in the clink in the first place. The court convenes and the prisoners are sent for. The soldiers return and report: "We found the prison securely locked

---

[46] Kellerman, Bill. 1987. "The Cleansing of the Temple: Jesus and Symbolic Action. pp. 256–261 in Jim Wallis (ed.), *The Rise of Christian Conscience*. San Francisco: Harper & Row. Quotation on p. 260.

[47] Berrigan, Phil. 1996. *Fighting the Lamb's War: Skirmishes with the American Empire*. Monroe, ME: Common Courage Press.

[48] Interview with Greg Boertje-Obed, conducted by the author, October 21, 2001.

[49] Recidivism refers to the tendency of criminals to relapse into their deviant ways.

and the prison guards at their post outside the gate, but when we opened the gate, we found no one inside." Everyone is baffled.

Word spread quickly, and the Sanhedrin is informed that "those folks you arrested are back at their preaching." They are brought back by the guards.... The charge is clear: "We gave you strict orders not to preach such a Savior, but you have filled Jerusalem with your teaching and you intend on charging us with the killing of this man." The defense is crystal clear: "Better for us to obey God than men." What ensues is bedlam. The authorities want to kill the prisoners, literally, but... the Council has the apostles whipped and orders them not to speak of Jesus Savior. Then, it says, "They set them free." The result: "The apostles went out from the Council rejoicing that they were considered worthy to suffer disgrace for the sake of the Name." Day after day, both in the Temple and in the people's homes, they continued to teach and to proclaim that Jesus is the Messiah. Not very repentant criminals. Recidivists, no doubt about it.[50]

Critics of the Plowshares movement argue that this is a biased, politicized reading of the early church. They note that in the book of Romans, the apostle Paul taught: "Let every person be subject to the governing authorities. For there is no authority except from God, and those that exist have been instituted by God" (Romans 13:1). In response, movement activists and supporters state that this passage must be read in light of Jesus's example, as well as the broader context of this text. Immediately preceding this statement, the apostle Paul declared:

Repay no one evil for evil, but take thought for what is noble in the sight of all. If possible, so far as it depends upon you, live peaceably with all. Beloved, never avenge yourselves.... No, if your enemy is hungry, feed him; if he is thirsty, give him drink; for by so doing you will heap burning coals upon his head. Do not be overcome by evil, but overcome evil with good. (Romans 12:17–21)

Thus, Catholic Left activists believe that Paul is not advocating blind obedience to the state but conditional cooperation with governments that act justly. Yet, as one theologian points out, government actions are rarely compatible with scriptural teachings:

States, politicians, kings, [and] presidents do not turn the other cheek. They do not love the enemy. The enemy is the one they prepare to kill, the one that they hate; it is the one they order people to kill. They do not give the enemy food and drink; they do not return good for evil. So is the closing paragraph of Romans 12 contradictory to Romans 13? Of course not. What is meant is [that] you obey governing authorities to the extent that they act consistent with the will of God. The extent that they

---

[50] McKenna, Megan. 1996. "The Angel of Recidivism," pp. 92–96 in John Dear (ed.), *Apostle of Peace: Essays in Honor of Daniel Berrigan*. Maryknoll, NY: Orbis Books. Quotation on pp. 92–93.

order something inconsistent with the will of God is evil.... Certainly no Christian in his/her right mind believes that if Hitler orders Christians to slaughter Jews and throw them in the furnace, to take Jewish children, mothers, and fathers and kill them by the millions, that that becomes God's will and that Christians are bound to obey. Let us not be absurd. The statement is clear cut and the statement is that when governing authorities say to do God's will, one does it. Anything else contrary to the will of God, one simply refuses.[51]

Some biblical scholars suggest that the most interesting aspect of this text is that such teachings were even necessary. Reading these epistles in a very different sociopolitical context, 2,000 years after they were written, it is easy to forget that the early Christian church was frequently in conflict with the Roman state – a point that is underscored by the fact that many of Paul's letters were written from prison. Because Roman imperial practices were in such contradiction with Christian beliefs, members of the early church were constantly defying the government. Thus, church leaders felt a need to temper this attitude of resistance by establishing a set of teachings on government subordination. Myers noted, "It is unfortunate that... [this] set of teachings, originally conceived as a counterpoint, has become so often the one-dimensional ethic for a church no longer in collision, but rather collusion, with the state."[52]

Tactical Legitimation in Court Trials

This biblical tradition of provocative, prophetic action is not the only justification that Plowshares activists use to legitimize their tactics. They also invoke international law, especially in court. By taking a closer look at two Plowshares trials, we can see how activists combine their religious convictions with legal arguments. Moreover, it will reveal how the Catholic Left melds a prophetic tradition that emphasizes faithfulness, regardless of outcome, with the instrumental aim of proving that weapons of mass destruction violate international law and must therefore be dismantled.

The Plowshares Eight Trial

Immediately following the first Plowshares action at the General Electric plant near Philadelphia, the eight participants were taken to jail and

51 As quoted on p. 82 in Dear, John. 1994. *The Sacrament of Civil Disobedience*. Baltimore: Fortkamp Publishing.
52 Myers, Ched. 1987. "By What Authority?: The Bible and Civil Disobedience," pp. 237–246 in Jim Wallis (ed.), *The Rise of Christian Conscience*. San Francisco: Harper & Row.

eventually brought before a judge who charged them with various felonies. The judge set bail at $250,000 for six of the activists, and stated that Daniel and Philip Berrigan would be held without bond. Eventually, four of them posted bail and were released to organize in anticipation of the trial. The other four stayed in prison, providing legal assistance and moral support to fellow inmates. After several months, the courts offered to release the remaining Plowshares activists on their own recognizance. When they refused, the courts expelled them against their will. About this time, the presiding judge called in the activists' attorney, Charles Glackin, and told him that he did not want to repeat the Harrisburg trial of 1972, where the media devoured the story of Catholic Left activists facing down FBI director J. Edgar Hoover. The judge offered to drop all charges and allow the activists one hour to make public statements.[53] The eight turned the offer down, insisting on a trial that would allow them to expose the first-strike capacity of these weapons and educate the population on international law.

When the trial began, the case was assigned to Judge Samuel Salus III. The activists chose to defend themselves, with the assistance of legal counsel. They opened their trial by explaining to the jury that they were innocent since their action was warranted by the "necessity defense." This defense – also known as the "justification defense" – holds that someone is allowed to break a law when imminent danger is present, when the normal channels of dealing with a threat are ineffective, and when that person is acting to prevent a greater harm. For example, a person who enters a burning house to rescue those inside is not guilty of trespassing since this action was done to save lives. Thus the Plowshares activists told the jury, "If you find that our intention was not criminal, then you must find us not guilty."[54] To support their case, they put together a team of expert witnesses to testify that General Electric's Mark 12A warheads pose an imminent danger. Specifically, the defendants planned to call Robert Aldridge (an engineer who had previously worked on first-strike weapons), George Wald (a 1967 Nobel Prize winner in physiology or medicine), and Robert J. Lifton, a psychiatrist who had studied the survivors of Hiroshima. All of these experts would explain the potential threat to human life that nuclear weapons pose – a danger that the Plowshares activists were trying to stop.

---

[53] Polner, Murray, and Jim O'Grady. 1997. *Disarmed and Dangerous: The Radical Lives and Times of Daniel and Philip Berrigan.* New York: Basic Books, p. 346.
[54] Quotation from the film *Inside the King of Prussia.*

Judge Salus decided, however, that the justification defense would not be allowed and that none of these experts could testify. He argued that nuclear weapons were not on trial and thus their testimony was irrelevant. Norm Townsend, one of the Plowshares activists' legal advisors, found this ruling preposterous. He stated:

Had this been a case where someone was holding a gun to your head, if you had ... destroyed the gun, you would have been permitted in a criminal trial to say why you destroyed the gun, why you damaged that property.... The United States has a gun to everyone's head ... and that gun can go off at any moment. We wanted to be permitted to show the jury that the gun is pointed at their heads.... It's not unreasonable for [the Plowshares Eight] to remove that gun, to destroy the gun, and present it in a way that's codified by Pennsylvania statute. The judge just arbitrarily, without any argument on the motion ... decided that what we wanted to do was totally irrelevant to the case.[55]

In addition to presenting the necessity or justification defense, the "Plowshares Eight" also proclaimed that they were innocent because they were upholding international law. They tried to call Richard Falk, Professor of International Law at Princeton University, to testify that U.S. nuclear weapons violate international treaties that prohibit nations from preparing for genocide or wars of mass destruction. The activists argued that they were justified in trying to destroy these armaments because the Nuremberg trials after World War II dictated that international law supersedes national laws, and those who know that their government is violating international laws must actively work to stop it. The Nuremberg laws therefore hold individuals accountable for their governments' actions and grants them the right to interfere with crimes against humanity. This, the Plowshares Eight argued, is precisely what they were doing – taking responsibility for ending the perilous situation that their government leaders created by producing, testing, and threatening to use nuclear armaments. Daniel Berrigan emphasized this personal responsibility when he addressed the jurors:

You have heard about [our use of] hammers and blood. These [nuclear weapons] are the hammers of hell ... that will break the world to bits.... We eight have been trying to take responsibility for them, to call them by their right name, which is murder, death, genocide, the end of the world.... We would like to assume responsibility for our world, our future, our children. And if that is a crime, then it is quite clear that we belong in their jails.... In the name of all the eight, I'd like to leave with you, friends and jurors, that great and noble word which is our crime: responsibility.[56]

---

[55] Quotation from the film *Inside the King of Prussia*.
[56] Quotation from the film *Inside the King of Prussia*.

Despite this appeal to international law, Judge Salus told the jury to disregard the argument because the Nuremberg principles were irrelevant. He instructed jurors to focus only on the issue of whether the defendants had damaged property and broken the law. The jury complied, convicting all eight of the charges against them.

The Plowshares Eight appealed the conviction by arguing that they were not allowed to present the "necessity defense" or call witnesses on their behalf. The Pennsylvania Supreme Court reversed the conviction in 1984, but the state set in motion more appeals that lasted for nearly a decade. Finally, in April of 1990, the eight were brought to court for resentencing. The presiding judge, James Buckingham, allowed the activists to call their expert witnesses. After listening to their testimonies, he announced his decision: all eight were sentenced to time served, plus twenty-three months of probation. He briefly added a personal comment, acknowledging that the defendants were acting on moral convictions and that he shared their concern about nuclear war. Despite the judge's sympathetic comments, Plowshares supporters knew that the nuclear arms race was escalating and thus the actions continued.

The Griffiss Plowshares Trial

In almost all subsequent Plowshares trials, activists have employed the same legal arguments that the Plowshares Eight tried to use – namely, that their actions are permitted by international law and that the necessity defense justifies such measures since they are taken to prevent greater harm. An additional strategy was used by seven activists who hammered on a B-52 bomber, converted to carry Cruise missiles, at the Griffiss Strategic Air Command Base in upstate New York in 1983. During a pre-trial hearing, the Griffiss Plowshares activists submitted a motion to dismiss the charges against them, arguing that they were upholding the constitutional prohibition against a national religion. Invoking the Catholic Left's belief that nuclear weapons had become "gods of metal," they asserted that reverence for militarism had become America's civil religion. One of the defendants, Elizabeth McAlister, explained their argument to Judge Howard Munson:

We are dealing with serious constitutional issues – namely, the issue of a national religion having been established in our country in violation of the First Amendment. The religion of national sovereignty or nuclearism is alive and flourishing.

Its existence, its pre-eminence, its rituals, gods, priests and high priestesses make serious encroachments on all of us ... violating our freedom of religion. ... The state religion not only compels acts that are prohibited by the laws of God but the state religion itself prohibits the free exercise of religion. The state religion compels a quality of loyalty focused on our acceptance of the existence of nuclear weapons as a necessity. Weapons we are expected to pay for, adulate, thank God for, become sacred objects of worship. Such worship is prohibited by the laws of God.

Likewise the state religion prohibits the acts of justice that God's law requires. The acts of justice include ... not killing or preparing to kill, but also the rescuing of victims of murder, or intercession on their behalf. In this time when nuclear weapons threaten all created life, ... in this time when 40,000 children die daily from hunger while the world spends 1.3 million a minute on annihilatory weapons, acts of rescuing victims or intercession on their behalf take the form of direct acts of disarmament. ... Then to use the laws of our land for the purpose of punishing people who carry out acts of nonviolent direct disarmament is unconstitutional. Such application of the law prohibits our free exercise of religion and violates Article I of the Constitution.[57]

The judge listened carefully to McAlister's appeal and asked for a copy of her statement. Later, he called the seven defendants back. He told them that he found their motion innovative and had given it a great deal of consideration, but ultimately he was denying their request because he was not convinced that the government intended to establish a national religion when the arms race started.[58] The charges stood and a trial was scheduled for the following month.

When the trial date arrived, the activists entered a plea of not guilty based on international law and the "necessity" or "justification" defense. The prosecution asked the judge to exclude these defenses, along with the accompanying testimonies. Judge Munson barred the Griffiss Plowshares participants from citing international law but he did allow them to call experts to support their claim that they were trying to stop an imminent and greater harm. The Plowshares activists called several witnesses. A Harvard psychologist, Dr. Henry Abraham, testified to the psychological damage that the arms race was causing. Cornell biologist Dr. Alan McNeil explained how the missiles could produce a nuclear winter, and Robert Aldridge detailed the characteristics of first-strike nuclear weapons. Princeton law professor Richard Falk spoke of the mandates of international

---

[57] Berrigan, Philip, and Elizabeth McAlister. 1989. *The Time's Discipline: The Beatitudes and Nuclear Resistance*. Baltimore: Fortkamp Publishing, pp. 133–134.

[58] Weber, Sarah Appleton. 1984. *Griffiss Plowshares Action and Trial*. Photocopy of manuscript made by Plowshares Support, Syracuse, NY.

law, and historian Howard Zinn described how civil disobedience is a long-standing American tradition and essential to a functioning democracy. [59]

After the defendants rested their case, the prosecuting attorneys asked the judge to strike the activists' justification defense. He complied, stating that they had failed to present sufficient evidence to support their claim that nuclear war was imminent and that other channels for addressing the threat were ineffective. Thus Judge Munson instructed the jury to disregard the expert witnesses.[60] The jury members then deliberated for nearly a day before returning a verdict. They found all seven defendants not guilty of sabotage but guilty of conspiracy and destroying federal property. They received sentences ranging from one to two years. Despite having the opportunity to present expert witnesses and submit a justification defense, the outcome of the Griffiss Plowshares trial was similar to the outcome of the Plowshares Eight trial, as well as the vast majority of Plowshares cases that followed.

Plowshares and the Media

To establish legitimacy of means, organizers must convince others that their tactics are justifiable. Plowshares activists have accomplished this through their theology of resistance and references to international law. Yet how have these justifications been disseminated to others? In most movements, activists work with the media to spread the word about their cause. Plowshares activists do as well, but in a limited manner since they are quite skeptical of conventional journalism.

Plowshares activists criticize the mainstream media for not providing in-depth information. Activists are rarely quoted in full and little background context is offered, thus reducing the action to a brief, sensationalized story. David Mackenzie stated, "The quality of coverage varies enormously. Although hostile reporting is rare, scrappy, skimpy, inaccurate or downright misleading copy is common."[61] To illustrate the point, he noted that one newspaper printed a two-sentence account of a Plowshares action with the heading "Priest Accused of [Air Force] Burglary." The religious motives

---

[59] Brennan, Claire. 1984. "Griffiss 7 Strategy Allowed," *The Post-Standard*, May 31, 1984, p. 8.

[60] Weber, Sarah Appleton. 1984. *Griffiss Plowshares Action and Trial*. Photocopy of manuscript made by Plowshares Support, Syracuse, NY.

[61] Quotation taken from the Trident Plowshares Handbook (third edition), available online at www.tridentploughshares.org/article1076.

and the political issues involved in the action were completely missing, giving the impression that this was a common property crime committed by a clergyman.

In addition, Plowshares participants view the mainstream media as controlled by the nation's power elite and driven by capitalist interests. In the activists' opinion, those who own the "mental means of production" are not likely to devote serious attention to the criticisms put forth by the movement. Ciaron O'Reilly noted: "Moderates have a false perception that the mainstream media is some kind of social service objectively reporting the news rather than having a radical perception of it as a highly centralized, profit-driven industry. . . . Freedom of the press is for those who own one!"[62] Although there have been some instances of positive coverage,[63] U.S. Plowshares members have occasionally been portrayed as extreme deviants, religious terrorists, political fanatics, and criminals. Thus, many members do not make extensive efforts to work with conventional newspapers or television stations because the movement may be depicted negatively and the story is likely to be reduced to trite sound bites.

Instead of using traditional media outlets, Plowshares activists are more likely to put out their message through independent, alternative channels where they have a greater capacity to control their public message. Since one of the goals of activists is to engage Christians in a discussion about the morality of war, they frequently submit articles or give interviews to Catholic periodicals such as *National Catholic Reporter* and Catholic Worker newsletters. They accept invitations to speak at colleges, religious gatherings, and peace movement events. Several have authored books about their experiences, typically published by religious presses or presses with a progressive orientation.[64] A few independent, low-budget films have been made as well, such as *Inside the King of Prussia*, which re-enacts the Plowshares Eight trial.[65] Plowshares activists also seek radio coverage. Tom Hastings noted, "Mainstream media are an uphill battle. Radio is best . . . [because] Plowshares do exciting actions for critically thought-through reasons, both

---

[62] Ciaron O'Reilly, personal correspondence with the author, January 24, 2007.

[63] This has been particularly true in the case of the three Dominican Sisters' action in Northern Colorado. The *Denver Post* closely covered their action, trial, and subsequent refusal to pay restitution, portraying the nuns as women of conscience.

[64] These include Common Courage Press, Fortkamp Publishing Company, Orbis Books, New Society Publishers, and so forth.

[65] Other films include *Gods of Metal* and *Conviction*.

of which tend to appeal to public radio producers."[66] In each of these venues, activists are able to elaborate on the issues, explain their motives, and justify their tactics.

Finally, for many Plowshares activists, legitimacy of means is best conveyed through interpersonal contact and discussion. This is where authentic dialogue can occur and understanding of tactics increases. One activist stated:

> Discussions with friends and family are probably the most effective media.... Other channels that can be used to increase participation are direct contact and discussions with the opponent during actions and trials.... Unfortunately, the protest movement is often looking more for publicity than for publicizing.... The main issue has become how to get in contact with the mass media and thereby strengthen one's own prestige.... To go on tour with a slide show, used together with discussion, is often a more effective 'mass media' than a few headlines.[67]

In the Plowshares movement, media coverage is not pursued for its own sake, but as a means of increasing awareness about the threat of nuclear weapons, conveying biblical teachings on non-violent resistance, and reaching the conscience of people so that they will take responsibility for disarmament. Since conventional media sources rarely accomplish this, Plowshares activists seek alternative methods to broadcast their message.

Conclusion

When Catholic Left activists engaged in property destruction, they knew that they would need to persuade others that this was a valid method of resistance. To establish legitimacy of means, they had to explain the value of conducting such symbolic, high-risk actions, particularly since they yield little in terms of achieving movement goals. Thus Plowshares activists and supporters developed a theology of resistance that calls people of faith to continue the biblical tradition of non-violent prophetic provocation. Although many would argue that the movement's theology is not orthodox, some have found these alternative religious views compelling. Enough people were persuaded that dozens of Plowshares campaigns followed the General Electric action.

[66] Tom Hastings, personal correspondence with the author, January 23, 2007.
[67] Herngren, Per. 1993. *Path of Resistance: The Practice of Civil Disobedience*. Philadelphia: New Society Publishers.

Appeals to international law constitute a second method for establishing legitimacy of means. While their prophetic mandate is central to their faith and witness, Plowshares activists also have their feet firmly grounded in this-worldly arguments about whether weapons of mass destruction are permitted by law and what responsibilities individual citizens bear for preventing nuclear war. They maintain that international law is on their side. If they can prove this in court, they believe that the movement can hold governments accountable, forcing them to dismantle their nuclear arsenals.

The movement's theological ideas and its legal arguments have been conveyed to thousands of people – mostly through public speaking events, religious publications, and independent media outlets. While many still find the movement's tactics questionable, legitimacy of means was established sufficiently that the Plowshares movement began to expand.

3

Sustaining Commitment

Taking advantage of the Freedom of Information Act, one Plowshares activist requested his file from the Federal Bureau of Investigation. The Bureau responded that it needed an advance payment for photocopying expenses since his file was nearly 400 pages long.[1] Similarly, when Philip Berrigan was arrested in 1997 for a Plowshares action in Bath, Maine, the prosecuting attorneys pulled his criminal record. It revealed that Berrigan had been arrested nearly forty times in the previous thirty years and had spent over ten years behind bars.[2] While these individuals may have more extensive records than other Plowshares activists, many movement partici-pants are repeat offenders who, time and time again, commit dramatic acts of civil disobedience. What enables these individuals to persistently resist over time? How do they sustain their commitment to peace work through the years and decades, especially when the consequences of their activism are severe? These questions deal with the issue of activist retention – the developmental challenge that organizers must address if they hope to main-tain their movement over the long run, avoiding the shift into abeyance or the complete termination of their movement.

Now nearly thirty years old, the U.S. Plowshares movement has demon-strated considerable endurance as a result of its ability to sustain activists' commitment. The movement's longevity is even more noteworthy consid-ering the broader disarmament movement subsided in the early 1990s as the Cold War ended. In fact, 35 percent of all U.S. peace organizations had completely ceased operations by 1992 due to dissipating public concern

---

[1] Informal conversation with activist, author's field notes, May 23, 2001.
[2] Philip Berrigan's Legal and Police Document, DePaul University Archives, Berrigan-McAlister Collection, Box 5.

about nuclear arms and an increased sense of peacetime security.[3] While most peace organizations saw their numbers dwindle during this period, Plowshares campaigns continued at a steady pace. In this chapter, I examine how the U.S. Plowshares movement has retained members and perpetuated their commitment, contributing to a trajectory of sustained persistence.

Movement Exiting and Persistence

Once individuals are drawn into a movement, their ongoing participation is hardly assured. There are many factors that can lead people to minimize their involvement or drop out completely. Activists may find that they have less time for protest activities as they take on new responsibilities, such as full-time careers or raising children.[4] Commitment to a movement can also diminish as people's convictions wane and their connections to other activists weaken over time. These trends are often related. As beliefs abate, people may withdraw from movement networks; similarly, if people are not strongly integrated into activist circles, the intensity of their convictions may fade. Relationships with movement outsiders may also facilitate decisions to leave, especially if they are with significant others who oppose this form of activism.[5] In addition, activists sometimes drop out of one movement in order to devote more time to other causes.[6] Finally, when movement participation incurs significant costs and produces high levels of psychological stress, activists are likely to experience burnout, which can lead to diminishing levels of commitment, and ultimately disengagement.[7]

[3] Edwards, Bob, and Sam Marullo. 1995. "Organizational Mortality in Declining Social Movements: The Demise of Peace Movement Organizations in the End of the Cold War Era." *American Sociological Review* 60: 908–927.

[4] Doug McAdam argues that those who are free from such responsibilities – or, in his words, are "biographically available" for activism – are more likely to engage in high-risk actions. To see how people sometimes overcome biographical unavailability to sustain their involvement in movements, see Downton, James, and Paul Wehr. 1997. *The Persistent Activist: How Peace Commitment Develops and Survives*. Boulder: Westview Press. Also see Nepstad, Sharon Erickson, and Christian S. Smith. 1999. "Rethinking Recruitment to High-Risk/Cost Activism: The Case of Nicaragua Exchange." *Mobilization* 4(1): 25–40.

[5] Aho, James. 1994. *This Thing of Darkness: A Sociology of the Enemy*. Seattle: University of Washington Press.

[6] Cress, Daniel, J. Miller McPherson, and Thomas Rotolo. 1997. "Competition and Commitment in Voluntary Memberships: The Paradox of Persistence and Participation." *Sociological Perspectives* 40: 61–79.

[7] Klandermans, Bert. 1997. *The Social Psychology of Protest*. Cambridge, MA: Blackwell Publishers.

While all these factors can undermine long-term activism, not everyone who is exposed to these countervailing forces stops protesting. So what distinguishes those who leave a movement from those who remain engaged? Not surprisingly, research shows that persistent activists have higher levels of commitment than those who drop out.[8] According to Steven Barkan, Steven Cohn, and William Whitaker, those who possess an enduring movement commitment tend to hold beliefs and values that are compatible with a social movement organization (SMO). They note that while "interest in achieving SMO goals and agreement with SMO ideologies often go hand in hand, that is not always the case. For example, although many feminists might agree with the goal of an anti-pornography SMO led by religious fundamentalists, the two groups would disagree on the reasons for opposing pornography and many other points."[9] Feminist members of this organization, therefore, are likely to be less dedicated than their fundamentalist counterparts. They also argue that those individuals who have close friendships with other activists and with movement leaders are more devoted. Additionally, Barkan and his associates posit that those who have great trust in their leaders, and those who believe the movement is effective, exhibit the highest degree of commitment.[10]

While strength of devotion is important, it is essential to recognize that movement commitment is a multifaceted phenomenon. Bert Klandermans notes that it is comprised of an *affective* component, reflecting the degree of emotional attachment to a movement, a *continuance* component – referring to the costs associated with leaving a movement that consequently encourage ongoing involvement – and a *normative* component, indicating the moral obligation individuals feel to continue working for movement goals.[11] These three forms of commitment emerge from

---

[8] Downton, James, and Paul Wehr. 1997. *The Persistent Activist: How Peace Commitment Develops and Survives*. Boulder: Westview Press; Klandermans, Bert. 1997. *The Social Psychology of Protest*. Cambridge, MA: Blackwell Publishers.

[9] Barkan, Steven E., Steven F. Cohn, and William H. Whitaker. 1993. "Commitment Across the Miles: Ideological and Microstructural Sources of Membership in a National Antihunger Organization." *Social Problems* 40: 362–73. Quotation on page 364.

[10] In addition to their 1993 article, also see Barkan, Steven E., Steven F. Cohn, and William H. Whitaker. 1995. "Beyond Recruitment: Predictors of Differential Participation in a National Antihunger Organization." *Sociological Forum* 10: 113–134.

[11] Klandermans' ideas (1997) are drawn from occupational psychology literature, specifically the following works: Allen, Nathalie J., and John P. Meyer. 1990. "The Measurement and Antecedents of Affective, Continuance, and Normative Commitment to Organization." *Journal of Occupational Psychology* 63: 1–18; Meyer, John P., and Nathalie Allen. 1991. "A Three Component Conceptualization of Organizational Commitment." *Human Resource*

independent sources. Affective commitment develops through pleasurable interactions with fellow activists and through material or cultural rewards gained from movement participation. Continuance commitment is formed when activists make extraordinary sacrifices for a movement, such as risking their own safety or forfeiting careers and relationships for a cause. This makes members more invested since a movement's failure would render these sacrifices worthless.[12] Normative commitment emerges from long-term socialization processes that instill beliefs that are consistent with the movement, as well as the moral imperative to fight injustices. The stronger these three forms of commitment, the greater are the chances that activists will remain part of a movement.

Commitment, however, is not static or fixed. All three aspects of dedication can dissipate with time. Affective commitment can decrease if the material rewards of participation diminish or if people no longer derive pleasure from activism. Similarly, normative commitment can fluctuate since convictions, particularly militant ones, may wane if they are not continually reinforced. And while high costs for participation might solidify continuance commitment by giving people a greater stake in the fate of the movement, activists may become embittered or disillusioned if they feel their sacrifices were made in vain. Therefore, retaining movement members over the long run entails an ongoing effort to strengthen all three components. If a movement is not steadily winning material gains, leaders must increase the cultural rewards of activism by keeping friendships strong. Leaders must also develop strategies and practices to rejuvenate moral convictions and reinforce the belief that the costs incurred are worthwhile.

In addition to strengthening commitment, the barriers to long-term movement participation must also be addressed. Activists need to counter the factors that undermine support and contribute to movement exiting. In a

---

Management Review 1: 61–89; Meyer, John P., Nathalie Allen, and Ian R. Gellatly. 1993. "Affective and Continuance Commitment to the Organization: Evaluation of Measures and Analysis of Concurrent and Time-lagged Relations." *Journal of Applied Psychology* 75: 710-720.

[12] This finding is also supported by Donatella della Porta's study of Italian and German underground groups. She argues that "the militants' very high initial investment reduced the likelihood that they would leave their organization.... They persisted in their involvement because surrendering implied 'losing' everything they had already paid as costs for entering the underground" (1992: 284). It is also consistent with Rosabeth Moss Kanter's (1968) study of utopian communities in which she found that those communes that required their members to make significant sacrifices had greater survival rates than those that did not.

comparative study of activists in the U.S. peace movement, James Downton and Paul Wehr found that a key characteristic distinguishing "persisters" from "terminators" was their ability to manage issues that disrupt movement engagement.[13] Persisters minimized the effects of opposition to their political work through a variety of coping mechanisms, such as humor and meditation. They also neutralized the impact of cross-pressures – negative reactions and criticism from others – by finding alternative sources of support. They implemented strategies to avoid burnout, such as regularly scheduled time for recreation. Moreover, they arranged their lives to accommodate activism, often pursuing careers in social change organizations or only accepting employment that offered a flexible schedule.[14] Those who successfully managed these issues were more likely to remain involved in peace activism over time. The task of obstacle management need not be a purely individualistic endeavor, however. Movement organizers can institutionalize strategies to help people address the issues that can derail long-term activism.

How have organizers in the Plowshares movement reinforced activists' affective, continuance, and normative commitment over the years? What types of practices have they implemented to sustain radical beliefs and revitalize affective ties that, without maintenance, can easily atrophy with time? How have leaders helped people overcome the obstacles to long-term, high-risk activism, enabling them to make significant sacrifices for the movement?

Commitment and Community

According to Plowshares persisters, community is a critical component to long-term war resistance. Although many live in their own intentional communities – such as religious orders or other faith-based groups – the majority have connections to Jonah House and the Atlantic Life Community. Table 3.1 indicates that 97 percent of respondents have visited Jonah House, nearly 94 percent have attended an Atlantic Life Community retreat, and more than 80 percent have volunteered or lived at a Catholic Worker house. Table 3.2 indicates that Plowshares activists believe that ties

[13] Downton, James, and Paul Wehr. 1997. *The Persistent Activist: How Peace Commitment Develops and Survives.* Boulder: Westview Press.
[14] Also see Lichterman, Paul. 1996. *The Search for Political Community: American Activists Reinventing Commitment.* New York: Cambridge University Press.

Table 3.1. *Plowshares Activists' Participation in Catholic Left Communities (percentages)*

Community participation	Yes (%)	No (%)	Total
Visited Jonah House	96.9	3.1	100
Attended Atlantic Life community gatherings	93.8	6.2	100
Volunteered at Catholic Worker	81.3	18.7	100

N = 54

Table 3.2. *Importance of Catholic Left Communities in Sustaining Activism (percentages)*

Community	Extremely important (%)	Very important (%)	Somewhat important (%)	Not very important (%)	Not at all important (%)	Total
Jonah House	68.8	21.9	9.3	0	0	100
Atlantic Life	43.4	20.0	23.3	3.3	10	100
Catholic Worker	55.2	34.5	6.9	3.4	0	100

N = 54

to these communities are essential to the longevity of their commitment. Almost 91 percent stated that Jonah House is extremely or very important in sustaining their faith and activism, and almost 90 percent shared the same sentiments about Catholic Worker communities. Close to two-thirds believe that the Atlantic Life Community is extremely or very important in maintaining their resistance to militarism. But why? What occurs in these communities that sustains commitment and counters the tendency to drop out?

Community as a Means of Reinforcing Normative Beliefs

These Catholic Left communities help retain participants and promote persistence because they strengthen normative commitment to movement goals and beliefs. In essence, they operate as "plausibility structures." This term was introduced by Peter Berger, who argued that beliefs about the supernatural, as well as other views at odds with mainstream society, would weaken under social pressures that deem such perspectives untenable. To maintain faith, people must form groups where they "huddle together with like-minded fellow deviants – and huddle very closely indeed. Only in a counter-community of considerable strength does cognitive deviance have a chance to maintain itself."[15] Berger's claim is supported by studies of doomsday groups such as *When Prophecy Fails.*[16] This work chronicles the events surrounding a woman who claimed to be receiving messages from outer space about an impending flood. On the predicted day of disaster, her prophecy failed to materialize. As a result, some of her followers lost faith, but others did not. The factor distinguishing the ongoing believers from the former believers was social support. One group had awaited the flood together; when the disaster did not occur, the leader reportedly received another extraterrestrial message stating that the city was saved because of their faithfulness. These participants not only accepted the explanation, they also became active proselytizers. Those who were isolated from the group, however, relinquished their faith in the prophet.

Community, therefore, can sustain radical and even highly improbable beliefs. It does so by providing interaction with "confirming others" and by offering explanations that legitimate beliefs and assuage doubts. Plausibility structures often implement rituals, such as prayer and group singing, to regularly reinforce alternative values and views.[17] Berger maintains that "it is only as the individual remains within this structure that the conception of the world in question will remain plausible to him."[18]

This type of supportive community is particularly important to Plowshares activists because they encounter significant opposition that can erode their convictions and instill doubts about the legitimacy of prophetic symbolic action. Some of this criticism comes from friends and relatives. For instance, one woman's spouse was initially very opposed to her participation in the movement. She recalled, "My husband thought I had been mesmerized by this group of people who were controlling my mind. He was really determined to stop me.... My brothers came over to my house one night and one said, 'Why don't you just put a cross on the front yard and hang yourself up there?'... Everybody thought I'd gone cuckoo."[19] Her experience is not uncommon, as Table 3.3 indicates that a sizeable number of

---

[15] Berger, Peter. 1969. *A Rumor of Angels.* Garden City, NY: Doubleday, p. 19.

[16] Festinger, Leon, Henry W. Riecken, and Stanley Schachter. 1956. *When Prophecy Fails.* Minneapolis: University of Minnesota Press.

[17] Billings, Dwight. 1990. "Religion as Opposition: A Gramscian Analysis." *American Journal of Sociology* 96: 1–31.

[18] Berger, Peter. 1969. *A Rumor of Angels.* Garden City, NY: Doubleday, p. 40.

[19] Interview with Molly Rush, conducted by the author, March 26, 2001.

Table 3.3. *Opposition Experienced by Plowshares Activists (percentages)*

Disapproval from	Yes (%)	No (%)	Total
Spouse	20	80	100
Friends	50	50	100
Parents	59.1	40.9	100
Children	26.1	73.9	100
Extended family	54.2	45.8	100
Colleagues	8.3	91.7	100
Church leaders	23.4	76.6	100

N = 49

activists faced opposition from family and friends. In fact, 89.8 percent of survey respondents stated that they faced disapproval from someone close to them.

Some Plowshares activists also received sharp words from strangers who were angered by their actions. For example, the Prince of Peace Plowshares group boarded the nuclear-capable Aegis destroyer ship USS *The Sullivans*, built at the Bath Iron Works (BIW) in Maine. The six activists hammered on the ship, poured blood, and were arrested. They were initially brought before a state judge who refused to jail them, calling Philip Berrigan a "moral giant and the conscience of a generation."[20] After their release, they were re-arrested by U.S. marshals and the federal government charged them with conspiracy and damaging government property. Once they were convicted, their lawyer, Maria Holt, received the following letter from a very hostile observer.

Dear Ms. Holt

I am incensed at your irresponsible defense of the traitors who desecrated *The Sullivans*, a proud vessel honoring the only family in American history that lost five sons at once in defense of your liberties. Your arrogant Me-generation has no appreciation of the sacrifices made by men like the Sullivan brothers on the sacred altar of liberty. The Berrigan mob might just as well go and urinate on the Viet Nam wall memorial or overturn gravestones at Arlington. In saner times, the Navy guard at BIW would have been armed and the vandals would have been shot on the spot. Having shot a lot of enemy soldiers whom I respected more, I would gladly volunteer right now to blow these ungrateful bastards away. Teenage vandalism is bad enough. Adult vandalism is an abomination.

[20] Wilcox, Fred (ed.). 2001. *Disciples and Dissidents: Prison Writings of the Prince of Peace Plowshares*. Athol, MA: Haleys. Quotation on page xvii.

People like the Plowshare gang are not "working to prevent the ultimate holo-caust," our <u>military</u> is.... The Plowshares mob isn't "brave." They're stupid and dogmatic and un-American. Otherwise, they would be doing something really worthwhile. Like working in India with Mother Theresa or helping suffering children in Angola, or teaching Central American natives alternative methods to slash-and-burn agriculture. But that's too much more like work and that doesn't suit their pathological need for imagined persecution. Hopefully, there are some people behind bars who are at least patriotic enough to beat these traitors into plowshares themselves so we won't have to house and feed a bunch of sick vandals for decades to come.[21]

To sustain radical beliefs and convictions in light of such opposition, Plowshares activists need reinforcement from one another, which they find in Catholic Left communities. Local churches typically do not provide suf-ficient support because many are apolitical or conservative and some are overtly antagonistic to their controversial style of peacemaking. One Plow-shares activist, who attends Mass in her neighborhood parish, described the dynamic in her congregation:

I am very aware of the hostility toward me. In [my] church, certain people won't give me the kiss of peace. I am still Catholic, more Catholic than I ever was, but I am so saddened by the behavior of our church hierarchy.... During the Gulf War, there was a parishioner who was going into the armed services and the deacon wanted to support her so he offered a prayer of petition for our troops in the Middle East. In church that day, my brother stood up afterwards and said, "And God bless the Iraqi people who are on the receiving end of these bombs that we think God is blessing." Now that caused an uproar. Some priests could have just let it go, but at the end of Mass, our priest said, "I will not tolerate the kind of outburst in *my* parish. This is not acceptable." So people started talking – outside the church, inside the church – and it wasn't all nice.... Yet I was grateful for it because we got some interested members of the church to start studying *Pacem in Terris* [papal encyclical "Peace on Earth"]. The church wouldn't announce it from the pulpit; they wouldn't grant the space in the church to have the study of *Pacem in Terris*. No – these folks have the flag on their lapels while they're serving communion. They'd probably serve you red, white, and blue communion if they could. That's how co-opted they are.... If that was all that I was getting from the church, I would not be in it. But... there are these [other] faithful communities, folks doing faith-based resistance, that bring the story of Jesus to life. So that's how I stay plugged in.[22]

Plowshares activists rely upon their plausibility structures to affirm their alternative understanding of scripture and their belief that picking up the

[21] Letter from Bob Jorgensen, DePaul University Archives, Berrigan-McAlister Collection, Box 36A.

[22] Interview with Clare Grady, conducted by the author, August 12, 2003.

cross means provocatively challenging the state, and even the church. Without the support of like-minded activists, participants could easily feel isolated and alienated, weakening their normative commitment. Consider the experience of one priest in the movement:

I'm on the total margins of the church, the margins of the Jesuits. I'm always, always in trouble. They've moved to kick me out many times simply over peace actions, Plowshares actions, and civil disobedience. About a month ago I was hauled into the archbishop of New Mexico's office because I was organizing a silent prayer vigil at Los Alamos on Hiroshima Day. He forbid me to appear there, even to pray, or I'd be kicked out of New Mexico. My whole life I have one episode like that after another. . . . It's really hard. It's so painful. I get tons of hate mail, even death threats. But the thing is, I'm a Christian and I read in the gospel that Jesus was harassed and persecuted every day he opened his mouth . . . and he's the guy I claim to follow. . . . Dorothy Day said that if you're not in trouble, then you need to reflect on your life. It's a measure of your discipleship.[23]

This priest also emphasized the fact that his faith is nurtured and sustained by his ongoing connections to Catholic Left communities. These friendships and ties provide support in the face of opposition, thereby counteracting the effects of cross-pressures and burnout that so often erode movement commitment. He reflected:

My family thinks I'm part of a cult. But it's not a cult; we are free to leave whenever we want but we choose to build friendships and relationships. Right from the beginning, Dan and Phil [Berrigan] said that the number one lesson they learned from Vietnam anti-war resistance is the importance of community. It is not possible to work for peace without community. I have literally heard them say this dozens and dozens of times. They say, "You'll never last unless you get with a community. We can promise you that." We've seen thousands of people walk away from the peace movement because they got burned out. They were on their own and they became despairing, distressed. They didn't have a group of friends to help them. Phil was with Jonah House, I am with Pax Christi groups, and Dan has this group in Manhattan. It's about ten people and for 20 years they have been meeting every two weeks. You might say, "That's ridiculous. Nothing can ever come of that." But it's the only way Dan and I survived in the end because we have this community that says, "You're not crazy. What you're doing is right." We have this little group that is 100 percent behind us. We can't get that within the Jesuit order. You have to meet with like-minded activists. All of the long haul activists have learned that.[24]

Many activists articulate the importance of community, but to what extent have these plausibility structures actually reinforced normative

[23] Interview with John Dear, conducted by the author, June 11, 2003.
[24] Interview with John Dear, conducted by the author, June 11, 2003.

Table 3.4. *Beliefs and Values of U.S. Plowshares Activists (percentages)*

Activity values	Extremely important (%)	Very important (%)	Moderately important (%)	Somewhat important (%)	Not at all important (%)	Total
Resisting war	87.1	9.7	3.2	0	0	100
Resisting injustice	87.1	9.7	0	0	3.2	100
Fighting for the poor and oppressed	87.1	9.7	3.2	0	0	100
Following one's conscience	86.7	10	0	3.3	0	100
Protecting the environment	74.2	22.6	0	0	3.2	100
Prayer	74.2	19.4	3.2	3.2	0	100
Works of mercy	67.7	29.0	3.3	0	0	100
Establishing gender equality in the church	65.5	17.2	6.9	6.9	3.5	100
Supporting fair labor practices	62.1	31.0	6.9	0	0	100
Changing the social order	61.5	15.4	19.2	3.9	0	100
Bible study	60.0	23.3	10	6.7	0	100
Simple lifestyle	58.1	29.0	9.7	0	3.2	100
Withdrawing from capitalism	51.7	13.8	13.8	13.8	6.9	100
Proselytizing	15.4	0	3.9	19.2	61.5	100
Believing in God without doubt	12.5	4.2	8.3	8.3	66.7	100
Charitable giving	10.7	14.3	21.4	21.4	32.2	100
Sexual purity	8.0	8.0	36.0	12.0	36.0	100
Attending church regularly	0	3.8	23.1	23.1	50.0	100
Theological orthodoxy	0	3.6	7.1	14.3	75.0	100
Voting	0	0	13.8	17.2	69.0	100

N = 32

commitment, keeping movement beliefs and moral convictions strong over time? To gauge commitment to Plowshares goals and values, I asked survey respondents to rank the importance of various activities from war resistance and fighting injustice to prayer, charitable giving, and voting. The results, summarized in Table 3.4, indicate that normative commitment is quite robust among movement participants. Not surprisingly, "resisting war," "resisting injustice," and "fighting for the poor and oppressed" were ranked the highest, with 96.8 percent indicating that it is extremely important or very important. Although respondents gave high marks to the defining traits of the Catholic Worker movement – works of mercy, supporting fair labor practices, withdrawing from capitalism, and changing the social order – these traits are clearly secondary. This finding reflects both continuity with the values of the Catholic Worker and a stronger connection to Jonah House and the Plowshares movement's emphasis on resistance.

What is perhaps most striking are the beliefs and values that are ranked as less significant. No one thought that attending church regularly was extremely important, and only 3.8 percent said it was very important. Half of all respondents stated that it was not important at all. Although many do worship regularly, they often hold services in their own intentional communities. This is partly due the hostility that some activists encounter in mainstream churches or, as one former priest stated, "Regular churches are boring. They've lost sight of the real, exciting message of the gospel."[25] Plowshares participants also maintain that theological orthodoxy is not critical because, as described in Chapter 3, they believe that traditional interpretations of scripture are inaccurate. One activist observed:

I think if you asked that question about theological orthodoxy you'd find that most American Catholics would say the same thing – no, it's not what's important. I'm sure it is more so in the Plowshares movement because we don't care if the Pope says, "I give you my full blessings on this war." There is the orthodoxy of the Just War theory, you know, but I'm sorry, I just don't accept it. I don't think Jesus Christ would accept it.[26]

Finally, voting was ranked the least important, which is also consistent with Catholic Left beliefs. Recall that Dorothy Day placed little value on voting, calling instead for a comprehensive social revolution. Philip Berrigan also argued that voting grants legitimacy to politicians, who are often culpable for bellicose military policies. He stated:

Don't vote, it only encourages them! Social change never comes from elections, Congresses, or pulpits, but from the streets, courts and prisons. Voting is an establishment measure, as corrupt as the establishment itself. . . . One could fairly claim that the Plowshares people have answered the question of voting. Or, to put it

---

[25] Informal conversation with Plowshares activists conducted during participant observation, documented in field notes from December 29, 2002.

[26] Interview with Lin Romano, conducted by the author, June 16, 2003.

another way, they vote with their lives, with their physical safety, and with their freedom.[27]

This view is still prevalent, as nearly 70 percent of respondents indicated that voting is not important at all. Mary Sprunger-Froese offered her perspective on the voting issue:

Most of us come from a radical perspective, meaning we want to get at the root of the problem. Our problems here in the U.S. aren't going to be dealt with by checking a box on a ballot because the root of our problem has to do with our priorities. If it's money that is running the country, my vote doesn't stand for much. We certainly saw that in the last election; it had a whole lot to do with money and corporate power.[28]

Another activist stated: "I haven't yet seen a candidate who isn't going to advocate evil when they're elected. So given a choice of evils, I'm not going to vote for a lesser evil."[29]

The survey results indicate that normative commitment remains strong among activists, but precisely how do these Catholic Left communities reinforce these beliefs? Plowshares leaders have implemented a variety of community practices to reinforce normative commitment and the moral obligation to resist war. Many of these practices are enacted at the Atlantic Life Community gatherings that occur several times each year. I attended the Feast of Innocents retreat that is held after Christmas to commemorate the events that followed Jesus's birth and the Magi's search for the Christ-child. According to scripture, Herod, the regional ruler, heard reports of a newborn king and feared that the child would pose a threat to his rule. Consequently, he ordered the slaying of all male children under two years old. Throughout the Feast of Innocents' retreat, contemporary political leaders were compared to Herod, and the slaughter of children in the Middle East was linked to the massacre of innocents at Jesus's birth.

The Atlantic Life Community also uses rituals to underscore movement beliefs and goals. Each morning and evening, retreat participants gather for song, prayer, and biblical reflection. At the start of the retreat that I attended, a nun discussed biblical commentaries that describe Herod as a cruel, ambitious leader who was willing to crush all challenges to his authority. Stating that the lust for power fuels violence and oppression, the nun asked everyone to eradicate these violent impulses in themselves and in society. After

---

[27] Berrigan, Philip. 1984. "The November Elections – To Vote or Else..." *Year One*, Vol. X, No. 3, July 1984. Quotation on pp. 3, 5.

[28] Interview with Mary Sprunger-Froese, conducted by the author, May 29, 2003.

[29] Interview with Lin Romano, conducted by the author, June 16, 2003.

the meditation, the singing began. Given the proximity to Christmas, many of the songs were political versions of holiday carols. For instance, we sang "The Twelve Days of Christmas" using the following alternative lyrics:

> On the first day of invasion my leader said to me,
>   They're the most dangerous nation in the world.
> On the second day's invasion my leader said to me,
>   They have weapons of mass destruction;
>   They're the most dangerous nation in the world.
> On the third day's invasion my leader said to me,
>   They won't allow inspections;
>   They have weapons of mass destruction;
>   They're the most dangerous nation in the world.
> On the fourth day's invasion my leader said to me,
>   They didn't sign the biological weapons treaty;
>   Won't allow inspections;
>   Weapons of mass destruction;
>   They're the most dangerous nation in the world.
> On the fifth days' invasion my leader said to me,
>   DEMAND REGIME CHANGE NOW!
>   Didn't sign the weapons treaty;
>   Won't allow inspections;
>   Weapons of mass destruction;
>   They're the most dangerous nation in the world.
> On the sixth (etc.)
>   All they want is oil;
>   They just can't be trusted;
>   They execute their people;
>   They helped to train Al Qaeda;
>   They invaded other countries;
>   They weren't fairly elected;
> On the twelfth day's invasion my leader said to me,
>   (Spoken) They plan to use the bomb
>   (Sing)
>   not fairly elected;
>   invaded other countries;
>   helped to train Al Qaeda;
>   execute their people;
>   they just can't be trusted;
>   all they want is oil;
>   DEMAND REGIME CHANGE NOW;
>   didn't sign the treaty;
>   Won't allow inspections;
>   Weapons of mass destruction;
>   and they're the most dangerous nation in the world.

Similarly, we sang "Silent Night, Holy Night" with the following words:

> Silent night, holy night
> All is not calm, all is not right
> Millions die from war and poverty
> Children living in misery
> Stop the violence, choose life
> Stop the violence, choose life
>
> Silent night, holy night
> The powers rule
> With force and might
> We must resist the darkness with light
> Keeping hope by day and night
> Proclaim God's reign of peace
> Proclaim God's reign of peace

The evening closed with a prayer written by Dominican Sisters Jackie Hudson, Ardeth Platte, and Carol Gilbert, who were in jail awaiting their trial for the Colorado silo action. Like the biblical meditation, the prayer reflects the retreat's theme of crying out against the government's (Herod's) slaughter of the innocents. The following excerpt illustrates how this ritual reinforces Catholic Left beliefs, thereby strengthening normative commitment.

ALL: Oh God, hear the voice of your servant. Hear the cry of your people.

LEADER: Philip Berrigan has been present in the wilderness of these Washington, DC. sites for decades. Listen to his voice crying, "Disarm! Disarm!"

ALL: We join our voices to his, to Dorothy Day, Catholic Workers, and Jonah House. "Disarm! Disarm!"

LEADER: Kathy Kelly has been present in Iraq many times since 1990. Listen to her voice crying, "Stop the sanctions! Stop the bombing!"

ALL: We join our voices to hers and to Voices in the Wilderness. Stop the sanctions! Stop the bombing! . . .

LEADER: Bruce Gagnon has begun the international movement to keep outer space as the sacred heavens. Listen to his voice crying, "No more wars in space! No wars from space! No wars through space!"

ALL: We join our voices to his and to the Global Network against the Nuclearization and Militarization of Space. No wars into space! No wars from space! No wars through space! . . .

LEADER: Cry out prophets of our times. Cry out at the top of your voice, herald the good news. Fear not to cry out and say to the cities of the world, "Here is your God in the midst of your struggle for justice, for peace."[30]

[30] From participant observations and field notes written by the author during the Atlantic Life Community Feast of Innocents retreat, December 27–29, 2002, Washington, DC.

Similar rituals are incorporated into many other events. For instance, some Plowshares activists commemorate Ash Wednesday – day of repentance – at the Pentagon. The traditional symbols are given new meaning, consistent with movement beliefs and aims. One Ash Wednesday gathering began with the following statement:

Today is Ash Wednesday. Traditionally it is a day of atonement. Again this year we begin the Lenten season with war in the world and the promise of a year of war (or more). We enter this season needing to repent for all that is done in our name. The weight is so intense that we gather for solidarity and for the strength to overcome the evil of war. We use the traditional symbol of ashes and the contemporary symbol of oil.[31]

After scripture reading, prayer, and a moment of reflection, a bowl of ashes and a pan of oil were brought forward. The leader stated, "Oil: Is this what we are fighting over? Is it worth all the human life, all the devastation of land and air and water? Ashes: What does war leave in its wake? Ashes. More ashes. Ashes and ruin. Everywhere ruin."[32] Then some of the oil was poured into the bowl of ashes, and the leader anointed the others' foreheads with the oiled ashes. Each person responded, "By accepting this sign of the cross, may we be liberated from our dependence on oil and from perpetual war! May it free us to interfere with the killing of millions."[33]

Such ritualistic enforcement is crucial because Plowshares activists often see no measurable results from their efforts. After decades of resistance, war has not been eradicated and nations have not dismantled their weapons of mass destruction. And it is unlikely that these goals will be accomplished in the near future. Under these circumstances, it might be easy to lose faith in the movement's aims and to question the necessity of ongoing action. As a plausibility structure, Catholic Left communities must therefore provide an alternative explanation that underscores the importance of such prophetic provocation, regardless of the outcome. This type of reinforcement was evident during the Feast of Innocents retreat when an activist offered a meditation on the biblical passage where Ezekiel has a vision of God giving him a scroll and commanding him to eat it. God said to him, "Go now and speak my words to the people... But they will not listen to you because they are not willing to listen to me, for they are hardened and obstinate" (Ezekiel 3:4, 7). This activist called on each person to be a prophet, stating

---

[31] DePaul University Archives, Berrigan-McAlister Collection, unmarked.
[32] DePaul Plowshares Archives, Berrigan-McAlister Collection, unmarked.
[33] DePaul Plowshares Archives, Berrigan-McAlister Collection, unmarked.

that every Christian has a duty to denounce war even if the world will not listen. The meditation provided affirmation that the movement is part of a highly valued prophetic tradition, thereby helping activists overcome doubts about the importance of their sacrifices and the need for continual resistance.

Community as a Means of Strengthening Relationships and Affective Commitment

In addition to reinforcing activists' beliefs and moral commitments, community practices foster member retention by strengthening friendship ties and emotional bonds. For example, one man stated that the Atlantic Life Community gatherings are like a family reunion. In fact, he said that he felt more at home at these retreats than he did during a recent family gathering where his cousin thanked him and stated: "As a multiple felon, and a married (former) priest, you make everyone else in the family look good by comparison."[34] As this statement reveals, the sacrifices Plowshares activists make for the movement gives them a sense of distinction from the rest of the population. Catholic Left communities offer a place where activists are surrounded by like-minded individuals, thereby granting them a sense of belonging. When people develop an awareness of the beliefs, values, and lifestyles they share with others, bonds of solidarity are forged.[35] Moreover, affective commitment – that is, the degree of emotional attachment to the movement – is strengthened through pleasurable interactions that occur during these retreats. One activist commented; "I've experienced an enormous amount of fun and warmth and friendship. These gatherings, the people, have helped me and . . . never fail to challenge and . . . inspire me. It's like getting my batteries recharged."[36]

Emotional ties to movement leaders are also important, as previous research indicates that activists who closely interact with leaders have higher levels of commitment.[37] Within Plowshares circles, such interaction occurs

---

[34] From field notes written by the author during participant observation of an Atlantic Life Community Feast of Innocents retreat, December 27–29, 2002, Washington, DC.

[35] Jasper, James. 1998. "The Emotions of Protest: Affective and Reactive Emotions in and around Social Movements." *Sociological Forum* 13: 397–424.

[36] Stephen Hancock, as quoted in the 1997 *Hope and Resistance Handbook*, pp.1–2.

[37] Barkan, Steven E., Steven F. Cohn, and William H. Whitaker. 1993. "Commitment Across the Miles: Ideological and Microstructural Sources of Membership Support in a National Antihunger Organization." *Social Problems* 40: 362–373.

both during retreats and through visits to Jonah House. As stated earlier, 97 percent of Plowshares activists have spent time at Jonah House, and many claim that this experience instilled deep respect for the leaders' tenacious life of resistance. This affection can be heard in one man's comments:

Phil Berrigan, Liz McAlister, Carl Kabat – their lives, actions, friendships, commitment to peace, and their sacrifices have deeply influenced my faith and activism. They have the ability to bring joy, hope, and love in this dying world. It is comforting to know that they aren't going to run away from the responsibilities of being human, of being Christians, and living up to the command to love. I wouldn't trade our time together for all the money the Pentagon protects.[38]

These relationships are critical in terms of sustaining commitment, as one woman noted:

At Jonah House ... I found people who are willing to read the scriptures each day and try to live according to the values of the scriptures regardless of the cost or the consequences. I found a community of people who would experiment, and were led by prayer and discernment. ... When I came to Jonah House, I met Sister Ardeth. She has been open and kind to me and has taught me about love by treating me in a loving way. When I begin to falter, I talk to Ardeth and she tells me of her struggles, and somehow I am strengthened by her perseverance.[39]

As activists become acquainted with leaders, many are inspired to emulate their example. Participants also feel greater pressure to remain involved in resistance; not only is there direct accountability to live out their convictions, but failure to do so might cause disappointment among the leaders they so admire.

Although these relationships may form initially in community, ongoing contact is necessary to sustain these bonds over time. Lack of communication, distance, and infrequent interaction can undermine friendships and deplete affective commitment. If weakened ties to movement networks foster termination, then one would expect that persistent, long-term activists would regularly spend time at Catholic Left communities so that emotional bonds can be rejuvenated. As shown in Table 3.5, survey respondents do demonstrate a strong degree of involvement in these communities. Nearly 60 percent have lived at a Catholic Worker house for more than a year and approximately 30 percent have lived at Jonah House for one or more years. The extent of continued contact can be measured roughly by the number of Atlantic Life Community retreats that activists have attended. According to

[38] Anonymous survey response answer, June 2001.
[39] Anonymous survey response answer, June 2001.

Table 3.5. *Extent of Activists' Involvement in Catholic Left Communities (percentages)*

Community	Percentage of Activists
Catholic Worker (involved in a Catholic Worker community for):	
1 month or less	18.2
2–6 months	9.1
6–12 months	13.6
1–5 years	13.6
5–10 years	13.6
10+ years	32.0
TOTAL	100.1
Jonah House	
Visited 1–4 times (but did not reside there)	24.1
Visited 5–10 times (but did not reside there)	20.7
Resided for 1–5 months	10.3
Resided for 6–12 months	13.8
Resided for 1–2 years	3.5
Resided for 3 or more years	27.6
TOTAL	100.0
Atlantic Life Community	
Attended 1–3 gatherings	26.7
Attended 4–7 gatherings	23.3
Attended 8–14 gatherings	20.0
Attended 15 or more gatherings	30.0
TOTAL	100.0

N = 54

the survey, almost three-quarters have participated in four or more Atlantic Life Community retreats; about one-third have been to fifteen or more. Although comparative data with movement dropouts is needed to substantiate the importance of regular contact in sustaining affective commitment and retaining members, these numbers indicate at least that persisters spend a fair amount of time with other Plowshares activists

Community and Ongoing Activist Socialization

Community practices also strengthen commitment by intensifying activist identity, which is derived from action, not merely from affiliation with an ideological position or a political group. Jonah House routinely organizes protest events, and acts of resistance are a ritualized part of the Atlantic Life Community retreats. At each gathering, "witness actions" are conducted at the White House and the Pentagon. Every retreat participant is involved in the planning process and given a specific task, from leafleting to holding banners or being the designated spokesperson.

During a retreat that I attended, the group staged a silent vigil and a die-in in front of the White House. Some members committed civil disobedience, "dying" in the restricted areas and spilling blood. Later, the group reconvened to evaluate the action. The conversation centered on the differential treatment by the police. Specifically, several people poured blood, but only one was charged with the more serious felony of defacing government property. One of the blood throwers commented that "I felt like Peter denying Christ because I didn't come forward to say that I had done it, too." He struggled between not wanting to give information to the police and not wanting to abandon the individual who was singled out. A Plowshares leader responded that it is typical police practice to try to divide the group. She then led community members in a brainstorming session on different methods of handling the situation. This discussion reflected movement socialization – that is, learning the rules and the protocol of protest. Moreover, the planning, implementation, and evaluation of the White House witness not only taught people how to be activists, it gave them a chance to engage this role, thus deepening their activist identity.

Community as a Site for Addressing Internal Disputes

Tensions and disagreements among activists can also undermine long-term movement commitment. Serious disputes can contribute to factionalization, and some individuals may drop out completely if they feel their concerns are not being taken seriously. Movement leaders must find some way to resolve these differences, or at least make them tolerable for the group. Community provides a context where divisions can be addressed. In the U.S. Plowshares movement, activists are quite unified in most of their beliefs and values. There are some topics, such as abortion, where there is disagreement. A sizeable number of other Plowshares activists advocate a "consistent ethic of life" that entails opposition to war, capital punishment, and abortion. Others support women's right to choose. At one Atlantic Life Community retreat, the women held a discussion on this topic. One activist described the meeting:

I had written this statement that said, no matter what my personal feelings about abortion are, I believe it should be legally protected and a safe procedure available to women. A lot of the Catholic women at the Atlantic Life Community signed it...but a lot didn't or said they had reservations. We eventually decided to hold a women's caucus on it. We had some very sensitive leaders who said you cannot make a political statement, you can only talk about your own experience. You cannot respond to somebody else. So the ground rules were very well done. And it was one of the most moving things that's ever happened because it didn't matter which side you were on. Women got up and told these incredible personal stories. It went on for hours and people were in tears...but there's no consensus on that one.[40]

Although the group has not reached consensus on this issue, the discussions have helped them accept this difference since those who are pro-choice feel that their concerns have genuinely been heard by those who are pro-life, and vice versa. In this way, the movement is able to live with a diversity of opinions. Some Plowshares activists have made public statements against abortions, while others have demonstrated for women's right to reproductive choices. One Plowshares participant, for instance, decided to take action when her bishop began leading marches to a local abortion clinic. She stood beside their processional holding a poster of the Virgin Mary with the following statement written on it: "God had one child and He was planned."[41]

Movement leaders need skills to constructively facilitate discussion over such potentially divisive issues but they also need a forum to address these topics. Community provides this context.

Overcoming Barriers to Long-Term Activism

To foster persistence, movements must reinforce commitment *and* address the barriers to long-term movement participation. One common obstacle is life responsibilities, such as careers and family obligations, which often make people reluctant to engage in high-risk or high-cost activism. Participation in a Plowshares campaign can easily result in job and income loss since activists almost always serve time in prison. How, then, are people able to join the movement? Are participants mostly young students who do not have jobs that would be jeopardized? Unlike the subjects of other studies

[40] Interview with an anonymous Plowshares activist, conducted by the author, June, 2001.
[41] Interview with an anonymous Plowshares activist, conducted by the author, May, 2003.

Table 3.6. *Characteristics of U.S. Plowshares Activists at Time of First Action (percentages)*

Age	%
Twenties	12.1
Thirties	48.5
Forties	21.2
Fifties	12.1
Sixties	6.1
TOTAL	100.0

(mean = 41.5, median = 39 years old)

Marital status	
Single	63.6
Married	27.3
Divorced	6.1
Widowed	0
Separated	3.0

Children	
Yes	33.3
No	66.7

Age of youngest child at time of action	
0–2 years old	9.1
2–5 years old	18.2
6–12 years old	18.2
13–17 years old	9.1
Over 18 years old	45.4
TOTAL	100.0

N = 36

of high-risk activism,[42] Plowshares activists are not typically college-aged youth. As Table 3.6 shows, the average age of American Plowshares activists at the time of their first action is approximately forty years. Additionally, one-third have children living at home. Given the need to provide for their families, how have they managed these responsibilities while remaining involved in the movement?

Assistance with Family Responsibilities

Several researchers have demonstrated that while families and full-time employment can be a barrier to movement participation, those who have a

[42] McAdam, Doug. 1988. *Freedom Summer*. New York: Oxford University Press.

108

strong activist identity and are deeply motivated may structure their lives to accommodate movement engagement.[43] Certainly this is true of Plowshares activists. Survey results indicate that this group is well educated – more than three-quarters are college graduates and 44 percent have advanced degrees (Masters, Ph.D., M.D. or J.D.). Many have placed such a high priority on war resistance, however, that they have given up professional careers to devote themselves to the movement. This is evident in the fact that over 58 percent of respondents are full-time volunteer activists. Only 29 percent have full-time jobs. Approximately 13 percent work part-time – most are self-employed or contract workers in manual labor or social service fields. This provides for basic living expenses while offering flexibility for protest activities. It is also consistent with the movement's emphasis on simple living, voluntary poverty, and downward social mobility (roughly 40 percent earned less than $10,000 annually in 2001). As a result, 90 percent of Plowshares activists responded in the survey that they did not lose their job as a result of their acts of resistance. This also explains why only 8.3 percent faced opposition from colleagues (see Table 3.3).

Although the potential loss of employment is not a serious barrier to long-term activism for most activists in the U.S. Plowshares movement, family responsibilities can be. Approximately 33 percent had children at the time of their first arrest. Instead of seeing it as a deterrent, many of them saw their children as the precise reason why they must resist weapons of mass destruction. Philip Berrigan and Elizabeth McAlister continued their life of war resistance while raising three children. They wrote:

So many experiences have taught us that children need to see commitment lived out by those who love them. We recall the terrible dislocation and alienation of German youth after World War II as they realized that their parents were silent in the face of Hitler's crimes in order to "protect" them. . . . Our resistance is perhaps our only armor against the hard "why" they will ask. . . . In preparations for war, as in war itself, pain, separation, death, breakup of families is the price. [Our children] have no more a birthright to normality than the orphans of Vietnam, than those starving in Southeast Asia, the Sahel, elsewhere, than the poor and dispossessed in the United States.[44]

---

[43] Downton, James and Paul Wehr. 1997. *The Persistent Activist: How Peace Commitment Develops and Survives*. Boulder: Westview Press; Lichterman, Paul. 1996. *The Search for Political Community: American Activists Reinventing Commitment*. New York: Cambridge University Press; Nepstad, Sharon Erickson, and Christian S. Smith. 1999. "Rethinking Recruitment to High-Risk/Cost Activism: The Case of Nicaragua Exchange." *Mobilization* 4(1): 25–40.

[44] Berrigan, Philip, and Elizabeth McAlister. 1989. *The Time's Discipline: The Beatitudes and Nuclear Resistance*. Baltimore: Fortkamp Publishing. Quotation on pp. 34–35.

Similarly, another woman explained why she participated in a Plowshares action even though her daughter was less than a year old.

Before my daughter was actually born, I saw pictures that the War Resisters League had put together, pictures that were taken after the bombing of Hiroshima and Nagasaki.... There was one of a woman in Nagasaki who had obviously just given birth, nursing her baby, and both of them were physically affected by the bomb. The look in their eyes was death and this infant wasn't more than a few months old. I was about to give birth in a few months and I'm thinking, this could be my baby. Dan Berrigan made this statement a long time ago that if people are as committed to peacemaking as those who are involved in warmaking, then we would be willing to do a lot more. These people, in the name of war, will give up their lives, leave their families. They are called heroes for going off to fight wars just after giving birth. So Dan's statement was really weighing on me.... The big factor that kind of tipped it for me was seeing these women ... crying out to be fighter pilots and go to combat ... during the Iraq build-up [to the Gulf War]. They were willing to leave their families to go kill people. I would be willing to leave my family in the name of ending war, in the name of disarmament, and justice.[45]

Catholic Left communities provide material assistance and family support to those involved in Plowshares actions, enabling them to go to prison with the assurance that their children are being cared for. Members of Jonah House, for example, raise their sons and daughters jointly and have implemented a policy of having only one parent imprisoned at a time. Although children still miss the parent who is incarcerated, they have an extended set of parents to ease the burden. Berrigan and McAlister stated that "[Our children] were born in a community committed to nonviolent resistance. They have been surrounded by people who love them, who are ... committed, self-sacrificing, deeply spiritual women and men. Each of the adults has developed a unique relationship with the children, has shared in their upbringing, has become co-responsible for them."[46]

Some critics may argue that these children will be psychologically damaged by their parents' actions. Although a systematic analysis of the emotional well-being of activists' sons and daughters is beyond the scope of this book, there is some anecdotal evidence indicating that many children do not harbor resentment. For example, within the Plowshares movement, no one has been separated from their parents more than Philip Berrigan and Elizabeth McAlister's children. Now adults, they speak affectionately about

---

[45] Interview with Michele Naar-Obed, conducted by the author, October 21, 2000.
[46] Berrigan, Philip, and Elizabeth McAlister. 1989. *The Time's Discipline: The Beatitudes and Nuclear Resistance.* Baltimore: Fortkamp Publishing. Quotation on p. 34.

their childhood and their parents. This admiration is evident in a letter that Jerry Berrigan wrote to his father:

Dear Dad,

... I decided to undertake writing to the people who have been present in my life, who have been formative and who have loved me. And I write to you, Dad, because you and Momma have been wonderful parents and I love you both very, very deeply. You have been constantly present in my life, you have nurtured me and allowed me to grow at my own pace while providing me with a rich example. You have said that we owe to each other our best version of the truth. And that is true – there is no gift more profound. Your life is testament to the best approximation of truth that I have ever come across or even heard of. It may make people uncomfortable, it may challenge them. It definitely challenged me and continues to. But it is a gift, and those who realize this cherish it beyond words. I give thanks that I was born to you and Mom. And, as the article in *The* [Catholic] *Agitator* indicates, I can only hope that your influence will not be wasted on me. ...

With mucho love from your only son,
Jerry[47]

Support During Incarceration

In addition to caring for their families, Catholic Left communities provide emotional support to Plowshares activists who are imprisoned. This is critical because the federal prison system often sends inmates to locations that are far removed from their homes. Because the movement's organizational infrastructure is comprised of an extended network of faith-based communities, there is often a group nearby that can regularly visit Plowshares prisoners. In addition, other members send letters, books, newspaper clippings of actions, and so forth. Long-term activists provide suggestions on how to handle difficult situations behind bars, as well as activities that make the prison experience not only bearable, but part of the movement's ongoing witness. For instance, many write articles for Catholic publications, form Bible studies and political discussion groups, and help other inmates with a variety of tasks. One activist commented:

I always used the time to write letters for people and be an amateur counselor to others ... teach GED classes. So [it's about] Matthew 25: "Feed the hungry, visit the sick and imprisoned." It seems to me that aside from the action, going to jail is a good thing for Christians to do. Of course, I'm defining Christian as widely as possible to include anybody who is attempting to lead a merciful, compassionate

---

[47] Letter from Jerry Berrigan to his father, Philip Berrigan, January 31, 1997. From the DePaul Plowshares archives, Box 10.

life. It seems that being in prison voluntarily – since very few other people are there voluntarily – gives you an opportunity to be a willing ear to people who rarely have anyone who is a willing ear. Illiteracy is rampant, and very few people are willing to help write letters and make themselves available to help out in a multitude of ways. People in jail could really use the assistance. So I always felt that my time in jail was well spent, helping people who wouldn't have gotten help from anyone else.... I feel like I did as much good, or more good, in jail than I did with [Catholic Worker] soup kitchen work. I think they are both very valuable ministries.[48]

Another woman echoed this sentiment:

So many people say, "How could you just waste your time like that, going off to jail?" I never felt like a minute of my time was wasted. There was so much work to be done for other people. I had moments that were personally difficult and threatening as well as moments when I was absolutely elated.... There was one woman who had really been trounced by the judge and she had a court appointed attorney who had no interest in her case. I spent a lot of time with her and helped her write a motion appealing her sentence; that got her out of jail basically. She said, "I'm going to show up at your sentencing." I was thinking – yeah, right. Well, she did. This poor, illiterate, inner city woman shows up at my sentencing to support me. So there's camaraderie that you can build in a jail and it's always a lesson in loving and caring for one another amidst all the abuse by the guards.

These stories are not intended to minimize the truly harsh conditions that Plowshares activists experience in prison. Some have been threatened, harassed, and assaulted by other inmates and many witnessed prison staff engaging in reprehensible behavior. Kathleen Rumpf, who now works in jail ministry, commented on her most recent experience in prison:

I thought I had seen it all but what I saw this time in Texas was something so diabolical.... This was a prison for women with health issues but what I saw was deliberate, calculated indifference. I saw stupidity, meanness, ignorance, people dying and them [prison personnel] trying to cover it up. I took care of a woman who had an entopic pregnancy. She had screamed and begged for help all night long.... I went to the hospital with her but by then it was too late.... Sometimes I saw tumors growing out of people; when they got there they went untreated, undiagnosed to the very end.... I consider these prisons and jails as weapons of mass destruction now because of the impact on the community, our infrastructure, the lives inside. It's the biggest civil rights abuse of this decade.[49]

---

[48] Interview with Bruce Friedrich, conducted by the author, July 30, 2003.
[49] Interview with Kathleen Rumpf, conducted by the author, May 29, 2003.

Sustaining Commitment

So what has enabled Rumpf to survive prison and to continue resisting war?

For me, what's most important are relationships. . . . It's getting the news clippings in the mail, getting a newspaper subscription that a friend provided. Trying not to live within a vacuum, staying connected while you're isolated from your community. . . . That kind of lifeline with people who are in like mind was very important to me. I never had to ask myself, am I wrong? I didn't need that kind of support but just sometimes to call up . . . or joke.[50]

Clearly these Catholic communities provide important moral support to activists while they are incarcerated. Yet they may also prepare activists for the austere, highly restricted conditions of prison life. This idea has been most clearly articulated by those activists who are, or were, members of religious orders. Father Carl Kabat, for instance, explained how his priestly training helped him handle a lengthy sentence:

I remember the first long sentence I received. We were basically expecting five year terms. I watched the other three [co-defendants] during the sentencing and a couple of them almost turned white. Paul got ten years, Whitefeather got eight, and Helen and I got eighteen years. But for me it wasn't so hard. I was trained in the old church, back before Vatican II. The major seminary helped prepare me because in many ways, it's like prison. When I was in seminary, you didn't leave the grounds for five or six years.[51]

Elizabeth McAlister and Philip Berrigan, both former members of religious orders, concurred:

In many ways, religious life prepared us well for prison. Indeed, in many ways, prison life seemed easier than the religious formation we recall. The parallels deserve some mention: There is in both a radical displacement from home and loved ones and periodic, formalized visiting time with them. There is in both the enclosure, the cell, and authorization to move about. One's possessions are as limited and circumscribed in prison as they are in religious life. We were prepared for the enforced celibacy of prison life and had learned better ways to live with that special kind of pain. One obeys in prison or meets heavy consequences of lock-down and privation. There are sanctions in religious life, too, for disobedience. . . . One prays in prison and in religious life or rapidly meets a death of spirit. And there are few diversions with which to excuse the failure to pray.[52]

---

[50] Interview with Kathleen Rumpf, conducted by the author, May 29, 2003.

[51] Interview with Carl Kabat, conducted by the author, April 6, 2001.

[52] Berrigan, Philip, and Elizabeth McAlister. 1989. *The Time's Discipline: The Beatitudes and Nuclear Resistance*. Baltimore: Fortkamp Publishing.

Monastic life uniquely prepared some Plowshares participants for prison. In turn, these activists shared their knowledge and insights with others, increasing the likelihood that they too would survive the experience with a willingness to embark upon another campaign.

Assistance with the Logistics of High-Risk Activism

Catholic Left communities also promote retention in the Plowshares movement by offering practical assistance, such as housing activists during trials and after incarceration. This has become particularly important since the U.S. government has recently prohibited some activists from returning to their home communities during their probationary period. Michele Naar-Obed, for instance, was granted early prison release but was banned from Jonah House since the court felt that the community would encourage her to violate the law again. Because her husband and daughter resided in Jonah House, they needed a new place to live until her probation was over. In an article entitled, "It Takes a Village to Do a Plowshares Action," Naar-Obed wrote:

It seems Plowshare activists are now being faced with a new and different tactic of oppression by our government.... Banishment from our homes and communities and forced separation from others that witness for peace seems to be the new method of punishment. Failure to adhere to these orders results in the real threat of extended prison time.... Under the new laws passed by Congress, that time can be very lengthy.... I view this as an extension of prison. The difference this time is the absence of razor wire....

It's unclear whether this new form of government oppression will affect all Plowshares activists.... What we do know from this experience is that the government has gotten meaner and seems to have developed the idea that if they can destroy community, they can stop resistance.... The challenge then is not only to the individuals doing the action, but to community as well.[53]

The extensive network of resistance communities provided a solution to Naar-Obed's situation. She and her family stayed with friends of the Norfolk (Virginia) Catholic Worker for six months and then later moved into the Catholic Worker community in Duluth, Minnesota.

---

[53] Unpublished article by Michele Naar-Obed, 1998, DePaul University Archives, Berrigan-McAlister Collection, Box 24.

Sustaining Commitment

Catholic Left communities have thus fostered retention by ensuring that emotional, spiritual, and material assistance will be readily available to those who make sacrifices for the cause. Through practical forms of support and ritualized community practices, Plowshares organizers have managed to reinforce commitment while simultaneously helping its members overcome the barriers to long-term, high-risk activism.

4

Death of a Charismatic Leader

There are many highly committed individuals in the Plowshares movement who have tenaciously resisted war, year after year, regardless of the consequences. But no one embodied this spirit of persistent resistance more than Philip Berrigan. For nearly four decades, he challenged military policies and called the church to reject war. Despite serving eleven years in prison, he did not stop engaging in prophetic provocation. Even when he was diagnosed with cancer, he continued denouncing weapons of mass destruction. Days before he died, he dictated a final statement to his wife. He said, "I die with the conviction, held since 1968 and Catonsville, that nuclear weapons are the scourge of the earth. To mine for them, manufacture them, deploy them, use them, is a curse against God, the human family, and the earth itself."[1] When he passed away at Jonah House on December 6, 2002, he left a legacy of radical religious peacemaking.

Philip Berrigan will undoubtedly be remembered as one of the most committed and controversial war resisters of his era. But his outspoken opposition to militarism did not begin until his midlife years. As a young man, he willingly went off to fight in World War II. In his autobiography, he wrote:

I longed to join my older brothers at the battlefront. I wanted to join the hunt for Adolf Hitler, to hack him into pieces, and to count the demons as they flew out of his wounds. I wanted to charge pillboxes, blow up machines gun nests, and fight hand-to-hand with my country's enemies. I was 19 years old. Willing, and most able, to be a warrior. . . . When I graduated from Officer Candidate School, I was a skilled killer, trained in the use of all small arms, clever with the bayonet, good with a submachine gun and the Browning automatic rifle. That is exactly what I was: a

---

[1] Statement sent by Elizabeth McAlister to the Plowshares email listserv, December 5, 2002.

highly skilled killer. And then, on August 6, 1945, the Enola Gay dropped "Little Boy" on Hiroshima, killing a hundred thousand Japanese. Three days later, the United States Air Force dropped "Fat Man" on Nagasaki. The Japanese capitulated, the war ended, and President Truman proclaimed to a grateful nation that the United States of America had discovered the secret of the universe. We cheered. We danced. We celebrated. . . .

Years later, my friend Thomas Merton would write "A Devout Meditation in Memory of Adolf Eichmann," a beautiful and provocative essay which explores the meaning of sanity in a world where sane men and women systematically slaughter their fellow human beings. Eichmann was a faithful servant of the Third Reich, doing his part to help kill six million Jews. . . . Adolf Eichmann didn't wake screaming in the night, the horrors of Auschwitz burning his brain. When he looked at food, he didn't see the bonewracked faces of starving Jewish children. Eichmann had a very good appetite, he slept well, he spoke clearly, and he wore clean clothes. Merton tells us that Eichmann "had a profound respect for system, for law and order. He was obedient, loyal, a faithful officer of a great state. He served his government very well." By all accounts, Adolf Eichmann was sane. . . .

Years after my return from the killing fields, I looked into the mirror of my own violence. What I saw there forced me to rethink and redefine the meaning of sanity. I realized that while I considered Adolf Eichmann a war criminal and despised him for participating in the Holocaust, we actually had a few things in common. Like him, I had only been following orders. Like him, I was sane enough to do my duty, and to do it well. Like him, I believed that wars are fought for noble reasons. We were both true believers, one a mass murderer, the other a killer on a smaller scale. . . . My world began to shift, rather slowly at first, more dramatically as I read and thought and prayed. . . . [W]hat, I wondered, did it all mean? Eventually, but not until the early sixties, I would conclude that war is the big lie, subordinated to, and entrenched by, lots of little lies.[2]

Once Berrigan came to this conclusion, he fully devoted himself to the task of abolishing war.

Loss of a Charismatic Leader

Berrigan was transformed from a soldier to a war resister, from an advocate of Just War theory to one of the most outspoken Catholic pacifists of the twentieth century. He publicly criticized the Catholic Church for its complicity and silence on the issue of war, but he was also deeply devoted to it, stating repeatedly that he would be a witness for, and sometimes against, the

---

[2] Berrigan, Philip. 1996. *Fighting the Lamb's War: Skirmishes with the American Empire.* Monroe, ME: Common Courage Press. Quotation on pp. 13, 20–24.

church for his entire life.[3] In the aftermath of his death, he was remembered as one who spoke truth to power, thereby keeping the prophetic tradition alive. In one eulogy, he was described as "a red-blooded American turned prophet, a good kid turned Christian revolutionary."[4] Another observed that his style was somewhat abrasive, but Philip Berrigan had "helped the church from becoming entirely a non-prophet organization."[5] Similarly, Coleman McCarthy wrote:

From the right and left, and the far reaches of both, critics have held forth. Some see the deeds of the Berrigans and those joining them in what are called Plowshares actions – civil disobedience or, more accurately, civil resistance – as street theatre that wins momentary applause but does little to change public policy. Others... see the Berrigans and those who join them in a long line of prophets, going back to Amos, Isaiah, Buddha and others who believed in the value of witness, and in paying heed only to the idea that being faithful counts more than being successful.... A question about Phil Berrigan has been: What did all those years in prison really accomplish? An answer can be found in the parable of the Buddhist spiritual master who went to the village square everyday. From sunrise to sunset he cried out against war and injustice. This went on for years, with no visible result. One day the master's disciples implored him to stop: "People aren't listening. They turn away. Everyone's insane," they told him. "It's time to stop." "No," said the master, "I need to keep crying out so I won't go insane." Praise Phil Berrigan. He died sane.[6]

Approximately 600 people journeyed to Baltimore for the funeral of this contemporary prophet. The memorial service was held at St. Peter Claver Church – the poor, black, urban congregation that Philip Berrigan had served during the late 1960s. It was the place where his imaginative and disruptive tactics began; he had even used the parish car to drive to Catonsville for the draft board raid. Thirty-five years later, people gathered in this church to remember the life of Philip Berrigan. With the pews packed and people standing in the aisles, his brother Daniel gave the homily, stating that "What we had at the end was a masterwork of grace and human sweetness. We gazed on him with a kind of awe. Dying, Philip won the

---

[3] Berrigan, Philip. 1996. *Fighting the Lamb's War: Skirmishes with the American Empire*. Monroe, ME: Common Courage Press.

[4] Schaeffer-Duffy, Claire. 2002. "The Life of an Inside Agitator." *National Catholic Reporter*, December 20, 2002, pp. 14–15.

[5] Schaeffer-Duffy, Claire. 2002. "The Life of an Inside Agitator." *National Catholic Reporter*, December 20, 2002, pp. 14–15.

[6] McCarthy, Coleman. 2002. "After Life of Resistance, He Died Sane: For Phil Berrigan, Being Faithful Counted More than Being Successful." *National Catholic Reporter*, December 27, Vol. 39(19): 18.

face he had earned at such cost."[7] Fellow Plowshares activist Father John Dear presided over the mass and friends offered humorous anecdotes and personal stories of how this man transformed their lives.

But what will happen to the Plowshares movement now that one of its key leaders is gone? During the memorial service, activists addressed this issue, calling upon their comrades to continue Berrigan's provocative tradition. During a time of sharing, one former Jonah House member expressed concern that the movement might fade, becoming nothing more than an obscure bit of history. She recalled how Jonah House residents often played board games for recreation. One night, they were playing Trivial Pursuit, when one of Berrigan and McAlister's daughters drew a card in an attempt to win the history category. The card read: "Name two priests who were arrested for destroying draft files during the Vietnam War." She proudly announced the answer: "Daddy and Uncle Dan." While the crowd of mourners laughed at the story, this woman challenged them to keep the movement strong so that Berrigan's life would not be trivialized over time.[8] In a similar appeal, a Baltimore Catholic Worker told the funeral participants that they would each have to contribute more in Berrigan's absence. He stated, "Phil Berrigan...was that rare combination where word and deed were one. Always. Everywhere. Steadfast. Rock solid....He was that tree standing by the water that would not be moved. Yes, Phil, *Deo gratias!* Thanks be to God for your life. For your spirit that is still with us. Now, with you gone to another place, all of us will have to do more. *Couragio* to you, Phil!"[9]

Philip Berrigan's daughters, Frida and Kate Berrigan, also encouraged people to sustain the movement that their father had led. At his funeral, the daughters offered the following eulogy that reflected their belief and hope that the Plowshares movement would not die with its leader:

One of the thoughts that resonated the most with us in the last days of Dad's life was that he showed us all what it means to be free. We visited our dad in many prisons.... We spent time with him in all these dead spaces meant to intimidate and beat down; spaces that repel and resist children, laughter, loving, and family; spaces meant to communicate a clear message of who is in charge; spaces with stupid rules

---

[7] O'Neill, Patrick. 2002. "Hundreds Gather to Mourn Death of Famed War Resister." *National Catholic Reporter*, December 20. Available online at http://www.natcath.org/NCR-Online/archives/122002/122002p.htm

[8] This story is taken from an audiorecording of Berrigan's memorial service on December 9, 2002, provided to the author by Per Herngren.

[9] As quoted in Zinn, Howard. 2003. "A Holy Outlaw." *The Progressive* 67(2): 14–15.

about how, when, and for how long to touch and hold; spaces where you talk into a phone and look through smudged plastic.

Some families would sit silently in the visiting rooms, some would play cards, some would fight. Those families ... seemed burdened by the thought and the experience that in jail everything is different; life does not go on as usual. You are not free to do as you please or be who you are. But our dad never seemed touched by that weight. Even in prison, even in those awful spaces, he was free. In prison, as in the outside world, his work and life were to resist violence and oppression, to understand and try to live by God's Word, to build community and help people learn to love one another.

When we visited our dad in prison we paid no heed to the spoken and unspoken rules. We filled those places with love, with family, with stories and laughter and strategizing. Dad showed us that freedom has nothing to do with where your body is and who holds the keys and makes the rules. It has everything to do with where your heart is and being fearless and full of hope.

When Dad died, after a long week of struggle, pain, and silence, he was completely free from discomfort and pain, free from a body that no longer worked, and free to live on in us, in all of you. He is still very present to us, and the work we do (all of us) – today, tomorrow, and for the rest of our lives – will keep our dad close to us.

He is here with us every time a hammer strikes on killing metal, transforming it from a tool of death to a productive, life-giving, life-affirming implement.

He is here every time a member of the church communicates the central message of the gospel (thou shalt not kill) and acts to oppose killing, rather than providing the church seal of approval on war.

He is here whenever joy, irreverent laughter, kindness, and hard work are present.

He is here every time we reach across color and class lines and embrace each other as brother and sister.

He is here every time we risk our freedom in an effort to secure justice and peace for all.

He is here whenever children are loved, respected, listened to, but not idolized, sheltered from the truth, or used as an excuse for not doing what is right.

He is here when we challenge comfort, silence, complicity, the easy way out.

He is here when we believe in every person's potential for good, regardless of background or labels.

He is here when we unlearn the violence and greed we are inculcated with as Americans, and practice peacemaking and reconciliation.

He is here when we engage in serious study of the gospels, mining their wisdom for tools to dismantle injustice.

He is here when we live in community, live simply, and share.

Thanks, Dad, for lessons in freedom, inside and outside of prison. And thanks to all of you for struggling towards freedom and working to build a just and peaceful world. Our dad lives on in you.[10]

10 Berrigan, Frida, and Kate Berrigan. 2003. "Fearless and Full of Hope: In Prison and Out, Phil Berrigan Lived for Freedom." *Sojourners* Vol. 32(2): 30–32.

Death of a Charismatic Leader

When the service was over, the crowd filed out of the church, forming a funeral procession behind the flatbed pick-up truck that carried Berrigan's simple wooden casket. The crowd solemnly proceeded through the streets of this tough Baltimore neighborhood – a rat-infested urban wasteland with extremely high unemployment rates and drug problems[11] – where members of Jonah House have lived for thirty years. These are the very conditions that compelled Philip Berrigan to speak out against escalating military expenditures while such poverty and social devastation exist in one of the most affluent countries in the world.

When Philip Berrigan was laid to rest, the Plowshares movement lost a skilled organizer, a respected guide, an eloquent spokesperson, an innovative strategist, and a compelling motivator. Yet his legacy as a prophet, a model of action, remains strong. This is evident in a poem, written by Father William Hart McNichols, that captures the sentiments surrounding Berrigan's death:

> ... Inside the infant whale lies
> the Prophet waiting for
> Sister Death who
> with infinite tenderness
> allows each of his earthly
> loves and followers to come kiss
> his hands or forehead,
> our tears and tears and tears
> on his pillow, on his
> glorious hand-made patchwork quilt.
>
> At exactly 9:30 p.m.
> (because even the clock moaned)
> on the feast of St. Nicholas the Wonderworker
> She came at last...
> ("and how do you like your
> blue-eyed boy Sister Death?")...
> and then the Lamb received His
> Prophet and Lover
> Faithful and True...
>
> We buried him
> after sunset in the
> frozen sea.
> You could see
> the skeletons rising and

---

[11] Field notes, Jonah House participant observation, October 21, 2000.

taking flesh just as
Holy Prophet Ezekiel
had been commanded,
had been promised . . .
We let fall our
dirt and roses on his
Flower Boat.
We followed it with our eyes full,
into the womb of the sea
of caskets.
And then
"there was silence
in heaven about the space
of half an hour."[12]

The Movement's Future

Although many Plowshares participants remain committed to Berrigan's prophetic tradition, one may question how the death of this charismatic leader will affect the movement's trajectory. Predicting the future of the movement is a risky and purely speculative endeavor. However, sociological theory and the collective action literature provide some basis for contemplating the long-term effects of leadership loss for U.S. Plowshares activists. One line of thinking builds upon the ideas of Max Weber, who asserted that leaders derive their power either through tradition, position within a bureaucratic structure (which he called rational–legal authority), or personal charisma.[13] Charismatic leaders gain authority because they are able to project deep conviction about the integrity and importance of their goals. These individuals possess a vocation, at times a messianic calling, for their movement's cause, and are able to convince followers that it is their duty to join and sustain the struggle.[14] Charismatic leaders are therefore especially important in the early stages of mobilization because they articulate the vision and beliefs of the movement and recruits others.[15] However,

[12] McNichols, William Hart. 2003. "Holy Prophet Philip Berrigan." Available at http://puffin.creighton.edu/jesuit/andre/berrigan.html.

[13] Gerth, H. J., and C. Wright Mills (eds.). 1946, pp. 297–301 in *From Max Weber: Essays in Sociology*. New York: Oxford University Press.

[14] Weber, Max. 1964. *The Theory of Social and Economic Organization*. New York: Free Press.

[15] Blumer, Herbert. 1969. "Social Movements," pp. 8–29 in Barry McLaughlin (ed.), *Studies of Social Movements: A Social Psychological Perspective*. New York: Free Press; Rothman, Jack. 1974. *Planning and Organizing for Social Change*. New York: Columbia University Press.

as time passes and the movement achieves some level of recognition, the original charismatic leadership is often replaced by a bureaucratic structure and institutionalized set of rules and norms. Once charisma is routinized, a movement is less susceptible to the disruption that can occur when a charismatic leader is lost because the established practices and bureaucratic authority are often sufficient to sustain the group during this period.[16]

The Plowshares movement, however, can hardly be described as a bureaucratized organization with a rational–legal form of leadership. Although many Catholic Left communities have established traditions, the movement remains a loosely coordinated set of decentralized groups. While their practices have been ritualized, the Christian anarchist culture of the movement has prevented it from becoming institutionalized. In other words, its leadership structure has remained primarily charismatic over the years and decades.

When charisma is not institutionalized, as in the case of the Plowshares movement, then a leader's death can cause problems that may ultimately undermine a movement. For instance, Zald and Ash stipulate that the loss of a charismatic figure is likely to trigger a decline in membership numbers as those "whose commitment was more to the man than to the organizational goal"[17] begin dropping out. To curb the depletion of their ranks, movement organizers must shift their appeals and incentive base "from gratifications related to the mythic stature of the leader and the opportunity to participate with him to the gratifications afforded by the performance of ritual and participation in a moral cause."[18] Failure to do this can lead to movement demise. Zald and Ash propose additionally that the death of a charismatic leader may cause increased factionalism because internal differences or power struggles are often kept in check by a shared deference to a revered leader. In short, their assessment is rather pessimistic. If charismatic leadership is not transformed into a bureaucratic form of authority, most movements will decline when that leader is no longer present.

Will Philip Berrigan's death portend the demise of this unique form of provocative, prophetic action? Of course, only time will provide a definitive answer. However, there are several indications that Zald and Ash's

[16] Zald, Mayer N., and Roberta Ash. 1966. "Social Movement Organizations: Growth, Decay, and Change." *Social Forces* 44 (3): 327–341.
[17] Zald, Mayer N., and Roberta Ash. 1966. "Social Movement Organizations: Growth, Decay, and Change." *Social Forces* 44 (3): 338.
[18] Zald, Mayer N., and Roberta Ash. 1966. "Social Movement Organizations: Growth, Decay, and Change." *Social Forces* 44 (3): 338.

predictions may not hold true for the U.S. Plowshares movement, and that it may in fact survive. First, its leadership is more stable than many other movements guided by a charismatic individual. This is because the Plowshares movement does not have a single leader, but several. Out of Catholic Left resistance to the Vietnam War, three key leaders emerged – Philip Berrigan, Elizabeth McAlister, and Daniel Berrigan. Each took on a particular role, which subsequently was transferred to the Plowshares movement. Ciaron O'Reilly observed:

Phil was a great organizer. He had one action and would recruit for the next. He was really focused, a driven activist. Liz is the community-builder, keeping the Atlantic Life Community networked. Dan's the artist, poet, the public face. He makes it marketable to liberals and other people. I don't think they were self-conscious about that at all but the trio worked in such a great dynamic.[19]

Although the other two will not replace Phil Berrigan, the shared responsibility of leadership means that the movement is not left without any guidance at all. As Georg Simmel noted long ago, triads provide greater stability than dyads or single individuals.[20]

The remaining leaders are not getting any younger, however. Daniel Berrigan is in his mid-eighties and McAlister is in her sixties. Can the movement sustain itself after all the members of this charismatic triumvirate are gone? The second reason why the Plowshares movement may survive, despite the eventual loss of all three leaders, is because Catholic Left leadership has been complemented by a solid infrastructure that has developed over the years, strengthening the movement's longevity. Jonah House has existed for over three decades and the Atlantic Life Community still meets at regularly scheduled intervals. The communities and traditions that the Berrigans and McAlister created may well outlive their creators, as is the case with Dorothy Day and the Catholic Worker movement. One Plowshares activist noted:

Phil was a force to be reckoned with. People had a lot of respect for Phil and would respond to him. If Phil said, "This is really important. I really need you here." You could count on people responding to that.... There's not one person who will assume that role now. It's not like Liz automatically steps into that role because he's not replaceable in that sense. But on the other hand, our community has enough strong voices and enough strong people that no, we're not going to

[19] Interview with Ciaron O'Reilly, conducted by the author, July 27, 2003.
[20] Simmel, Georg. 1950. "The Triad," pp. 145–169 in Kurt H. Wolff (ed.), *The Sociology of Georg Simmel*. New York: Free Press.

wither and die. Jonah House is strong enough without Phil and Phil wouldn't have it any other way.... He was all too aware that any one of us could have been killed at any time, including him. Our work is bigger than who we are. So I don't think the movement will suffer in that sense. We certainly suffer from the loss of Phil, who was an incredible resource and a wonderful human being. But as a movement, we'll continue to grow strong.[21]

The third reason the movement may persist is that the declining levels of commitment that coincide with a charismatic leader's death may be countered by Plowshares theology that emphasizes the need for ongoing prophetic action. When an inspirational leader dies, as Zald and Ash note, organizers have to transfer participation incentives away from association with an icon toward the satisfaction of fighting for a just cause. When Plowshares activists and theologians developed a biblical justification for their tactics, they drew the attention of recruits toward the message rather than the messengers. Although participating in an action with Phil Berrigan undoubtedly held great appeal for some, many will still find deep fulfillment in emulating Christ's temple action and delivering their prophetic message.

Some Plowshares activists are skeptical on this point, however. Although "resistance theology" is widely accepted by the U.S. Catholic Left, beliefs do not automatically translate into action. Often a leader must persuade, encourage, or cajole people to practice what they preach. One priest observed that Philip Berrigan was highly effective at moving people from moral conviction to action:

Phil got involved and really was part of every action.... There is nobody like him in the United States. There just simply isn't.... He was a tough guy. You looked at him and he was like Jeremiah. Not like Dan reading poetry and quoting the meaning of the book of Revelation. Phil was, "You get out there and start hammering or else you are not living up to what God calls us to do." ... He was a very imposing, strong character and we all really, really looked up to him. I loved him dearly but he was like Moses or Ezekiel or something. So ... Phil was organizing these things. That's what he did full-time – going and bringing groups together. Liz was not doing this; it was Phil. So I don't know what it's going to mean. It's possible that there will not be many Plowshares actions because he was such a strong personality and working at this full-time. There's no other Phil out there doing this.[22]

Although no one at present has taken on the recruiter role as comprehensively as Philip Berrigan did, the strength of members' continuance

---

[21] Interview with Lin Romano, conducted by the author, June 16, 2003.
[22] Interview with John Dear, conducted by the author, June 11, 2003.

commitment may provide a fourth reason why the movement might persist despite the loss of this leader. As discussed in Chapter 4, continuance commitment forms when activists make extraordinary sacrifices for a cause, thereby increasing members' investment in a movement since its collapse or failure would render these sacrifices worthless.[23] Several studies support this claim. For instance, Donatella della Porta studied Italian and German underground groups and found that "the militants' very high initial investment reduced the likelihood that they would leave their organization.... They persisted in their involvement because surrendering implied 'losing' everything they had already paid as the costs for entering the underground."[24] Similarly, in a study of successful and failed utopian communities, Rosabeth Moss Kanter found that those communes that survived required some degree of sacrifice and personal investment from their members, giving them a greater stake in the fate of the group.[25] Strong continuance commitment, therefore, may temper the decline of activism that typically follows a leader's death. Plowshares activists underscore this point, noting that their sacrifices often instigate a personal transformation that makes it difficult to return to "normal" life. One man reflected:

There's a point of no return.... There comes a point when we know too much to ever go back.... For seven years I worked as a social worker in the hollows of Appalachia, doing what some might say are works of mercy. I did it for the government and I got paid well...but I could not go down that road again and be at peace with myself.... A single man living in a whole house by myself, with a very comfortable lifestyle, very proximate to people who were in dire poverty. That discrepancy would just gnaw at me.... It would grate on me every single day, not to mention that it doesn't do anything about the need for resistance.[26]

Finally, Zald and Ash suggest that a movement's likelihood of survival is dependent on its degree of exclusivity or inclusivity. Inclusive movements require minimal levels of involvement and only a general degree of support. In contrast, an exclusive group requires that a "greater amount of energy and time be spent in movement affairs...[and] it more extensively permeates all

[23] Klandermans, Bert. 1997. *The Social Psychology of Protest*. Cambridge, MA: Blackwell Publishers.

[24] della Porta, Donatella. 1992. *Social Movements and Violence: Participation in Underground Organizations*. Greenwich, CT: JAI-Press, p. 284.

[25] Kanter, Rosabeth Moss. 1968. "Commitment and Social Organization: A Study of Commitment Mechanisms in Utopian Communities." *American Sociological Review* 33: 499–517.

[26] Interview with John Heid, conducted by the author, July 24, 2003.

sections of the members' lives."[27] When exclusive movements make high demands, as the Plowshares movement does, fewer people are likely to join. Those who do are typically extraordinarily devoted to the movement's goals and are willing to do whatever is necessary to achieve them. In addition, these participants tend to be like-minded.[28] This helps a movement survive because the homogeneity of the membership diminishes the potential for internal disputes that can arise when a charismatic leader dies.

I have cited five reasons why Philip Berrigan's death might not lead to the eventual demise of the U.S. Plowshares movement, but some activists voice doubts about its ongoing viability without him. Father John Dear, for example, notes that the risks and costs associated with the movement make it distinct from other forms of peace activism. When I mentioned that the Catholic Worker movement has continued to flourish long after the death of Dorothy Day, Father Dear argued that there are important differences between the Catholic Worker and Plowshares movements. He stated:

Actually, the numbers of houses of hospitality are twice now [what they were] when Dorothy died and that's really beautiful. But Dorothy, by the 1970s, was in *Life* and *Time* magazines. They called her a living saint and she was getting awards. The official church was beginning to recognize her. The pope sent her messages and now he's going to canonize her. . . . [Being involved in the Catholic Worker is] very hard and very painful but it doesn't mean you're going to be locked behind bars for 25 years. You can leave the house and have a beer. Phil is nowhere near as acceptable as Dorothy was by 1980 and certainly as she is now. In fact, Phil is very marginalized. . . . I don't know that anyone can do what Phil did because it's so hard. If I said to you, "Sharon, look. Let's secretly meet and in a few months, quit your job and we'll go to prison [for a Plowshares action] for 20 years. Leave your family and your kids." You'd just laugh. I mean, it's totally absurd.

But you know, the world is in such bad shape and these Plowshares actions are so powerful because you're literally doing what Isaiah said and it certainly was the most profound experience of my life in every way. So maybe they will live on, maybe they will. I hope they will. There was an action in New York and the Pit Stop Plowshares in Ireland [a few months after Phil died]. And Amy Goodman on the radio show *Democracy Now* has been promoting him a lot. That's very encouraging and I never expected that. Dan [Berrigan] has been saying that after Thomas Merton and Dorothy Day's deaths, it has taken years for good people and thoughtful people

[27] Zald, Mayer N., and Roberta Ash. 1966. "Social Movement Organizations: Growth, Decay, and Change." *Social Forces* 44 (3): 331.

[28] Taylor, Verta. 1989. "Social Movement Continuity: The Women's Movement in Abeyance." *American Sociological Review* 54: 761–775.

to begin unpacking the meaning of their lives for the wider community. Dan has said [that] it will be a couple of decades before we recognize who Philip Berrigan was.[29]

The death of this charismatic leader will undoubtedly shape the U.S. Plowshares movement, yet the precise effects and consequences are difficult to predict. One thing is fairly clear, however. To survive and persist, Plowshares activists will have to successfully deal with this shift in leadership, just as they resolved earlier developmental challenges.

[29] Interview with John Dear, conducted by the author, June 11, 2003,

PART II

The International Plowshares Movements

5

Intermittent Resistance

THE GERMAN, DUTCH, AND AUSTRALIAN PLOWSHARES MOVEMENTS

When hundreds of activists gathered in Baltimore for Philip Berrigan's memorial service, they joked that this was perhaps the largest gathering of convicted felons that had ever occurred outside of the U.S. correctional system. These mourners came from all over the United States and as far away as the Netherlands and Sweden. Even those who could not attend the funeral found other ways to commemorate Berrigan. One fitting tribute occurred at Shannon Airport, near Limerick, Ireland. Two days after Berrigan passed away, 400 people gathered to protest the use of this airport as a refueling station for U.S. military planes in transit to Afghanistan and Iraq. After several protest speeches were made, six members of the Dublin Catholic Worker walked up to a large sculpture surrounded by a pool of water. They poured red dye into the water, replicating an action in which Berrigan made the White House fountains appear to be filled with blood. Next, they transformed the airport sculpture into a monument to Berrigan and the victims of the Iraq war. They pasted photos of Iraqi children and painted the words "THE WAR STOPS HERE – PHIL BERRIGAN R.I.P." Then they stated:

We come to Shannon Airport today to bring the works of darkness into light.... We employed the symbols of blood, water, and images of Iraqi children. Over half a million Iraqi children under the age of five have been killed due to the continuing US/UK bombardment and sanctions.... We attempt in a humble and nonviolent way to speak truth to power in an environment of spin, lies, and cheerleading for massacre. Bottom line – the war machine has decreed the theft of Third World oil to be more sacred than the blood of Iraqi children. We reject this equation.... We act in solidarity with Iraqi children under fire and brothers and sisters imprisoned for peace and justice sake.... [We act in solidarity with] Dominican nuns Ardeth Platte, Carol Gilbert, Jackie Hudson, facing 30 years for conducting a citizen weapons inspection and disarmament action at a nuclear missile silo in Colorado, USA. . . . We act in memory and celebration of the life of Phil Berrigan.[1]

Several individuals involved in this action later returned to the Shannon airport to launch the first Plowshares campaign in the Irish Republic.

How did Berrigan's influence spread across oceans? How did the Plowshares movement expand from a small group on the East Coast of the United States into a movement spanning three separate continents? Collective action researchers argue that movements diffuse by two means. First, activists overseas may get information about the initiating movement through indirect means such as news reports, web sites, and films.[2] Second, those abroad may have direct relationships with activists in the originating movement. Through these friendships, they learn more about the struggle and then emulate it in their own country. In most cross-national movements, diffusion usually occurs from a combination of both direct and indirect ties.

In this chapter, we will examine how the Plowshares movement diffused internationally. Moreover, we will explore the challenges that organizers faced as they attempted to launch movements in their home countries. In West Germany, the Netherlands, and Australia, activists were not able to successfully address the developmental tasks of creating a movement infrastructure or gaining legitimacy of means. Thus, after dramatic starts, these incipient Plowshares movements faltered, resulting in a trajectory of intermittent resistance. To understand why these nascent movements failed to fully mobilize, we must examine briefly the history of Plowshares actions in these countries.

West Germany

The first Plowshares action outside the United States occurred in December 1983 at a U.S. army base in Schwäbisch-Gmünd, West Germany. This action was instigated by Dr. Wolfgang Sternstein, who was raised by an abusive father who had been a dedicated member of the Nazi party. Sternstein's

---

[1] This is taken from an announcement, written by Ciaron O'Reilly, entitled "IRELAND – Resistance in Memory of Phil Berrigan, in Solidarity with Iraqi Children." This account of the Shannon airport action was posted on the international Plowshares listserv on December 10, 2002.

[2] Strang, David, and John H. Meyer. 1993. "Institutional Conditions for Diffusion." *Theory and Society* 22: 487–511.

early childhood experience motivated him to break the cycle of violence in his own life. He commented, "Later on I realized that this decision was important, but not sufficient. The social heritage of violence is overwhelming. It moulds your character into the role of victimizer or victim, victor or vanquished, master or servant."[3] This decision led him to search for alternatives to violence. "From the beginning, I realized that it is not enough to say no to hatred and violence," he said. "We need a constructive alternative to violence as a means of conflict resolution. Moreover, we need a constructive program as a completion or counterpart to nonviolent resistance."[4]

To find alternatives to violence, Sternstein began reading the teachings of Jesus, Gandhi, Kierkegaard, Martin Luther King, Jr., and others. During the Vietnam War, he heard about the draft board raids. Intrigued with the Catholic Left's unique form of faith-based resistance, he paid keen attention to media reports of the Plowshares Eight action at the GE King of Prussia plant. Then, in September 1983, Sternstein had the opportunity to meet Philip Berrigan, who had been invited to West Germany, along with a number of other prominent activists, to participate in a blockade in Mutlangen where thousands of protesters were trying to stop the deployment of Pershing II missiles. This meeting began a lifelong friendship between the two men.

Inspired by his encounter with Berrigan, Sternstein began planning a Plowshares action in West Germany. Two other activists, Herwig Jantschik and Karin Vix, joined him. To gain greater publicity, they decided to openly announce their campaign but they did not disclose the exact date when it would occur. They also embarked on a six-week march from the North Sea coast to southern Germany. Along the way, they distributed a booklet explaining the basis of their convictions and a short history of the U.S. Plowshares movement. To show its support, Jonah House sent Carl Kabat to join the march. During the journey, Dr. Sternstein's wife asked Father Kabat if he would participate in the action; she said it would be a great comfort to have an experienced Plowshares activist involved. Kabat agreed, and on December 4, 1983, Kabat, Sternstein, Jantschik, and Vix armed themselves with hammers and bolt cutters and entered the U.S. Army base in Schwäbisch-Gmünd, where they began disarming a Pershing II missile launcher. They were quickly apprehended, arrested, and later released on

---

[3] Survey response from Dr. Wolfgang Sternstein, July 10, 2001.
[4] Survey response from Dr. Wolfgang Sternstein, July 10, 2001.

their own recognizance. Over a year later, the four were brought to court on charges of attempted sabotage, trespassing, and destruction of property. Kabat had since returned to the United States and did not attend the trial, but the other three were convicted. Sternstein and Jantschik were sentenced to ninety days in prison or a $900 fine, while Vix received a sixty-day sentence or a fine of $225.[5]

The next German action occurred in December 1986. This time, Sternstein acted with Suzanne Mauch-Fritz and Heike Huschauer. Huschauer had lived in the United States from 1968 to 1970, when the movement against the Vietnam War was in full force. Like Sternstein, she had first heard about the Catholic Left through indirect ties, following media accounts of the draft board raids. Later, after returning to West Germany, she read about the Plowshares Eight action at General Electric. She recalled, "When I learned about the first action, I immediately felt, 'that's it!' . . . For me, I felt from the very first moment on, this was the most convincing form of activism."[6] Huschauer was already deeply involved in the opposition to nuclear missile deployment in West Germany, devoting thirty to seventy hours a week to the peace movement. When the opportunity to join a Plowshares action arose, she was ready. She recalled: "I tried all the conventional forms of resistance before I participated in a Plowshares action. It was a sort of stepladder, an escalation of actions."[7]

The three Germans were also joined by Stellan Vinthagen of Sweden. Direct relational ties to members of Jonah House played a critical role in building this German-Swedish alliance. Philip Berrigan and Carl Kabat were already acquainted with Sternstein but they were also linked to a Swedish activist, Per Herngren, who had participated in a Plowshares action at a Martin Marietta plant in Florida. When Vinthagen wanted to conduct a Plowshares action in Europe, he contacted Herngren, who put him in touch with Jonah House. Jonah House knew that Sternstein was planning another action, and soon the three Germans and Vinthagen began meeting on a regular basis. They decided to target Schwäbisch-Gmünd again, attempting to damage the tractor-rig of the Pershing II launch box as well as the crane that maneuvers the missile into firing position. Vinthagen explained the reason behind their decision:

---

[5] The account of the "Plowshares Number Seven" action is derived from Sternstein's own account, along with Art Laffin's (2003) chronology in *Swords Into Plowshares: A Chronology of Plowshares Disarmament Actions, 1980–2003*. Marion, SD: Rose Hill Books.

[6] Survey response from Heike Huschauer, August 16, 2001.

[7] Survey response from Heike Huschauer, August 16, 2001.

That crane was one of a number that were made in Sweden. We also started a campaign against that factory in northern Sweden afterwards. So there was a good connection in terms of Swedish complicity in nuclear weapons despite official policy against nuclear weapons.... That's always been a secondary thing when we do an action; [we try to determine] what are the issues? Where can we challenge the culture of obedience? Where can we make the links between our complicity and the problems of people in the Third World, people living in war and oppression? For us in Sweden, it has been the weapons trade that was the obvious link, how our profit making is linked to war and suffering.[8]

After months of preparation and multiple meetings, the four entered the U.S. Army weapons depot in Schwäbisch-Gmünd. They hammered on the crane, pounded on the launcher's generator, and poured blood upon the rig. After approximately thirty minutes, they found a guard and submitted to arrest. They released a statement saying, "With awareness of our responsibility, we understand that we are the ones who make the arms race possible by not trying to stop it."[9] They were charged with trespassing, sabotage, and damage to government property, and then released. Nearly three years passed before they were brought to trial, convicted, and sentenced to two to four months in prison.

The second Plowshares action not only challenged the deployment of nuclear weapons in West Germany, it also facilitated the formation of the European Plowshares movement's infrastructure. Wolfgang Sternstein, Stellan Vinthagen, and Per Herngren (who was deported back to Sweden after serving one year in a U.S. prison) decided to plan more actions. As Vinthagen recalled:

You could say out of this... Plowshares action in Germany, a community grew because we continued to meet and decided to create a Hope and Resistance network to have regular international contact. During the Swedish-German action, we had been talking about "What's the next step, the next Plowshares action?" Then there was Dutch interest and it became clear to us that we needed some kind of European network to sustain questions, interests, experience, and personal contacts around Plowshares issues and to find ways to interpret and change our inspiration from the United States into something that works here.[10]

This small group began sponsoring "Hope and Resistance" retreats, patterned after the Atlantic Life Community gatherings. Both Sternstein and

[8] Interview with Stellan Vinthagen, conducted by the author, June 24, 2003.
[9] From "Pershing to Plowshares" chronology description, found at http://www.plowsharesactions.org
[10] Interview with Stellan Vinthagen, conducted by the author, June 24, 2003.

135

Herngren had attended these retreats in the United States and shared their knowledge about how this network sustained the American Plowshares movement. The U.S. infrastructure was thus used as a model, with European adaptations.

Although Sternstein helped organize this European network, he was not able to cultivate an ongoing Plowshares movement within his own country. In fact, there were no other Plowshares campaigns in Germany after the 1986 action. Why? Two factors appeared to have undercut German activists' ability to build a movement that could expand. First, it was difficult to establish "legitimacy of means" since the population was unaccustomed to this form of activism. Germany had no comparable tradition of radical non-violent resistance and thus this type of action was culturally unfamiliar. In Sternstein's words, "We lack such great figures like Thoreau, King, the Berrigans, or movements like the abolitionist movement, the civil rights movement, and the movement against the Vietnam War."[11] Indeed, the handful of Germans who did participate were often those, like Huschauer, who had been exposed to the more radical protest traditions in the United States. Additionally, since Germany is largely a secular nation, the theological justifications that compelled American activists to engage in prophetic provocation – regardless of the likelihood of success – had little resonance in the German context. It was not easy to persuade people to undertake risky actions if they did not believe they would actually contribute to the abolition of nuclear weapons.

The second reason that the German Plowshares movement did not shift into the expansion stage was the lack of intentional communities that could help potential activists bear the costs of high-risk campaigns. As discussed in Chapter 4, many U.S. Plowshares activists live in faith-based resistance communes in which members care for one another's children and share material resources, thereby minimizing concerns about family responsibilities that might be neglected if someone received a long prison sentence. Without this type of support, Germans were understandably apprehensive about the consequences of Plowshares activism.

For these two reasons, Sternstein decided to shift to lower-risk tactics. As people gained activist experience, he hoped that they would eventually become more committed, develop into a resistance community, and ultimately engage in higher-risk actions. With this plan in mind, in 1989 he founded EUCOMmunity, which sponsored demonstrations, vigils,

---

[11] Survey response from Wolfgang Sternstein, July 10, 2001.

blockades, and other forms of direct action at the site of the U.S. European Command (EUCOM) headquarters for American forces. Located near Stuttgart, EUCOM coordinated many of the military attacks on Libya in 1986 and provided logistical support for more than 90 percent of the actions in the 1991 Gulf War.[12] Sternstein and others started an annual act of civil disobedience at EUCOM. Called "de-fence actions," activists used bolt cutters to remove part of the facility's fence. They then entered the site to plow the ground, sow seeds, plant flowers, or share a meal.

Although Sternstein successfully mobilized numerous de-fencing actions, resulting in roughly 100 hundred arrests, he was not able to transform this small group of activists into a community of resistance that paralleled those in the United States. Vinthagen commented:

I think the conclusion of some key organizers like Wolfgang was that they wanted to do other kinds of actions that weren't so high risk. There were clear discussions during a couple of the Hope and Resistance retreats about whether high-risk actions were putting people off and whether you could really do it here in Europe.... We talked much about the difference between the United States and Europe but [one of the big issues] was that people were not living in communities. That was a major problem in Plowshares in Europe. We were creating a very strong community when we were meeting [for retreats] and some of us were very close friends, but feeling that kind of community from long distance. So some people made the decision that they would focus on low-risk actions instead, which I think was reasonable, but it didn't produce the link that we hoped for.[13]

German Plowshares organizers were therefore not able to form a stable movement infrastructure or establish legitimacy of means. Without the support of international communities or a theology that instilled long-term commitment, this small group of activists was particularly vulnerable to shifting political opportunities – that is, the changes in the social and political environment that create unfavorable circumstances for protesters. The end of the Cold War and the perception of world peace made it very difficult for German Plowshares activists to recruit participants during the 1990s. In a letter to Phil Berrigan in 2001, Sternstein wrote:

You know my ambition to find a way...to launch a campaign to get rid of the 66 American nukes still on German soil. I worked rather hard on that subject in the last two years, developing a strategy, proposing the project to individuals and

---

[12] Sternstein, Wolfgang. "The EUCOMmunity: Tiny Steps Towards a Nuclear Free World." Unpublished, undated report, DePaul University Plowshares Archives, Berrigan-McAlister Collection.

[13] Interview with Stellan Vinthagen, conducted by the author, June 24, 2003.

organizations, etc. But I have to confess my complete failure. There was no interest at all, no consciousness of the threat of a nuclear holocaust, not to speak of the already ongoing war against the poor. People are occupied with daily business, daily struggle for life, daily pleasure and daily entertainment. The few intellectuals who are able to see it are tired, frightened or discouraged.... I recognize a basic dilemma: people don't feel concerned of the approaching disaster (in the eighties it was different because they thought it was imminent) and as soon as the crisis is real they may become concerned, but then it is too late.[14]

German activists were also adversely affected by another significant change in the political environment: the rise of the Green Party. Although a sizeable proportion of the population supported the idea of abolishing nuclear weapons and nuclear power plants in West Germany,[15] many felt that the Greens would represent these concerns and work toward these goals through conventional political means. This led some activists to believe that they no longer had a personal responsibility to eliminate nuclear weapons through direct action; this was now the duty of their elected parliamentary representatives, who used institutional processes.[16] But when it became evident that the Green Party was only making nominal gains and symbolic achievements, many became disillusioned. Sternstein summed up the situation:

People are deeply disappointed and inclined to resignation. As a consequence, there is no media coverage anymore, which again weakens the movement. This analysis may be too simple. There are certainly other factors, e.g. the disintegrating social influence of the globalized economy, the end of the Cold War, the new strategy of NATO, the ideology of warfare for human rights, etc. Nevertheless, the disintegrating influence of the Greens on social movements is, in my opinion, the worst.[17]

Despite his remarkable personal commitment, Wolfgang Sternstein and the other German activists were not able to successfully accomplish the

---

[14] Letter from Wolfgang Sternstein to Phil Berrigan, May 1, 2001. DePaul University Archives, Berrigan-McAlister Collection.

[15] Sternstein wrote that in a 1999 poll, 90 percent of the German respondents supported the initiative to abolish weapons of mass destruction. From Sternstein's survey response, July 10, 2001.

[16] This is consistent with David Meyer's argument that as movements begin to institutionalize and enter mainstream political processes, their momentum subsides, thereby contributing to the decline of collective action. For further information, see Meyer, David S. 1993. "Institutionalizing Dissent: The United States Structure of Political Opportunity and the End of the Nuclear Freeze Movement." *Sociological Forum* 8(2): 157–179.

[17] Sternstein, Wolfgang. "German Country Report" sent to the Hope and Resistance retreat, 1999. From the personal files of Per Herngren, Hammarkullen, Sweden.

micro-foundational tasks of establishing a movement infrastructure and legitimacy of means. Not only did this hinder recruitment attempts, it also meant that this newly formed movement was more profoundly affected by shifting political opportunities. While U.S. peace groups also experienced a less favorable climate in the 1990s – as people no longer perceived nuclear weapons as a grave concern and attention was shifting to other global issues – the American Plowshares movement persisted during this era. Intentional communities of resistance provided a context to hold people accountable, to keep emotional and relational ties strong, and to reinforce the belief that the prophetic message must be delivered regardless of the outcome. In short, a strong infrastructure and highly developed theology of resistance were sufficient to enable the U.S. movement to overcome the factors that can undermine ongoing collective action. The lack of these factors in the German movement meant that its trajectory was brought to an abrupt halt.

The Netherlands

In the early 1980s, hundreds of thousands of Dutch citizens attended demonstrations to stop the deployment of nuclear weapons in the Netherlands. These actions were largely initiated by two religious peace groups – the ecumenical Inter-church Peace Council (IKV) and Pax Christi Netherlands, a Catholic organization.[18] But by the mid-1980s, mass protests began to decrease. They declined further in 1987 when the Intermediate-Range Nuclear Forces (INF) treaty was signed, eliminating ground-launched Cruise and Pershing missiles in Europe. As the demonstrations subsided, a small group continued to inhabit peace camps that had been formed outside the Woensdrecht U.S. Air Force base. The campers held daily vigils at the base entrance and formed direct-action affinity groups to draw attention to the fact that while the INF treaty eliminated ground-based missiles, the North Atlantic Treaty Organization (NATO) was expanding and modernizing sea- and air-launched nuclear missiles.[19]

One of these affinity groups called itself the North Atlantic De-fence Movement. It had twelve members, including Frits Ter Kuile, who spent almost a year in prison for defying the Netherlands' required military service, Co van Melle, a physician who worked with undocumented refugees

[18] Wittner, Lawrence S. 2003. *Toward Nuclear Abolition: A History of the World Nuclear Disarmament Movement, 1971 – Present.* Stanford: Stanford University Press.

[19] Interview with Heleen Ransijn, conducted by the author, June 20, 2003.

and the homeless, and Kees Koning, a priest. Koning had once served as a military chaplain, but resigned when he was asked to convince soldiers to support limited nuclear battle strategies. Subsequently, he worked in a homeless shelter before departing for India, where he lived for five years. Later he returned to Holland to care for his dying father, but when he tried to move back to India, his request for a visa was denied. He felt exiled in the First World, and struggled against the structural violence and apathy that he encountered in Europe. Dutch activist and theologian Heleen Ransijn recalled: "He had been moved so deeply by what he saw and experienced in India that he just couldn't come back to the Netherlands and take up his normal life again. It had become impossible for him."[20] Koning ultimately joined the Emmaus community, located in the Sisters of Love monastery in Eindhoven, Netherlands. He got permission to live in a small shed in the garden, where he rolled out his sleeping bag at night, as he had done in India. He devoted his time to recovering and selling items discarded by the affluent, sending the profits to various projects in the Third World.[21] Recognizing that the wealth and power of developed nations was linked to expanding militarism, Koning joined the North Atlantic De-fence affinity group, although, in Ter Kuile's words, "being fully in a group was not really Kees' style; he lacked the patience for it."[22]

Koning, Ter Kuile, van Melle, and other affinity group members planned an action for the first anniversary of the INF treaty. On December 8, 1988, they entered the Woensdrecht Air Force base, where they tried to damage the missile bunkers. They released a statement saying, "The Cruise missiles won't be destroyed but given a new military destination. We oppose these new steps in the arms race. . . . We demand that the money destined for new arms be spent instead on producing food for the hungry, detoxifying toxic waste dumps and cleaning polluted water."[23] The activists were quickly apprehended by the police and thrown into jail. Dutch authorities released all of them after a day, except for Koning, who was held for another week because the police suspected that he was involved in an earlier action at

---

[20] Interview with Heleen Ransijn, conducted by the author, June 20, 2003.
[21] Ter Kuile, Frits. 1996. "In Memoriam Kees Koening." *The Daily Hammer: Newsletter of the Ploughshares Support Network*, October 1996, No. 13: 13.
[22] Ter Kuile, Frits. 1996. "In Memoriam Kees Koening." *The Daily Hammer: Newsletter of the Ploughshares Support Network*, October 1996, No. 13: 13.
[23] Laffin, Arthur J. 2003. *Swords Into Plowshares: A Chronology of Plowshares Actions, 1980–2003*. Marion, SD: Rose Hill Books.

the base. While in jail, Koning read the book *Swords into Plowshares*, edited by U.S. Plowshares activists Art Laffin and Sister Anne Montgomery. The book inspired him to use similar tactics in the Netherlands.

Koning immediately began planning a Plowshares action at the Woensdrecht base. He decided to target the NF-5 fighter planes that the Dutch government was shipping to Turkey as part of a NATO-aid program to defeat Kurdish nationalists. Emulating the U.S. Plowshares movement, Koning planned to hammer on these planes and pour blood. He asked his friend and fellow activist Co van Melle to draw his blood. As Koning explained his intention, van Melle told him that he should not undertake this action alone; on the spot, he volunteered to join Koning.[24] The next day – January 1, 1989 – the two men entered the base, where they struck the fighter planes with sledgehammers. Heleen Ransijn noted:

This Plowshares action caused quite a shock at that moment in the Netherlands because nobody had ever done anything like that. There were all kinds of reactions. Some people thought they were crazy and out of their minds. . . . Yet it started making me think in different ways. In one sense, you could say that damaging something, anything, whether it's a fighter jet or a nuclear missile, is a form of violence. . . . But on the other hand . . . perhaps it's a small crime to damage something which is so lethal and so devilish. It would constitute a bigger crime to just let it exist or, even worse, to let it be used.[25]

Frits Ter Kuile also stated:

The fact that an ex-military chaplain and a physician, both with gray hair, instead of "young, unemployed activist-scum" did such an action, and did it openly, really made the news and triggered a campaign against arms shipments to Turkey. The sale of the planes was discussed and debated in the media, parliament, and in the cabinet, but in the end, the Netherlands remained loyal to NATO and sold the planes to Turkey.[26]

Koning and van Melle were charged with trespassing and sabotage of equipment that resulted in $350,000 of damage. Approximately six weeks later, they were brought to court and allowed to bring in expert witnesses to testify on their behalf. Those who took the stand included a former officer in the Dutch Air Force, a Kurdish lawyer who spoke of the human rights

[24] Interview with Susan van der Hijden, conducted by the author, June 24, 2003.
[25] Interview with Heleen Ransijn, conducted by the author, June 20, 2003.
[26] Ter Kuile, Frits. 1996. "In Memoriam Kees Koning." *The Daily Hammer: Newsletter of the Ploughshares Support Network*, October, No. 13: 13.

abuses in Turkey, and Philip Berrigan, who traveled from Jonah House to attend the trial. Koning and van Melle were convicted, and van Melle was sentenced to seven months (with three months suspended), followed by a probationary term of two years. Koning received eight months (with two months suspended) and two years probation. The two men contested the conviction and were released pending a new court date for their appeal.[27]

This Plowshares action received widespread media coverage throughout the Netherlands, inspiring others to continue the resistance. On February 9, 1989 – the day that Koning and van Melle went to trial – activists Ad Hennen and Rolland van Hell broke into a Dutch military base, using axes to disarm Hawk missiles. Then a spate of Plowshares campaigns occurred in quick succession over the next months. In March, Koning struck again. On Good Friday, he entered the Volkel nuclear base and took a pickaxe to another fighter plane destined for Turkey. When he went to trial in May, the prosecutor asked the judges to sentence him to eighteen months in prison. Ironically, however, he had smashed the precise plane that he had previously tried to damage, and the judges ruled that he could not be charged twice for destroying the same plane. Consequently they released him but he was not yet ready to retire his sledgehammer. In July 1989, on the anniversary of the first nuclear detonation, Koning broke into the Netherlands' Valkenburg Air Force base. He hammered upon a P-3 Orion nuclear-capable airplane while other activists plowed an area of the base and planted seeds, attempting to transform it from a place of death to a place for new life.[28] Later, Koning returned to the Volkel nuclear base, where he used his sledgehammer to damage a communications tower.

The North Atlantic De-fence affinity group continued for some time, providing support to Koning during these various actions. It eventually disbanded toward the end of 1990 when a government infiltrator generated internal dissension.[29] Another Plowshares action would not occur on Dutch soil for more than a dozen years. Yet the affinity group members remained active in various causes during this time. Koning joined the Gulf War Peace Team, traveling into the Kurdish part of Iraq. He also participated in a human rights delegation in Turkish Kurdistan and later joined

---

[27] Laffin, Arthur J. 2003. *Swords Into Plowshares: A Chronology of Plowshares Actions, 1980–2003.* Marion, SD: Rose Hill Books. p. 41.

[28] Laffin, Arthur J. 2003. *Swords Into Plowshares: A Chronology of Plowshares Actions, 1980–2003.* Marion, SD: Rose Hill Books. pp. 41–42.

[29] Ter Kuile, Frits. 1996. "In Memoriam Kees Koning." *The Daily Hammer: Newsletter of the Ploughshares Support Network,* October, No. 13: 13.

civilian interventions in Bosnia.[30] Frits Ter Kuile organized a peace pilgrimage for Europeans, who marched from St. Mary's Trident base in Georgia to the Nevada nuclear test site. While planning the campaign, Ter Kuile spent time with U.S. Plowshares activists and Catholic Workers in Washington DC and New York City. After the St. Mary's pilgrimage, Ter Kuile participated in civilian interventions in the Balkans and then moved home to join the newly formed Catholic Worker community in Amsterdam.[31]

Although various activists continued their war resistance into the 1990s, it seemed that the Dutch Plowshares movement had come to an end when Kees Koning died in 1996. Fellow activists and members of his religious order held a vigil in his small garden shed. Ter Kuile recalled the memorial and some of the challenges Koning faced during his struggle for peace:

Once a right-wing group burned down his shed and Kees lost his books and sleeping bag, and [in 1995] a molotov cocktail missed his shed, but burned down the Emmaus part of the monastery. Kees more or less put up with the attacks, both on a physical level and on a right-wing media level, [with] the publicity, and so on. He quietly continued to live as he thought was best. Living simply, working at Emmaus and in his vegetable garden, direct disarmament and civil intervention in war zones provided only partial answers to the burning questions of how to live best in this world of injustice and suffering, and Kees became more and more silent.... July 22nd, Kees was in his garden, laid down, put a piece of wood under his head, and passed over. There was a night vigil around his coffin in his shed, and during the funeral service we put ears of wheat on his body, the grain that has to die and fall into the earth. Someone also gave him a little bolt cutter on his journey, and his best buddy gave him the Plowshares movement symbol of two people hammering a sword into a plowshare, cut out in wood.[32]

Even after his death, Koning continued to be an important figure in the radical faction of the Dutch peace movement, inspiring others to use Plowshares tactics. In 2000, Susan van der Hijden of the Amsterdam Catholic Worker began planning a disarmament campaign, along with seven others. However, when it became evident that the others only wanted to do support work, van der Hijden decided to participate in a British Plowshares action

---

[30] Ter Kuile, Frits. 1996. "In Memoriam Kees Koning." *The Daily Hammer: Newsletter of the Ploughshares Support Network*, October, No. 13: 13.

[31] Ter Kuile, Frits. 1996. "Woensdrecht-Nevada-Balkan-Amsterdam!" *Jeannette Noel House Newsletter*, Christmas 1996. From the DePaul University Archives, Berrigan-McAlister Collection, Box 15.

[32] Ter Kuile, Frits. 1996. "In Memoriam Kees Koning." *The Daily Hammer: Newsletter of the Ploughshares Support Network*. October 1996, No. 13, p. 13.

instead. Another Dutch activist, Barbara Smedema, was not deterred by the prospect of acting alone. In 2003, she followed Koning's example by taking a sledgehammer to the communications tower at the Volkel Air Force base. Smedema recalled how she was drawn to these controversial tactics when, many years earlier, she had first heard about the Plowshares movement in the Netherlands: "When I lived in a town in the north of Holland where I went to study, there was the students' church, a progressive, good church.... The first time I went there, the clergyman told a story about a priest who damaged an airplane, a fighter jet that was sold to Turkey to attack the Kurdish people. The priest smashed it with a sledgehammer and when I heard the story, I thought, 'Wow! That's fantastic!'"[33]

What led this woman to carry out a solo action after a thirteen-year hiatus in the Dutch Plowshares movement? Smedema explained:

It's best to start with the International Court of Justice. In 1996, they were asked to make an advisory opinion about whether nuclear weapons are legal or not.... What they said is that it is illegal to use nuclear weapons and to threaten [other nations] with them. There is only one exception: when a country is in danger of annihilation.... So the judges made this loophole but they said that all countries should make a very great effort to get rid of all nuclear weapons because they are the greatest danger to life on earth. After that, there were many movements of people in European countries that have nuclear weapons from the U.S. They said, okay, we have nuclear weapons here so we'll go onto the military bases to look for them.... We did civilian inspections ... [because] we wanted the world to know that the weapons are here and they should be put away, abolished.... People also went back to the Nuremberg trials, which say that people are obliged to do something against this. So that's where I started with the renewed fight against nuclear weapons.[34]

Once Smedema decided to take more dramatic action for disarmament, she targeted the Volkel base because it houses the U.S. military's regional communications center, which facilitates the coordination of the American nuclear missile fleet. She commented: "In Volkel, there is one place where they have a bunker and a communications radar installation. In that bunker, there are always American soldiers who are responsible for the nuclear weapons and communications with the United States.... I thought that if they don't have their communications system, they can't go to war.[35] So, on February 9, 2003, Smedema scaled the base fence. When she reached the communications tower, she climbed onto the bunker and smashed the

[33] Interview with Barbara Smedema, conducted by the author, June 21, 2003.
[34] Interview with Barbara Smedema, conducted by the author, June 21, 2003.
[35] Interview with Barbara Smedema, conducted by the author, June 21, 2003.

antennae. Then she cut the electrical cables that power the radar installation. She was arrested after roughly twenty minutes, but she had informed the press in advance and they filmed the whole action. That night, while Smedema sat in jail, news programs throughout the Netherlands aired footage of her wielding a sledgehammer in an attempt to stop war.

Smedema was charged with property damage, endangering air traffic, and assaulting a police officer. Smedema was angered by the last charge, which she claimed was fabricated to discredit her commitment to nonviolence. She stated:

They charged me with kicking a police officer, a woman, which was a false accusation.... When a police officer says you did something like that, the judge believes them. You're basically already convicted. I was really pissed off about that because I think it was the strategy of the prosecutor to treat me like a common criminal and not someone who was doing a political action.... I really didn't want to be convicted of something I didn't do so I really fought against it....[36]

Eventually, Smedema was found guilty of all the charges and was sentenced to seventy-eight hours of community service. Since she had already spent six weeks in jail, the judge determined that this was equivalent to seventy-eight hours of community service, and she was released.

Although Smedema was inspired by U.S. Plowshares activists, her connection to them is minimal, and primarily mediated through indirect ties. Whereas Koning had initially read written accounts of the U.S. movement, he later developed a direct relationship with Philip Berrigan, who served as an expert witness in his trials. Koning's status as a radical Catholic priest undoubtedly furthered his identification with the American Plowshares movement. In contrast, Smedema's information about her U.S. counterparts was passed on through Koning and others. She stated: "I'm really inspired by the U.S. Plowshares movement but Kees was more into reading about what the Plowshares movement is about [whereas] I know it through other people's accounts.... I'm still thinking about whether I really see myself as a Plowshares activist or not because I often see Plowshares activists as religious people and I'm not religious."[37] Her secular orientation has resulted in a weaker identification, leaving her uncertain about whether or not she is reviving the Dutch Plowshares movement. In fact, other Dutch activists ask whether one can even speak of a *movement* per se. Rather, they posit that it is more accurate to describe Plowshares actions in

[36] Interview with Barbara Smedema, conducted by the author, June 21, 2003.
[37] Interview with Barbara Smedema, conducted by the author, June 21, 2003.

the Netherlands as a handful of individuals who have emulated the tactics of the Berrigans.[38]

Whether it was an attempted movement or simply a series of campaigns, the Dutch Plowshares trajectory reflects a rapid sequence of actions, giving the initial impression that a movement was about to prosper and expand. Yet almost as quickly as it started, the actions ceased, with only periodic efforts over the next decade or so. Why did this group start out with strong potential, only to dissipate rapidly, leading to this trajectory of intermittent resistance?

Like their German counterparts, Dutch activists did not establish a local infrastructure that could serve as the foundation for an expanding movement. In the United States, Plowshares activists built upon Catholic Worker communities, using them as a recruitment network and a model for new intentional communities. Some U.S. Catholic Workers were even rejuvenated by the Plowshares movement, leading a handful to shift their emphasis from traditional works of mercy to war resistance.[39] But there was no equivalent network of faith-based radical activist communities in the Netherlands. There is one Catholic Worker community in Amsterdam, but it was just starting up as the first Plowshares actions got under way. Moreover, since the Amsterdam Catholic Workers were primarily focused on establishing their community and assisting undocumented refugees, they were simply unable to take on the tasks of organizing and supporting acts of resistance. Although the Netherlands had a strong history of peace camps, these camps could not provide much infrastructural support for the Dutch Plowshares movement because participants tended to be transient and turnover was fairly high. Without a pre-existing foundation, Dutch Plowshares activists would have to build their own infrastructure, but they were not interested in doing so. Thus, an affinity group served as the basis for these early Dutch Plowshares actions. However, they quickly discovered that a group of twelve is easier to divide than an entire network of communities. When the North Atlantic De-fence affinity group split because of government infiltration, there was no wider support system to help it recover.

A second explanation for the Dutch movement's trajectory of intermittent resistance was that the leadership of the movement was never clearly

---

[38] Interview with Heleen Ransijn, conducted by the author, June 20, 2003. Interview with Krista van Velzen, conducted by the author, August 15, 2004.

[39] Interview with Carmen Trotta, conducted by the author, August 8, 2003.

defined. The media focused on Koning, whose charisma and prophet-like appearance made him the de facto leader. But unlike the Berrigans, Koning did not take on the task of building a movement by forming communities, recruiting others, and developing retention practices. Barbara Smedema remarked: "The media made him the leader [since] he had done the actions. But it was really an anarchistic, democratic movement. When you saw him, he really was a bit like a prophet... but it wasn't like he was a leader."[40] Although others could have stepped into that leadership role, no one appeared committed to building and expanding the movement. Krista van Velzen, a Plowshares activist who was subsequently voted into the Dutch parliament, commented: "In general, the peace movement in the Netherlands, especially after the Cold War, never really had an aim to grow.... There is a group of people doing direct actions but... they've never been focused on making the direct action movement bigger."[41]

Finally, many Dutch activists did not view themselves as part of a prophetic biblical tradition that encourages ongoing action regardless of the effects or consequences. Although some activists were deeply religious, they did not explicitly integrate their theological beliefs into the movement. Van Velzen stated that this type of biblically based action is rare in the Netherlands:

I was reading magazines so I knew about the [U.S.] Plowshares movement. But I always found the whole Christian connection, from my background, a bit dodgy. The combination of reading the Bible and drawing conclusions out of a Bible, it never crossed my mind that would be a way to do things, you know? ... But through the years as I was becoming a more politically-aware person, a more activist-minded person, I was just very surprised to see that there are people who would actually be political out of a Christian philosophy.... Then I paid a visit to the U.S. and I was staying at Jonah House. There are some nuns living there and they're so down to earth, normal. I stayed there for a while and in the evening they did scripture study and I was like, "Oh, no. Enough." ... But they were discussing the position of women in modern society, based on Rachel or one of the women in the Bible. It was really interesting and then after probably ¾ of an hour, one of the nuns said, "Okay, let's forget about it." They just tossed aside the Bibles and there was wine and beer coming to the table. I was like "Wow! Look at this!" I was just really amazed.... We don't have many people like that [in the Netherlands] – you know, very strong Christian believers doing radical actions.[42]

[40] Interview with Barbara Smedema, conducted by the author, June 21, 2003.
[41] Interview with Krista van Velzen, conducted by the author, August 15, 2003.
[42] Interview with Krista van Velzen, conducted by the author, August 15, 2003.

In short, the Dutch Plowshares movement did not have a stable infrastructure, a committed leadership that devoted itself to movement development, or a sustaining theology. As with the German activists, this meant that Dutch Plowshares participants were more vulnerable to external forces that could derail or subvert a budding movement. In the Dutch case, state-sponsored repression caused the collapse of the initial movement. In the U.S. context, government infiltration and repression has also occurred. American activists, however, had developed a sufficiently stable network of communities that the collapse of one would not undermine the entire movement. Thus, once again, the U.S. Plowshares movement indicates that a strong micro-foundation can sometimes overcome adverse macro conditions. The Dutch case illustrates the vulnerabilities that young movements face if they do not successfully resolve these developmental challenges.

Australia

Halfway around the world, a similar trajectory of intermittent resistance was occurring in Australia. The Australian Plowshares movement emerged from a small group of pacifist, anarchist Catholics who, despite their shared beliefs, had no ties to the U.S. Catholic Left in the beginning. One Australian organizer, Ciaron O'Reilly, described the movement's origins:

In '77 ... I went to the university and there was this guy ... who was sort of like the Tom Hayden of Australia – a very strong anarchist, very charismatic ... articulate. So a group of us who were Christian protesters, he pretty much demanded – what are you for? What are your politics? We hadn't really thought beyond protest. So we started a group called Two or Three Gathered in His Name, which was Christian anarchist pacifism. We were also anti-abortion, which made us very marginal on the Left.... We were doing that for a couple of years before we even knew the Catholic Worker existed. Then someone gave me a copy of the New York Worker [newsletter] ... We were attracted by their Christian anarchism. We thought we were the only ones in the world but [we discovered] there's actually a tradition out there. So we just started writing. I remember writing the New York Worker with all these questions.[43]

Initially these Australians gleaned most of their information about the U.S. Catholic Left through indirect links such as books, films, and Catholic Worker newsletters. Yet the more they learned, the more they were inspired

---

[43] Interview with Ciaron O'Reilly, conducted by the author, July 27, 2003.

by these radical religious activists and began to model themselves after them. O'Reilly continued:

I think that was the beginning of having a sense that there is a politic implicit in Christianity.... So then I used to go to the university library, dredging up all these books. There was nothing really in Australia. Most Catholics who began working with the poor became co-opted by the social welfare system. They end up managing the poor. Most Catholics in Australia who start screaming for justice end up getting co-opted by the Labor Party. There's not a radical tradition [there].... There were people experimenting with base Christian community stuff in Australian suburbia, which wasn't going to go anywhere. The Third World stuff just didn't seem applicable and it seemed like these people [the U.S. Catholic Left] were coming up with something as intense in the First World. That's what Ched Myers talks about – there'll be a theology of liberation from the Third World and a theology of repentance and resistance [in the First World]. That seemed to make sense to me.... [So] in '82 we formed a [Catholic Worker] community.... We were very intense young people and we opened the house to anyone.... We wouldn't take any money from the government so we built this oven in the back yard and made bread and soap and beer and candles and we used to sell that around the neighborhood. Then we started a shop [called Justice Products]. We started selling anything made by cooperatives and prisoners. We sold a lot of Nicaraguan coffee in the 80s. So we did three things: community building (we lived with a common purse, financed ourselves through cooperative work), hospitality (taking aboriginal people in and visiting them in jail) and then direct action.[44]

This new Catholic Worker community in Brisbane soon attracted other like-minded individuals. These included Joanne Merrigan, a grade school teacher at a local parochial school. Based on her reading of scripture, Merrigan began questioning the legitimacy of war when she was a teenager. As an adult, she also became committed to a simple, environmentally sound lifestyle and social justice activism. Yet, as she put it, "By the time I got my first job teaching at age 21 ... I had never met anyone else who agreed with my ideas."[45] She also felt somewhat alienated from the counter-culture of the secular peace movement. So when she attended a Hiroshima Day rally in 1983 and met members of the Brisbane community, she felt an immediate connection. She recalled: "I found that I had so much in common with them...that I became a regular visitor to their house and attended all the vigils and rallies they organized. I joined the community when I left teaching at the end of 1984."[46]

---

[44] Interview with Ciaron O'Reilly, conducted by the author, July 27, 2003.
[45] Survey response from Joanne Merrigan, August 23, 2003.
[46] Survey response from Joanne Merrigan, August 23, 2003.

A few years later, Merrigan moved into a Catholic hospitality community in Sydney, where she met Anthony Gwyther. Gwyther had read about the U.S. Plowshares movement during his seminary studies and was particularly moved by an article describing the eighteen-year sentences that two Plowshares activists had been given in 1984. Then, as Gwyther read Ched Myers' theological works, he became convinced that direct acts of disarmament were the best Christian response to militarism.[47] Eventually, Merrigan and Gwyther decided to use the tactics and symbols of the U.S. Plowshares movement. They were joined by Marie Grunke, a Blessed Sacrament nun. Merrigan described the first Australian Plowshares action:

Two of us had been arrested in October 1987 at an Air Force base near Sydney, vigiling and pouring our own blood on a U.S. supply plane.... In November 1987 we heard that the USS *Leftwich* was coming to Sydney and would be open to the public in late December.... Three of us met regularly for about a month, praying, reflecting, and planning our witness. We chose to go on board the ship on the 28th of December (Feast of Holy Innocents), pour our own blood on the weapons launchers, and hold up a banner stating how many children were dying of hunger every second and reading "Beat Swords into Plowshares." Two of us hammered on the weapons launcher.... The third person [Sister Marie Grunke] decided that she would not do that, but that she was prepared to accept the same penalty as us.[48]

To everyone's surprise, no legal action was taken against them. After they used their hammers, spilled their blood, and read their statement, they were simply escorted off the ship without being arrested.[49] The authorities did take action, however, when Anthony Gwyther conducted a second Plowshares campaign in August 1991 at the Darwin Australian Air Force base. After pouring blood and hammering on a B-52 bomber, he was charged with trespassing and criminal damage. Gwyther was convicted and sentenced to three months in prison.[50]

As Merrigan and Gwyther organized in Sydney, the Brisbane Catholic Workers continued their works of mercy. But in contrast to the Sydney

---

[47] Survey response from Anthony Gwyther, July 25, 2003.
[48] Survey response from Joanne Merrigan, August 23, 2003.
[49] Laffin, Arthur. 2003. *Swords Into Plowshares: A Chronology of Plowshares Actions, 1980–2003.* Marion, SD: Rose Hill Books, p. 37.
[50] Laffin, Arthur. 2003. *Swords Into Plowshares: A Chronology of Plowshares Actions, 1980–2003.* Marion, SD: Rose Hill Books, p. 48.

150

group, which faced minimal sanctions for its campaigns, the Brisbane activists experienced state harassment. O'Reilly recalled:

We were pretty targeted. We got a lot of special branch harassment. . . . They raided the house in relation to our prison work. There had been a riot and we were advocating for the prisoners. They claimed that they received letters demanding prison reform or foot and mouth disease would be released. They raided three houses, two individual prison activists and the Catholic Worker, looking for animal pathogens and they confiscated our typewriter and our trash.[51]

Eventually, the harassment and the demands of community life took its toll. O'Reilly continued: "We kept rolling along and it went for about three years and then everyone collapsed from exhaustion."[52]

The Brisbane Catholic Worker house was eventually re-established years later, but during this hiatus several members traveled to the United States, where they built direct ties to American Catholic Left communities. Ciaron O'Reilly, for instance, spent time at Catholic Workers in Los Angeles, Las Vegas, and Des Moines. Later, he lived at Jonah House, where he began planning a Plowshares action with Moana Cole, a Catholic Worker from New Zealand. Bill Streit and Sue Frankel of the Dorothy Day Catholic Worker in Washington D.C. eventually joined them. On January 1, 1991, the four entered the Griffiss Air Force base in New York. Frankel and Streit hammered on a B-52 refueling plane while O'Reilly and Cole poured blood and painted phrases on the runway, including "Isaiah strikes again" and "Love your enemies – Jesus Christ." They were arrested, convicted, and sentenced to twelve months in prison.[53] Since Cole and O'Reilly were not U.S. citizens, they also had to appear in immigration court. As a result of these hearings, Cole voluntarily returned to New Zealand and O'Reilly was deported back to Australia.

Shortly after they returned home, O'Reilly and Cole formed a Catholic Worker house in New Zealand. Both then moved to Australia in 1994 to focus on the country's military, economic, and political complicity in the East Timor war. They started the Greg Shackleton Catholic Worker community, named after an Australian journalist killed in East Timor during the Indonesian invasion. This new group decided to target the Petroz

[51] Interview with Ciaron O'Reilly, conducted by the author, July 27, 2003.
[52] Interview with Ciaron O'Reilly, conducted by the author, July 27, 2003.
[53] Laffin, Arthur. 2003. *Swords into Plowshares: A Chronology of Plowshares Actions, 1980–2003.* Marion, SD: Rose Hill Books, p. 46.

Corporation, which had taken advantage of the Indonesian occupation to pursue a drilling program. The Catholic Workers held vigils and liturgies outside the Brisbane Petroz building, hoping to have a dialogue with employees. When this yielded little response, they shifted from protest to direct action. O'Reilly recalled:

Their 23rd floor office in this tower of concrete and steel from which they operated appeared so sterile and distant from the blood being spilt. Their public relations strategy viewed dialogue as a means of managing dissent. We decided to reach into the symbols and sacraments of our tradition to speak some truth to power. From our studies of Scripture we had increasingly come to view Jesus' practice of exorcism as a dynamic confrontation with the powers of death and domination in the world, such themes as are explored in depth by the theologian Walter Wink. On the anniversary of the Díli massacre we gathered in Brisbane's Anzac Square.... Four of us gained access to the basement car park ... [and] rode the elevator up to the 23rd floor, which opened on to the Petroz offices. As the lift doors opened, my brother Sean engaged the Petroz secretary in conversation about East Timor while the rest of us strode past into the boardroom. We had brought with us containers of human blood that we had donated to the action. We poured this blood over the boardroom table and the Petroz logo to symbolize the EastTimorese blood that had been spilt as a result of corporate decisions made around this table. We pasted the office walls and exploration maps with photographs of Timorese slain, starving and wounded. We then carried out a rite of deliverance, or exorcism, naming the spirits of Petroz for what they were, spillers of blood, reapers of profit, destroyers of villages, homes and lives. We cast out any control Petroz and its agents of state and law had over our behavior, any hopes they maintained for our silence and complicity in the face of 200,000 Timorese dead. We then knelt in prayer.[54]

After spending several years on the East Timor issue, some Catholic Workers decided to focus more on weapons of mass destruction, particularly by exposing Australia's role in producing nuclear arms. In 1998, on the fifty-third anniversary of the nuclear attack on Nagasaki, Treena Lenthall and Ciaron O'Reilly revived the Plowshares tradition in Australia when they poured blood and used hammers to dismantle uranium-mining equipment at the Jabiluka mine site. They left a statement proclaiming, "The nuclear weapons assembly line begins here at the Jabiluka uranium mine. Today we end it here with this nonviolent act of disarmament – the prophecy of Isaiah. The road from Jabiluka leads to Nagasaki, Hiroshima, Chernobyl.... With this act of disarmament, we prepare the way of the Lord – a

---

[54] O'Reilly, Ciaron. 2001. *Remembering, Forgetting: A Journey of Resistance to the War in East Timor*. Sydney, Australia: Otford Press, p. 21.

path of nonviolent resistance towards justice and peace."[55] Lenthall was convicted of criminal trespass and one count of damage to an excavator; O'Reilly was found guilty of trespass and two counts of damage. They were sentenced to time served (approximately six weeks) and ordered to pay about $7,000 in restitution – which they refused to do. As a result, they served an additional sixty-six days in prison.[56]

The Jabiluka campaign was the third Plowshares action in Australia. The first occurred in 1987, the second in 1991, and the last one was carried out in 1998. Like the movements in Germany and the Netherlands, the Australian movement engaged in intermittent acts of resistance without ever fully mobilizing. Paralleling the other two cases, the Australian Plowshares trajectory was partially shaped by the fact that activists were not able to sufficiently address the developmental tasks that are necessary for a movement to expand. Specifically, establishing legitimacy of means was challenging because this type of radical faith-based war resistance was culturally unfamiliar to most Australians. Australian Plowshares activists therefore found that they were not always well received by members of the secular peace movement, who were at times suspicious of their religious roots. Additionally, Australia is a widely secular society, and even Australian Catholics were, for the most part, unaware of the radical Catholic tradition in the United States. Thus, many found these tactics shocking and impractical. O'Reilly stated:

Some of it's cultural. Utopianism is stronger in America. . . . and America is the only part of the First World that is at all church-going. I think I saw a statistic that said 44 percent of Americans are church-going[57]. . . . And the Left isn't as hostile to faith-based activists whereas in Australia, Britain and Ireland, a lot of the Left are angry ex-Catholics. So if you get up and say you're Catholic . . . you're too hip for the straights, too straight for the hips, too spikey for the fluffies, too fluffy for the spikies, too Christian for the anarchists, too anarchist for the Christians. It's very new. . . . But when I was in jail [in the U.S.], anyone born before 1950 knew about the Berrigans and Vietnam.[58]

---

[55] Laffin, Arthur J. 2003. *Swords Into Plowshares: A Chronology of Disarmament Actions, 1980–2003*. Marion, SD: Rose Hill Books, p. 68.

[56] Laffin, Arthur J. 2003. *Swords Into Plowshares: A Chronology of Disarmament Actions, 1980–2003*. Marion, SD: Rose Hill Books, p. 68.

[57] According to the results of the World Values Survey conducted at the Institute for Social Research at the University of Michigan, O'Reilly is correct. Forty-four percent of U.S. citizens attend church regularly.

[58] Interview with Ciaron O'Reilly, conducted by the author, July 27, 2003.

Australian Plowshares activists partially accomplished the second developmental task – building a movement infrastructure. Although they successfully formed local resistance communities that provided support, they were at a relative disadvantage compared with the U.S. movement, which inherited a pre-existing structure from the Catholic Worker and Jonah House. In contrast, Australian activists had to devote significant time and energy to creating and stabilizing these communities, and although they had some sense of how Catholic Left communities in the United States function, this knowledge was initially gleaned through indirect ties and thus was rather limited. O'Reilly commented: "[In the beginning] we had no real life connection to them and we made life harder for ourselves. We should have gone straight over there [to the U.S.] to check it out and then come back and started it."[59]

Developing community diverted activists' energy away from the tasks of recruiting new participants. Because their numbers remained small and they had no wider network of support within Australia, this handful of Plowshares activists was therefore susceptible to the countervailing pressures that undermine commitment. As members traveled abroad or spent time in jail, there were few to carry on the work of the community, and consequently some of them burned out. Without a firm foundation, state-sponsored repression also took a toll.

In short, without a stable infrastructure or legitimacy of means, it became difficult for Plowshares activists to expand the movement. Nonetheless, it was possible to launch a few actions. O'Reilly observed: "I think in whatever situation you can experiment with community building, acts of mercy and resistance, whether you're in jail or whether you have an infrastructure or not."[60] But experimenting is not equivalent to successfully building a movement. The Australians, Dutch, and German activists have faired better at experimentation than long-term mobilization.

---

[59] Interview with Ciaron O'Reilly, conducted by the author, July 27, 2003.
[60] Interview with Ciaron O'Reilly, conducted by the author, July 27, 2003.

6

Internal Tensions and Implosion

THE SWEDISH PLOWSHARES
MOVEMENT

The roots of the Swedish Plowshares movement can be traced to Syracuse, New York. This is where Per Herngren, an activist from Gothenburg, Sweden, was sent in 1983 to participate in an international peace organization exchange program. During his time in Syracuse, the Griffiss Plowshares action took place at an Air Force base just a short distance away.[1] In support of the arrested activists, a celebration was held and Herngren attended. In Sweden, he had seen the film *Inside the King of Prussia* about the Plowshares action at General Electric, but Herngren knew little about the movement at that point. He recalled:

None of those for whom we were celebrating were actually there: they were behind bars at a police station nearby. But many of the people active in the Plowshares movement were there. The party was a lot of fun. It was packed with people and I had to squeeze my way into a place on the floor. I found myself in the middle of a discussion about all the mistakes and weaknesses of the Plowshares movement. I knew almost nothing about the movement, but I managed to pick up a little during the discussion. After the party I lay awake all night. Finally I made up my mind. I contacted one of the people that had been most critical during the discussion. . . . I asked her if they would have any use of a Swede in the next group.[2]

Several months later, on Easter morning in 1984, Herngren and seven others entered a Martin Marietta plant in Orlando, Florida. Using hammers, the group destroyed components of the Patriot missile launcher and poured

---

[1] Interview with Per Herngren, conducted by the author, December 5, 2002.
[2] Herngren, Per. 1993. *Path of Resistance: The Practice of Civil Disobedience*. Philadelphia: New Society Publishers, pp. 32–33.

blood. Before they were arrested, they left an indictment that charged Martin Marietta with violating international law and God's law.[3]

Establishing Movement Infrastructure and Leadership

Swedish news agencies gave extensive coverage to Herngren's subsequent trial and incarceration. When he was deported after a year in the U.S. correctional system, he was fairly well known in Sweden, and received considerable support. Encouraged by this response, Herngren set out to build a European Plowshares movement. One of his first steps was to contact Wolfgang Sternstein in West Germany. Herngren recalled: "I knew about Wolfgang from Jonah House and I was looking for him because he was the only one I knew [in Europe] who had been interested in working with the Plowshares movement at that time.... So Wolfgang was recruiting in Germany and I was recruiting in Sweden [along with Gunn-Marie Carlsson]."[4] Out of these efforts, the 1986 German–Swedish action was born, as discussed in the previous chapter.

The European Hope and Resistance Network

Drawing from their knowledge of the Atlantic Life Community (ALC) and its Faith and Resistance retreats in the United States, Herngren, Sternstein, and others constructed a parallel European Plowshares network. They implemented some changes, however, to adapt it to the European context and the more eclectic views of the participants. Stellan Vinthagen explained: "One of the things we came to quickly was that *faith* and resistance is not our base. Some people were Gandhians or pagans and some were Christians; or like me and a number of people from Sweden, some were atheists or at least agnostics. So we felt like *hope* and resistance was more appropriate."[5] European Plowshares organizers made other alterations as well. For instance, many of the Faith and Resistance retreats in the United States thematically follow the Christian liturgical calendar. They also have established rituals, such as biblical meditations, prayer, and regular "witness" actions at the White House and Pentagon. The European activists similarly had times of

---

[3] Laffin, Arthur J. 2003. *Swords Into Plowshares: A Chronology of Plowshares Disarmament Actions, 1980–2003.* Marion, SD: Rose Hill Books.
[4] Interview with Per Herngren, conducted by the author, December 5, 2002.
[5] Interview with Stellan Vinthagen, conducted by the author, June 24, 2003.

156

meditation, but they were not necessarily a reflection on Christian texts. Vinthagen stated:

A similar thing [that we used] was text reflection but for us the Bible was not the centerpiece....It could be the Bible, and very often it was, but I would say that definitely in one out of two cases it was something else....We also decided to not end the retreat with an action, which I realize for the Plowshares gatherings in the United States is normal. We wanted to have a kind of retreat...that really focused on personal contact, celebration, evaluation, theoretical reflection, and not being occupied with any action planning because we were doing that at another time.[6]

As participation in the European Hope and Resistance retreats grew, the nature of these gatherings changed. Herngren observed: "In the 1980s, the Swedish-German group did have prayer and text reflection, that kind of thing, so it was very similar to the United States. Then we had a more secular group in the early 1990s. We still used the structure of text reflection, but then the Plowshares movement grew bigger...and they held meetings using different styles."[7] To enhance involvement in these meetings, activists implemented organizational rules and procedures that diverged from the U.S. Plowshares tradition. Specifically, they changed the Atlantic Life Community's format of large group discussions, meditation, and planning, choosing instead to adopt a small group system. At the start of each gathering, participants divided into "base groups" comprised of at least one person from each country. These groups functioned as a support structure for the duration of the meeting. The retreats also included a series of workshops on topics ranging from parenting and activism, resistance in prison, and feminism and non-violence, to juggling, massage, and salsa dancing. In all of these group activities, interactions were guided by specific practices aimed at maximizing democracy and limiting oppressive interpersonal dynamics. These guidelines, adapted from other movements that use democratic decision-making,[8] are outlined in the *Hope and Resistance Handbook*, which states:

We don't work in large groups (over ten people) – either for workshops or decision-making. This is because discussions in large groups tend to be dominated by just a few people. We use smaller groups because they are more democratic.... Of course,

---

[6] Interview with Stellan Vinthagen, conducted by the author, June 24, 2003.

[7] Interview with Per Herngren, conducted by the author, December 5, 2002. Further clarified in personal correspondence with the author, November 29, 2005.

[8] For further elaboration of these techniques and the role of consensus-based decision making in social movements, see Polletta, Francesca. 2002. *Freedom Is an Endless Meeting: Democracy in American Social Movements*. Chicago: University of Chicago Press.

small groups do not guarantee an absence of oppression. Just because we're into nonviolence, it doesn't mean that we're pure and perfect. Far from it. It's really important to explore and help change our own oppressive and self-oppressive behavior. These are some roles that we sometimes use within a workshop: **Vibes-watcher** who observes emotional undercurrents and feeds them back to the group when s/he thinks that they are strongly affecting the process.... **Sexism-watcher** who observes and feeds back any sexist behavior. **Oppression-watcher** who observes and feeds back any sort of oppressive behavior.... Other roles in the workshop include a **time-keeper** and a **fika-facilitator** (ensuring coffee and tea breaks). Each workshop should also appoint a **note-taker** or a **note-gatherer** who ensures that the report coordinator gets the exciting notes from the exciting workshop.[9]

Eventually, the Hope and Resistance retreats also included a formal business meeting.

The European Plowshares network is therefore markedly different from the U.S. Atlantic Life Community in a number of ways. First, the religious emphasis is notably weaker because participants are more heterogeneous than their North American counterparts. Second, the governance structure is much more explicit in the Hope and Resistance network. In the United States, the Atlantic Life Community emerged from the 1970s organizing efforts of Philip Berrigan, Elizabeth McAlister, and other Catholic Left activists. The early gatherings were influenced by the spiritual commitments and experiences of these leaders, many of whom had been members of religious orders, and thus biblical meditation and prayer, along with opportunities to put faith into action, became a standard part of the retreats. These activities eventually became ritualized, but they evolved organically without explicitly establishing retreat rules and procedures. A third distinction between the European and U.S. communities is evident in the relative emphasis of each group's gatherings. The Hope and Resistance network is more focused on the task of building a European Plowshares movement. The Faith and Resistance retreats in the United States are oriented to the reinforcement of a normative commitment to sustaining resistance over the long haul. Each group, however, recognizes that these retreats are a critical means of keeping relational ties and emotional bonds strong.

Establishing a Swedish Resistance Community

In addition to building this European Plowshares network, activists were working to build a movement within Sweden. To accomplish this, they

---

[9] Hancock, Stephen. 1997. *Hope and Resistance Handbook*, p. 6, from the personal files of Per Herngren.

held regular retreats, recruiting people from pre-existing groups and organizations. Per Herngren spread the news through the Swedish Fellowship of Reconciliation, Gunn-Marie Carlsson sought participants from a national women's peace group, and Stellan Vinthagen traveled to various peace camps.[10] Swedish organizers also formed a local intentional community, emulating the infrastructure of the U.S. Plowshares movement, which combines grassroots resistance communities with a broader network of activists. Vinthagen commented:

The major influence [on community building] definitely came from the U.S. Plowshares [movement]. It grows from our commitment to creating a movement that is able to sustain itself for decades. . . . The only thing that makes that possible is if you are able to sustain a life of resistance and . . . I can't really imagine how that is ever possible on an individual basis when you live a normal, bourgeois life and you need to sustain yourself in this capitalist society. So you need to create your own society. . . . A small part of that is to create community groups that are doing actions but another thing is to create an alternative economy, childrearing, other kinds of schools, all that stuff in order to be able to challenge these powerful forces that sustain the power structure of today.[11]

By 1989, Swedish activists had established Omega, an intentional community focused on war resistance. It was located in Hammarkullen, a neighborhood outside of Gothenburg that is largely populated by immigrants. Vinthagen described the beginning of the Omega experiment:

It was an intentional community focusing on living together in resistance, supporting each other in prison time, sharing economic resources. . . . We wanted to live in Hammarkullen since you could say it is a global village of people coming from war and poverty. We wanted to be in proximity of that environment to be reminded of the reasons that we are struggling. . . . So in 1989 we set up Omega as a kind of support to sustain our resistance. We also wanted to create a resistance locus, a place where people can come to get . . . experience and inspiration for this kind of action and then move on to other movements. Omega worked from 1989 to around 1992 in a very well-functioning way, sustaining and supporting us who were living there with surprisingly few conflicts.[12]

Complementing the Omega community was a group of activists who lived in the surrounding area. Because not everyone wanted to reside in an intentional community or focus their efforts primarily on acts of civil disobedience, this affiliated group enabled people to support the movement

[10] Interview with Per Herngren, conducted by the author, December 5, 2002.
[11] Interview with Stellan Vinthagen, conducted by the author, June 24, 2003.
[12] Interview with Stellan Vinthagen, conducted by the author, June 24, 2003.

without full involvement in Omega or a Plowshares action. Over the course of several years during the 1990s, fifty to sixty people moved to Hammarkullen to be involved with one of these two Plowshares-related communities.[13]

Cultural Adaptations

These community members and retreat participants began planning Swedish Plowshares campaigns. In many ways, their efforts closely paralleled U.S. actions, with an emphasis on long, careful preparation and a commitment to using prison as an ongoing witness. But Swedish organizers did make several changes to adapt the movement to their own cultural context. First, they decided against the use of blood. As Herngren explained: "From the beginning, we never used blood...[because] blood does not have the same kind of meaning to Protestants as it does in the Catholic tradition....People wouldn't really understand it here."[14] Activist Hasse Leander articulated other pragmatic reasons for this decision:

The most apparent difference is that in the U.S. blood is used as a symbol in connection with the disarmament of weapons. The blood comes from the activists themselves and is poured from babies' bottles over the weapons and other equipment.... In Sweden, blood has been very scarcely used in civil disobedience actions. One group used pig's blood in an action against Bofors. They did a die-in and poured blood over themselves. When the guard dogs arrived it became quite nasty. The dogs became tense and aggressive from the smell of pig's blood. The action didn't work very well, partly due to the blood.... It is difficult to say how people understand the symbols in an action. However, I think blood can actually be dangerous from a contamination point of view and it gives also associations to religious fanaticism which creates an unnecessary polarization to the opponent.... I find it difficult to agree with the use of blood in general and especially when it is not used in an extremely careful way.[15]

The second cultural adaptation was necessitated by the fact that Sweden has no nuclear weapons. Organizers therefore had to broaden their focus to the weapons trade industry. Leander noted: "In Sweden, the Plowshares

---

[13] Interview with Stellan Vinthagen, conducted by the author, June 24, 2003.

[14] Interview with Per Herngren, conducted by the author, December 5, 2002.

[15] Leander, Hasse. 1997. "The Ploughshares Movement in Sweden and the U.S.: A Comparison." *The Daily Hammer: Newsletter of the Ploughshares Support Network*, No. 14 (Winter): 10–12. Quotation from p. 12.

movement is mainly focused on exports of conventional weapons, but also on the very production of weapons, and the whole [policy] of military defense is questioned."[16] Vinthagen added: "We are challenging the profit making in killing.... Sweden is one of the ten biggest weapons exporters in the world. We have exported weapons to all wars since 1945. We have supplied weapons to Iran and Iraq, Pakistan and India. One of the most perverse things that capitalism is doing is making profit off the suppression of other people."[17]

In the third cultural adaptation, the symbolic meaning of Plowshares actions was altered slightly. Whereas both the U.S. and Swedish movements seek to abolish war, many Swedes did not see their task as prophetic enactment but rather challenging the obedience mentality that enables militarism to continue. They hoped to convince their fellow citizens that they have the power to change these policies if they are willing to pay the price for disarmament. Vinthagen commented: "We are trying to symbolically ... take responsibility to disarm.... At the core of our culture [is the belief] that we should obey and we don't have the power – we are just a small people.... We are actually showing where the power is.... The power holders just have power when we are obedient. In my view, a Plowshares action is a very simple way of challenging that [obedience]."[18] Likewise, Herngren observed:

In Plowshares actions, we use hammers to disarm weapons. My hammer symbolized for me the paradox of militarism. A Pershing II missile can annihilate my home town of Gothenburg, Sweden. There are no weapons that could stop such an attack. But my small, ridiculous hammer made it impossible to fire that particular missile. And similarly, it isn't raw strength that can stop the arms race.... The arms race could not continue without the obedience of citizens, which is caused mainly by people's fear of the consequences of disobedience. But there are no methods of control today that could be used against an entire population that is prepared to take the consequences of their disobedience. Therefore, vulnerability to the consequences becomes the prerequisite of breaking obedience's hold on us.[19]

---

[16] Leander, Hasse. 1997. "The Ploughshares Movement in Sweden and the U.S.: A Comparison." *The Daily Hammer: Newsletter of the Ploughshares Support Network*, No. 14 (Winter): 10–12. Quotation from p. 10.

[17] Interview with Stellan Vinthagen, conducted by the author, June 24, 2003.

[18] Interview with Stellan Vinthagen, conducted by the author, June 24, 2003.

[19] Herngren, Per. 1993. *Path of Resistance: The Practice of Civil Disobedience*. Philadelphia: New Society Publishers, pp. 96–97.

Once people become aware that they have a choice between obeying or disobeying, complying or resisting, perceptions begin to change. Herngren continued:

To some extent we allow others to control our behavior due to our interpretation of what is generally perceived as being possible.... For example, it is considered self-evident that only governments in disarmament negotiations can decide which weapons should be destroyed. When workers at a weapons factory or other people suddenly start disarming weapons on their own, our view of what is possible and who can act changes.[20]

The fourth and final cultural adaptation that distinguishes the Swedish movement from its U.S. counterpart is the degree of openness. U.S. activists plan and execute their campaigns in secrecy; in contrast, Swedish activists inform the police and factory owners in advance about their actions. Only the date and time are kept confidential. Whereas U.S. Plowshares organizers personally invite trusted individuals to participate, Swedish organizers send out announcements that new Plowshares groups are being formed and are open to all. Leander explains the rationale behind the decision to operate openly:

Of great importance is the difference in the relationship to relatives. The secrecy of the Plowshares movement in the U.S. is here quite troublesome, I think. A wife or a husband of an activist can remain uninformed of an action until it happens. The same with parents, other relatives and friends. When the action happens there is sometimes a strong emotional reaction among close relatives and friends, which is hard to deal with. In Sweden, Plowshares groups often invite relatives and close friends to special meetings. The group gives information about its plans (apart from the date of the action) and gives space for discussion and questioning. It can often be difficult to be criticized by people who are close ... but the meetings have proved good. The relatives have felt calmer when they realized that they are not alone in their questioning. The most important purpose these meetings serve is probably that they give a possibility and encourage relatives to keep in contact with each other. Thanks to these meetings, many relatives have been able to communicate with other people who are in the same boat, so to speak, and thus felt less lonely with their problem of having a person close to them in prison.

Part of the explanation is that the differences in the Plowshares movements mirror the differences between the American and Swedish societies. Sentences are much longer in the U.S. and conspiracy charges are common, and it presents itself

---

[20] Herngren, Per. 1993. *Path of Resistance: The Practice of Civil Disobedience*. Philadelphia: New Society Publishers, pp. 13–14.

immediately to let as few people as possible know anything about actions before-hand. Conspiracy charges mean that people are charged with conspiracy for having the knowledge that an action is being planned but not going to the police with that information. Many people in the American Plowshares movement think it is irresponsible to let people, who themselves have not chosen to take the risk, know about an action beforehand. One way of coping with this is to let the action be public in advance (except the date). When I told my father I was planning to do a Plowshares action, his response was to call the police to stop it. "Go ahead," I said. "We have already contacted them."[21]

Swedish Plowshares Actions Begin

With these cultural adaptations in place, activists began planning cam-paigns to end the Swedish weapons trade. Gunn-Marie Carlsson and Hen-rik Frykberg attempted the first Swedish Plowshares action in 1988 when they camped out at the Uddevalla harbor for several days. They were awaiting the arrival of a freight train loaded with Swedish anti-aircraft missile launchers that would be transferred to a ship destined for India. When the train reached the harbor, the two activists strapped on their hammers and crawled across the beach in the dark of night. When they were just a few meters away from the artillery, a security car's head-lights came on, illuminating the scene. Carlsson and Frykberg dropped their hammers and were promptly arrested. They were released after ten hours.[22]

About a year later, Anders Grip and Gunilla Åkerberg went to the rail-road yards in Kristinehamn where Swedish weaponry was transported by train to the coast. They located the equipment used to load weapons and were able to hammer upon and damage it. Afterward, they hung banners that read, "Violence and oppression depend upon our obedience and pas-sivity," and "We must dare to be disobedient."[23] Security officers soon apprehended them. But as they drove the two activists to the police sta-tion, some of the officers expressed their support, and even suggested other

---

[21] Leander, Hasse. 1997. "The Ploughshares Movement in Sweden and the U.S.: A Compar-ison." *The Daily Hammer: Newsletter of the Ploughshares Support Network*, No. 14 (Winter): 10–12. Quotation from p. 11.

[22] From the Swedish Plowshares movement chronology, found at http://www.plowshares.se/aktioner/svenskaaktioner.shtml.

[23] Laffin, Arthur J. 2004. *Swords Into Plowshares: A Chronology of Plowshares Disarmament Actions, 1980–2003.* Marion, SD: Rose Hill Books, p. 42.

sites for future Plowshares actions. Grip and Åkerberg were then held in custody overnight and released the next day. Eventually they were brought to court, convicted, and ordered to pay $10,000 in restitution to Bofors, the manufacturer of the weapons. When the activists refused to pay, Bofors rescinded its request for restitution.[24]

Numerous other Plowshares actions were carried out over the next few years. In the spring of 1990, three Swedes entered a weapon manufacturing plant in Eskilstuna. They hammered on a Carl-Gustaf bazooka and then distributed a statement to plant employees that read, "Swedish weapons are used in warfare all over the world. It is the responsibility of each and every one of us to contribute to disarmament. By disarming Swedish weapons, we hope to break through paralysis and powerlessness and instead help achieve peace and justice."[25] The following year, Anders Grip, Per Herngren, and Stefan Falk conducted another Plowshares action at the Eskilstuna factory. The three men wielded their hammers, damaging two grenade launchers and an AK-5 automatic rifle. During their subsequent trial, they were found guilty of property damage and unlawful entry. Falk and Herngren were ordered to pay fines and Grip was sent to prison for one month.[26]

Swedish Plowshares activists turned their attention next to the Saab Corporation's military aircraft factory in Linköping, where the company was producing the reconnaissance plane known as JAS. On June 22, 1993, Pia Lundin and Igge Olsson hammered upon the wings of one JAS plane, causing an estimated $200,000 in damages. Two days later, Thomas Falk and Hasse Leander broke into the hangar, planning to damage three of the four remaining JAS planes. They intended to leave the last one untouched, symbolizing the need for others to complete the task of disarmament. However, they were arrested before they were able to carry out their action. They were eventually convicted on charges of attempted sabotage and intent to conduct malicious damage. Within a few months, all four (Lundin, Olsson, Falk, Leander) were sentenced to one year in prison. Additionally, they were ordered to compensate Saab with $80,000 for the damages. The four refused to pay the restitution but began negotiating with Saab representatives to raise $80,000 for a water project in India. At first, Saab was open to

---

[24] Laffin, Arthur J. 2004. *Swords Into Plowshares: A Chronology of Plowshares Disarmament Actions, 1980–2003*. Marion, SD: Rose Hill Books, pp. 42–43.

[25] Laffin, Arthur J. 2004. *Swords Into Plowshares: A Chronology of Plowshares Disarmament Actions, 1980–2003*. Marion, SD: Rose Hill Books, p. 45.

[26] Laffin, Arthur J. 2004. *Swords Into Plowshares: A Chronology of Plowshares Disarmament Actions, 1980–2003*. Marion, SD: Rose Hill Books, p. 47.

the suggestion. But when the Plowshares activists said that they would continue their resistance until the factory stopped producing weaponry, Saab terminated the negotiations.[27]

Internal Tensions Arise

Plowshares actions at Swedish military installations and weapons factories continued steadily over the next few years.[28] It appeared that the movement had shifted into the expansion stage and was ripe for growth. However, trouble was brewing within the movement, especially around issues of leadership, gender, and strategy.

Leadership

Internal divisions first began to surface in the Omega community. Some residents wanted to focus more heavily on resistance, while others saw their primary calling as social service.[29] Thus there were divergent views regarding the community's purpose and priorities. Although differences of opinion are common in movements, the tensions within Omega became destructive. Criticisms became highly personal, harsh accusations erupted, and rumors spread – many of which centered on the movement's key organizers. Vinthagen recalled:

When people initially came to it, they felt like "Yes – finally there is a movement that is taking a strong stand for feminism, anarchy, and challenging the state and the military!" They felt they had come to the right place [because] they were sick and tired of lots of other movements that were not ready to break the law. And we introduced feminist methods into meetings early on – with consensus decision making, task sharing, sexism observers and vibe watchers – all those things. So they felt they had found a home but after a while…this kind of romantic feeling of

---

[27] Laffin, Arthur J. 2004. *Swords Into Plowshares: A Chronology of Plowshares Disarmament Actions, 1980–2003*. Marion, SD: Rose Hill Books, p. 52.

[28] On January 27, 1994, activists Calle Hoglund and Karna Rusek hammered on the nose cone of a military aircraft at the Såtenäs F7 base. In the spring of 1997, Cecilia Redner and Marija Fischer targeted the Bofors plant in Karlskoga, where they attempted to damage a naval canon that was designated for Indonesia. Next, three Swedish activists (Annika Splade, Stellan Vinthagen, and Ann-Britt Sternfeldt) were arrested in September 1998 when they dismantled production equipment at the Barrow Shipyard in Great Britain where a Trident submarine was being constructed.

[29] This same tension has occurred in numerous Catholic Worker communities in the United States. Some Catholic Workers feel that they should devote most of their time and energy to the works of mercy, whereas others also want to engage in war resistance.

being at home passed.... They started to react [to leadership]. I think that is very good; it's part of the development of the movement. But it becomes very difficult to handle in a small movement when attacks are happening covertly. I guess some people probably didn't dare to openly challenge us because they didn't feel they had the position or whatever to do that. But that process destroyed the community. It destroyed the small Plowshares movement that we had.[30]

The Omega community collapsed shortly thereafter.

Another Swedish Plowshares activist addressed the role that leadership issues played in the movement's struggle to expand. He noted that participants shared a strong ideal of how they wanted to structure their leadership, but implementing this model posed significant challenges. He noted:

[Some activists] were really strong academically and intellectually, criticizing the existing movement for being too dependent on leaders like Gandhi and King, and maybe also the Berrigans. [They advocated that] we should create an anti-authoritarian movement with a consensus decision making process, leadership rotation, and everything. At the same time, [these same activists] were taking a very strong leadership role.[31]

Gender

Tensions around gender dynamics also arose, as feminist activists voiced concern about the extent of men's influence. Anna-Carin Pihl interviewed a number of women in the Swedish movement and summarized their views in a 1996 movement newsletter. She wrote:

A third of the Plowshares activists in the U.S. are women.[32] A third of participants in Plowshares groups in Europe are women. In Sweden... one can count the number of female Plowshares activists on the fingers of one hand. The public faces are men, the "leaders" in this non-hierarchical movement are men. Why?

One answer of course lies in the size of the movement. On the whole there is no resistance culture in Sweden the same way there is in the U.S. All together, four Plowshares actions have been carried out in Sweden. Two women have taken part, according to the definition of "Plowshares activist." (But according to one of the women interviewed the number is larger, as many women take part as supporters,

---

[30] Interview with Stellan Vinthagen, conducted by the author, June 24, 2003.

[31] Interview with Hasse Leander, conducted by the author, June 27, 2004.

[32] According to Art Laffin's chronology of Plowshares actions in the United States the percentage of men participating in the campaigns is 57.6 percent compared with 42.4 percent women. Moreover, in personal correspondence with the author (November 19, 2005), Per Herngren noted that men were in the majority of hammerers, but women constituted a majority of the supporters.

media contacts, photographers, etc. "A manifestation of the division of the participants, created by men: the strong heroes do the hammering, the rest appear in the background, not as valuable," she says and stresses the importance of seeing the whole picture, rather than praising the hammerers to the skies.)

But this is not the full truth. Women are a minority in the movement. No one thinks they are more cowardly than the men. Instead, many ask if it's not the boyish adventures lurking in the background – the forms of preparation for actions seem to be typically "male": lying in bushes, spying on routines at weapons factories, cutting fences, smashing up weapons, etc. . . . Stories of adventure are everywhere in traditional boy's culture. . . .

Maybe part of the answer lies in men's desire for a career? Many women believe that is the case. "Men wholeheartedly and passionately devote all their time to what they believe in. In our patriarchal society, the right to aim for the stars has always been and is still reserved for men. Why should this not also be true for the Plowshares movement?" . . . . Another woman strongly criticized the fixation in the movement with the prison sentence. "The longer the sentence, the more heroic they are." . . .

But the feminist ways of working in groups seem to satisfy most of the women: go-arounds, consensus and the absence of hierarchies benefit both men and women. However, one woman writes: "The people who speak most, whose words are listened to, who take up the largest space and who take most initiatives are, also in this movement, men." Another: "We all agreed happily that we wouldn't have leaders. But loose structures and informal leaders are more difficult to call into question than formal ones. Inevitably, some people come to dominate. We discussed it but unfortunately the establishing of the existence of the problem doesn't always lead to any improvement." . . .

The classic gender roles of women monopolizing emotions and men shutting emotions out seem to exist as strongly amongst Plowshares activists. [One woman stated]: "In my group there was no space for solving difficult emotional conflicts. The men wanted to do the action at any cost. Most important was the goal, not the dynamics of the group and that we were all part of it. The women both wanted to and were able to talk about fears and hesitations, our own resistance to doing the action, whereas the men said, 'This is not the place for therapy.' As a consequence, two left the group. The question is if it is our responsibility to change the men."[33]

Strategy: Expressive vs. Instrumental Orientations

Another source of tension dealt with the question of whether the movement should shift its strategy from the primarily symbolic acts that characterize the U.S. Plowshares tradition toward the formation of a broad-based

---

[33] Pihl, Anna-Carina. 1996. "Daughters of Lilith." *The Daily Hammer*, March 1996. Translated by Lotta Kronlid, pp. 10–11.

movement. Swedish activists held numerous discussions about the relative emphasis on witnessing versus winning.[34] In contrast to U.S. activists, who consider these apostolic works an important form of witness regardless of the outcome, a sizeable number of Swedes wanted to be politically effective. Leander, who spent time in the U.S. Plowshares movement, discussed these differences:

There is a widespread idea amongst Plowshares activists in the U.S. about not worrying about what is effective or about attaining results. They mean that it is not possible to judge what is effective, but that the results lie in the hands of God. The only thing they can do is to witness about the truth. In Sweden, most people think that Plowshares actions and other civil disobedience are important just because it makes the nonviolence work more effective. . . . I think that if activists in Sweden noticed that the actions didn't lead to change, most of them would think about doing it differently. . . . In Sweden and Europe I have taken part in many discussions about how the movement can grow. Plowshares activists in the U.S. don't seem to view it like this. As far as I have understood it, there is not much interest in how their actions are received by the rest of the society, if they really work as a challenge. The important thing is to enflesh the Gospels.[35]

While some Swedish activists wanted to focus on witness actions, many decided to increase effectiveness by building a mass movement. However, this required the expansion of their ranks. To recruit new participants, Plowshares activists sponsored disarmament camps modeled after Great Britain's Greenham Common peace camps. They distributed flyers inviting "environmental activists, feminists, Plowshares members, syndicalists, anarchists, socialists, liberals, atheists, new agers, and Christians"[36] to participate. In the summer of 1992, 200 people attended – some for just a day or two – but only a small minority engaged in civil disobedience. The next

---

[34] For further discussion of this tension between expressive and instrumental orientations, see the following: Epstein, Barbara. 1991. *Political Protest and Cultural Revolution: Nonviolent Direct Action in the 1970s and 1980s*. Berkeley: University of California Press; Hertzke, Allen. 1988. *Representing God in Washington: The Role of Religious Lobbies in the American Polity*. Knoxville: University of Tennessee Press; Pagnucco, Ronald. 1996. "A Comparison of the Political Behavior of Faith-Based and Secular Peace Groups," pp. 205–222 in Christian S. Smith (ed.), *Disruptive Religion: The Force of Faith in Social Movement Activism*. New York: Routledge; Ruzza, Carlo. 1990. "Strategies in the Italian Peace Movement." *Research in Social Movements, Conflict, and Change* 12: 111–138; Yoder, John Howard. 1992. *Nevertheless: Varieties of Religious Pacifism*. Scottsdale, PA: Herald Press.

[35] Leander, Hasse. 1997. "The Ploughshares Movement in Sweden and the U.S.: A Comparison." *The Daily Hammer: Newsletter of the Ploughshares Support Network*, No. 14 (Winter): 10–12. Quotation from p. 12.

[36] From the Swedish disarmament camp invitation, personal files of Stellan Vinthagen.

summer, Plowshares organizers required that campers stay for a minimum of one week. As a result, the camp drew only sixty participants, half of whom participated in direct disarmament actions. The third peace camp was held in 1995. The numbers dropped to twenty-five because organizers clearly stated that the purpose was to plan acts of civil disobedience and thus campers were expected to stay for the entire three weeks and participate in direct action campaigns.[37]

The peace camps' declining numbers indicated that the costs associated with the Plowshares movement were prohibitive since many potential supporters were not willing to commit civil disobedience or go to prison. Based on this concern, a suggestion was made to redesign the movement in two ways: (1) incorporate more low-risk forms of participation, and (2) change the infrastructure from intentional resistance communities to a national, formalized membership organization. One activist explained why the intentional community structure was ineffective in Sweden, necessitating this organizational overhaul:

The intentional community movement is much bigger in the U.S.... There is a difference in context also. Sweden is a country where the ... average person here is a member of five or six organizations, maybe more. You're a member of the union, a sports organization, some nature group, a solidarity thing. Once a year you pay your membership and you get mailings. You're not so active; sometimes you go to a meeting, perhaps, but that kind of activism is very common here.... Most of the day-to-day work is done by people employed by the organization. So there are a lot of formal organizations but not these kinds of grassroots communities of resistance.[38]

In addition, intentional communities had little religious resonance in Sweden, whose Protestant tradition has no comparable form of communal monastic life. This is a sharp contrast to the U.S. movement where, according to my survey, nearly 60 percent of Plowshares activists have lived in a Catholic Worker community for one or more years and roughly one-third are, or were at one time, members of a Catholic religious order. Thus the notion of giving up personal possessions and living communally was not as foreign to them as it was to most Swedes, who were less likely to join a movement that required such living arrangements.

[37] From the country reports of the 1995 Hope and Resistance gathering in Valley Farm, Great Britain, held December 3–8, 1995. This information was also confirmed by Stellan Vinthagen in an interview conducted by the author on June 24, 2003.

[38] Interview with Hasse Leander, conducted by the author, June 27, 2003.

By 1995, a sizeable segment of the movement agreed to the proposed changes, and they established a formal member organization called *Svärd till Plogbillar* (Swords into Plowshares). It resembled a traditional social movement organization, publishing newsletters and sponsoring annual meetings. Leander stated: "We created the organization ... to open it up for people to get involved without moving into community or being part of a Plowshares group in which they risked jail. So that was an important aspect since many people wanted to widen the possibilities for people to get involved. Eventually we had 150, 200 members."[39] But not all Swedish Plowshares activists agreed with this change in strategy and form. In fact, some did not join *Svärd till Plogbillar* but continued to plan Plowshares actions in the traditional manner, focusing on the symbolic, high-risk act of hammering upon weapons. Others got involved in British campaigns against Trident submarines or worked within the Swedish Fellowship of Reconciliation. A small group changed its emphasis to animal rights, using the tactics of property destruction at animal testing laboratories. As a result, the movement began to splinter.

Even those who supported the new *Svärd till Plogbillar* organization found that these changes did not solve the activists' problems. The disputes over gender, strategy, and leadership continued, causing a great deal of distress and tension among activists. Vinthagen commented:

We came to the conclusion that we need a more formal structure so we took the step ... to create a support organization where there is clarity of decisions, a yearly meeting, clear membership, different working groups for different issues. We still had a consensus decision making process built into it. But instead of being the solution to these conflicts and being the integrating engine of a new generation coming into the movement, it became the central place for these conflicts to be played out. Around 1997, 1998 the newsletters of the organization were only debates around conflict issues inside the movement, so it was putting off people who were interested in joining.[40]

By 2000, Swedish Plowshares activists had not found any satisfactory means of resolving their issues. Frustrated and exhausted, the members decided to take a break, suspending the organization. This decision effectively marked the end of Sweden's formal Plowshares member organization.

In little more than a decade, two attempts to build a movement infrastructure had failed. Since the collapse of the Omega community and the

---

[39] Interview with Hasse Leander, conducted by the author, June 27, 2003.
[40] Interview with Stellan Vinthagen, conducted by the author, June 24, 2003.

Svärd till Plogbillar organization, there have been periodic efforts to re-establish grassroots communities. In the spring of 2002, Annika Spalde and Per Herngren formed a Catholic Worker house in Hammarkullen. Because roughly two-thirds of the neighborhood's residents are immigrants, Spalde and Herngren devoted their efforts to refugee assistance, as other European Catholic Workers have done.[41] They rented an apartment with a spare bedroom, and for a short time they housed a Romanian refugee. Later, an American Catholic Worker joined them, and the guest-room was no longer available, limiting the hospitality they could offer. Moreover, because the Swedish government provides ample social services, the level of need was minimal. The lack of space, the low demand for assistance, and the differences of opinion that arose among community members caused the Hammarkullen Catholic Worker to quickly disband. A few individuals from the group still offer prison support and operate a soup kitchen one day a week, but they no longer live together as an intentional community.[42]

Undeterred by the failure of the Hammarkullen Catholic Worker, Herngren then tried to create a Swedish version of Jonah House. With a few others, he formed the Fig Tree Community in 2003. One of the community members was Susan van der Hijden of the Amsterdam Catholic Worker, who explained why this type of resistance community was crucial. She stated: "We don't have a center like [Jonah House] in Europe, where people can come and meet others willing to do Plowshares actions. . . . And there's a bigger need for that right now [than a Catholic Worker] because for every peace and resistance person there are maybe 100 people doing social work."[43] Unlike Jonah House, however, the Fig Tree does not have a shared living facility. Instead, members sponsor some communal activities, such as a weekly meal and reflection time, and each person devotes roughly twenty hours a week to resistance work such as organizing trial support, planning actions, and so forth. But the Fig Tree community never expanded beyond a handful of activists who meet occasionally. And without a common house or a pooled income, members had to support themselves. For some, like van der Hijden, this was problematic because her lack of fluency in Swedish and her status as a foreigner made it difficult to find employment; she ultimately had to return to Amsterdam. Thus the vision

---

[41] Interview with Per Herngren, conducted by the author, December 5, 2002.
[42] Field notes taken from conversations at the Fig Tree community, June 23–28, 2003.
[43] Interview with Susan van der Hijden, conducted by the author, June 24, 2003.

of a European Jonah House that could facilitate the rebirth of a vibrant Swedish Plowshares movement never materialized.

Factors Shaping the Swedish Plowshares Movement Trajectory

By 2004, the Swedish Plowshares movement was essentially over. Although a small cadre still performs citizen inspections of weapon sites,[44] no act of military-related property destruction has occurred on Swedish soil since 1997. How do we account for the movement's demise when it initially appeared to have great potential as Swedish activists steadily carried out disarmament campaigns, year after year, culminating in nearly a dozen actions?[45] The trajectory of the Swedish movement differs from both the sustained resistance found in the United States as well as the intermittent, sporadic actions in Australia, the Netherlands, and Germany. The Swedes were able to form a movement that did expand to some degree, but very early on they encountered challenges that caused the movement to struggle and falter for over a decade, before ultimately collapsing. By taking a closer comparative look at the Swedish and U.S. Plowshares movements, we can gain insight into the differences between them and how this influenced their choices and divergent trajectories.

Charismatic versus Constructed Leadership

While U.S. Plowshares organizers put a lot of effort into establishing legitimacy and retaining members, Swedish activists struggled most with the developmental tasks of creating a movement infrastructure and a workable form of leadership. The Swedes initially replicated the U.S. movement's infrastructure; when they realized it was not working well, some altered it to reflect a more traditional Swedish movement organization. Despite numerous efforts, they never found a suitable solution to this dilemma. The inability to meet this challenge – and the conflicts that the task

---

[44] In May of 2003, several individuals inspected a Saab manufacturing site in Linköping, Sweden, to determine how many JAS strategic fighter jets were being produced and where they were located within the plant. After two hours inside the JAS plant, the activists were arrested and one was charged with preparations for sabotage. Because this was primarily an inspection and no action was taken to destroy the weaponry, I do not consider it a Plowshares action.

[45] Laffin, Arthur J. 2003. *Swords Into Plowshares: A Chronology of Plowshares Disarmament Actions, 1980–2003.* Marion, SD: Rose Hill Books.

172

generated – heavily influenced the Swedish trajectory, ultimately causing the movement to implode. In some respects, this is rather surprising since the Swedes had a much more clearly articulated model of leadership and decision-making than their American counterparts have. Moreover, they established a specific set of rules and procedures to ensure that the movement remained democratic and non-hierarchical. Why did this become such a point of contention and struggle for Swedish Plowshares activists but not for those in the United States, who have never explicitly designed a leadership system?

The task of establishing leadership may be less contentious when charismatic figures arise (and movements coalesce around them) than when nascent groups construct a leadership system. Charismatic leadership not only describes the compelling, passionate character of an individual's convictions and commitment but, as Weber suggests, charisma is also defined by the effect that a leader has on an audience. By definition, charismatic leaders are able to inspire others with the fervor and courage needed to challenge powerful opponents. They are able to persuade others that it is their duty to join the cause.[46] Indeed, without followers' recognition of a leader's unique gift, charisma does not exist.[47] Consequently, charismatic leaders already possess legitimacy among their followers, who are in awe of them. In fact, many recruits join a movement precisely to be closer to such individuals, or to emulate their example.

As charismatic leaders, Philip and Daniel Berrigan are admired by many activists in the United States and also Europe. They are seen as wise guides and venerated mentors to less-experienced activists. In a letter written to Philip Berrigan, for instance, one British Plowshares activist joked: "You're probably a little sick of people writing and telling how wonderful you are and how your witness is so inspiring. So I won't go on about that (although of course you are and it is – there, I sneaked it in!)."[48] Indeed, many activists claim that the Berrigans have changed their whole understanding of faith and life.

---

[46] Nepstad, Sharon Erickson and Clifford Bob. 2006. "When Do Leaders Matter?: Hypotheses on Leadership Dynamics in Social Movements." *Mobilization* 11(1): 1–22.

[47] Weber, Max. 1946. "The Sociology of Charismatic Authority." pp. 245–252 in Hans Gerth and C. Wright Mills (editors and translators), *From Max Weber*. New York: Oxford University Press.

[48] Letter from Chris Cole to Philip Berrigan, January 19, 1998. DePaul University Archives, Berrigan-McAlister Collection, Box 27.

Another reason that the Berrigans' leadership was not contested is because they possess a substantial amount of symbolic capital. Bourdieu uses this term to convey the prestige, honor, and social distinction that grants people authority and influence.[49] For the Berrigans, symbolic capital was derived from their extensive activism, including participation in the civil rights and anti-Vietnam War movements. By the time the first Plowshares action occurred at General Electric, the Berrigans were seasoned resisters with nearly twenty years of experience. More significantly, however, was the distinction they acquired from long prison sentences. Just as Nelson Mandela and Vaclav Havel's clout increased from years of incarceration, the Berrigans also gained honor in the eyes of their supporters as they suffered for their cause. When the costs of activism are high, those who are willing to pay the price, without flinching or being deterred, develop symbolic capital. Finally, the Berrigans' ability to command a following was strengthened further by the fact that Philip and Daniel Berrigan and Elizabeth McAlister had all been members of religious orders. They were thus perceived as legitimate moral authorities, especially by the many Catholics in the movement.

This combination of charisma and symbolic capital – derived through experience, suffering, and the moral authority afforded to clergy – meant that no official decision-making process was needed to determine who should guide the U.S. Plowshares movement. This does not mean that the American movement is conflict-free or that rank-and-file Plowshares activists never challenge the leadership. In their own writings, Plowshares leaders have confessed their mistakes and openly discussed the struggles of living in community.[50] Nevertheless, most activists have deferred to them out of respect for their legacy, experience, knowledge, and wisdom.

In contrast, most Swedish activists were drawn to the Plowshares movement because of its message and tactics, not because of the charisma of its organizers. Moreover, the initial leaders of the Swedish movement did not

[49] The concept of symbolic capital is developed by Pierre Bourdieu (1991) in *Language and Symbolic Power*. He posits that people may possess economic capital (material wealth) along with symbolic capital (prestige, honor, and social distinction) and cultural capital (knowledge, skills, and technical and educational credentials). One type of capital is readily transformed into another. In our article "When Do Leaders Matter?" (note 46), Clifford Bob and I argue that these forms of capital and others determine who rises to lead a movement.

[50] See Philip Berrigan's autobiography, *Fighting the Lamb's War* (1996, Monroe, ME: Common Courage Press), and Philip Berrigan and Elizabeth McAlister's book, *The Time's Discipline: The Beatitudes and Nuclear Resistance* (1989, Baltimore: Fortkamp Press).

have the same degree of symbolic capital. Their level of activist experience did not equal that of the Berrigans, nor were the sanctions they suffered as severe.[51] In addition, their occupational status did not grant them greater moral authority than others in the movement. Whereas the strong Catholic identity in the U.S. movement bred respect for the ecclesiastic vocation and prophetic leadership of the Berrigans, the feminist-anarchist identity of many secular Swedish activists led them to question the authority of leaders. Vinthagen confirmed: "We didn't have any kind of real profession; . . . We were in the beginning just students and [some of us former leaders] are men. That didn't really work when you are meeting up with young feminist anarchists."[52]

Whereas U.S. activists perceived themselves as joining a movement created by the Berrigans, Swedish Plowshares participants saw themselves as equal partners who were building the movement collaboratively. Although Swedish organizers endorsed this approach and introduced techniques of democratic decision-making to the group, they also had worthwhile experiences to share, given their previous involvement in Plowshares actions. Furthermore, they were deeply dedicated to the movement and thus spent a lot of time and effort determining which strategies the movement should take. They forcefully presented these ideas at movement meetings, causing some to feel that they dominated discussions. Vinthagen acknowledged that he did sometimes exert excessive influence. He stated:

I'll give you one example of where I think we weren't aware of our strong influence: the disarmament camps. [Another leader] and I had the same kind of basic picture of what Plowshares is, what is important, how the movement should develop and what a camp should look like, but we had slightly different perspectives on the details. Both of us are quite strong persons in putting energy into what we believe is best for the movement so we would come to the planning meetings for the disarmament camp with written statements beforehand on what we should do. . . . Since others did not come to the meetings prepared in the same way, we kind of monopolized the situation.[53]

As a result of this dynamic, participants challenged the de facto leadership positions that some individuals held. Despite the feminist methods that the group implemented – such as appointing sexism watchers, vibe watchers, oppression watchers – the disputes continued. These conflicts ultimately

---

[51] Laffin, Arthur. 2003. *Swords Into Plowshares, A Chronology of Plowshares Disarmament Actions, 1980–2003.* Marion, SD: Rose Hill Books.
[52] Interview with Stellan Vinthagen, conducted by the author, June 24, 2003.
[53] Interview with Stellan Vinthagen, conducted by the author, June 24, 2003.

divided participants, and thus the Swedish Plowshares movement confirms Zald and Ash's assertion that "The more the ideology of the movement organization leads to a questioning of the basis of authority, the greater the likelihood of factions and splitting."[54]

Factors Limiting and Exacerbating Internal Dissension

The conflict over leadership, gender dynamics, infrastructural form, and strategy eventually tore the Swedish movement apart. While U.S. Plowshares activists are in general agreement over these issues, they have other topics of dissension, but they have never escalated to the point of threatening the movement's existence. Why were Swedish activists so susceptible to intra-movement conflicts, whereas their American counterparts have kept them to a minimum? I propose that three factors have helped limit dissension in the U.S. movement while exacerbating problems in the Swedish context.

Heterogeneity. The first factor contributing to divisions within the Swedish movement is that participants were much more heterogeneous than American Plowshares activists are. The most obvious form of diversity is found in religious views. In the U.S. movement, 96.7 percent of Plowshares activists believe in God, compared with 63.6 percent of European participants. Even among those Swedish activists who identified as Christians, most were from Protestant backgrounds. Thus the culture of the Catholic Left – including its rituals, theology, and practice – did not provide a shared foundation or collective identity for Swedish participants as it does in the U.S. movement. Surprisingly, though, these religious differences did not become a serious source of division in the Swedish movement. Vinthagen, an athiest, noted: "I've never, not a single time, felt any kind of aggressive assertion of beliefs from Christians in the Plowshares movement. So it was never an issue."[55]

Instead, heterogeneity contributed to the Swedish movement's fragility because it made the organization more inclusive, bringing in a variety of views about the direction the movement should head, the strategies that should be used, and the legitimate sources of authority. These ideological

[54] Zald, Mayer N., and Roberta Ash. 1996. "Social Movement Organizations: Growth, Decay and Change." *Social Forces* 44(3). Quotation from p. 337.
[55] Interview with Stellan Vinthagen, conducted by the author, June 24, 2003.

differences permeated numerous decisions that the group faced. For example, Plowshares activists initiated dialogue with representatives from the Swedish weapons manufacturer Bofors, hoping to persuade the company to cancel its exports to Indonesia, where the weapons were used in the brutal occupation of East Timor. Discussions between activists and the company went on for over two years, but they caused significant dissension among the members of *Svärd till Plogbillar*. One faction considered such dialogue an essential component of non-violence, whereas others regarded it as co-optation. These ideological divisions took a toll on the movement, confirming Zald and Ash's argument that "There are two major internal preconditions for splits and the development of factions, heterogeneity of social base and the doctrinal basis of authority."[56]

Relationship to the State. The second reason the U.S. movement remains relatively unified has to do with its view of the government. As Lewis Coser noted decades ago, external threats foster in-group cohesion.[57] In the United States, Plowshares theology posits that the American government is an imperialistic, bellicose empire. Internal movement differences wane in comparison with the urgent need to fight unjust U.S. policies. The Swedish state, however, is not perceived in such negative terms. Because Swedish activists do not view their government as intrinsically evil, they did not experience the same unifying effect. Vinthagen noted:

The United States is in the center of the kind of problems Plowshares activists are confronting. Sweden is seen as one of the more progressive, democratic, socialist countries that exists. You can't talk about living in the belly of the beast like you do in the United States so that creates another kind of culture of resistance. . . . We don't equate the state with evil. Not at all. Here the state is good. . . . For those in the Plowshares movement in Sweden, our view is the same as Phil Berrigan's but the problem is just that Sweden is a softer version of the evil of militarized capitalism in Western-centric patriarchal culture. . . . But it's also that the state is more interested in listening to the criticism.[58]

Hasse Leander further underscored this point. "In the U.S. you live in this world empire where you have huge military spendings, nuclear weapons,

---

[56] Zald, Mayer N. and Roberta Ash. 1996. "Social Movement Organizations: Growth, Decay and Change." *Social Forces* 44(3). Quotation from pp. 336–337.

[57] Coser, Lewis. 1956. *The Functions of Social Conflict.* New York: The Free Press. Also see Aho, James. 1994. *This Thing of Darkness: A Sociology of the Enemy.* Seattle: University of Washington Press.

[58] Interview with Stellan Vinthagen, conducted by the author, June 24, 2003.

and huge social problems, so it's really easy to see the state as more or less evil.... In Sweden, the state is not that way.... I think most activists in Sweden...don't see the Swedish state as Babylon.[59] In short, the U.S. government's greater moral culpability in perpetuating war and nuclear weapons has made it a more formidable opponent, and activists must therefore set aside their differences to stop it.

Not only is the Swedish government perceived as more humane, it is also more receptive to Plowshares activists. In fact, some believe that the Swedish government helped undermine the movement by co-opting it to some degree. As David Meyer argues, when dissident groups are incorporated into institutionalized politics, they often lose their radical edge as they are subsequently forced to adhere to the rules and norms of the political establishment. Activists may also believe that they now have greater influence and thus may cease their use of disruptive and unruly tactics, relying on professionals to represent their views.[60] This occurred to some extent with the Swedish Plowshares movement. Vinthagen commented:

Today you will find people that have been part of our movement are now in parliament. You will find people like me who make careers at universities or as writers. We end up on TV shows. We end up on lists of the most powerful people in Sweden.... I think it's similar to Holland, and in some sense Germany, that if you are in opposition to the government here, you become an advisor to the government. You are co-opted. They give money even to the most angry anarchist groups, if they will accept it.... It's clever in terms of a power play because you have a stronger hold on the opposition when you say, "We will give you money in order to sustain your opposition but we won't accept this or that. We will put you in prison. But we're interested to know what you think about our latest proposal on this or that. And by the way, we're organizing a big conference on this issue. Could you send some delegates?"... That creates a totally different environment to do radical politics.[61]

Costs of Activism.   Finally, high levels of sacrifice constitute the third factor that has minimized internal tensions in the American Plowshares movement. The risks and costs involved in Plowshares activism in the United States mean that participants truly need one another. U.S. activists are almost invariably found guilty of the crimes they are charged with, and

---

[59] Interview with Hasse Leander, conducted by the author, June 27, 2003.

[60] Meyer, David S. 1993. "Institutionalizing Dissent: The United States Structure of Political Opportunity and the End of the Nuclear Freeze Movement." *Sociological Forum* 8(2): 157–179.

[61] Interview with Stellan Vinthagen, conducted by the author, June 24, 2003.

consequently most spend time in prison. They are separated from loved ones and exposed to the brutal conditions that exist in the American correctional system. They rely on the network of Catholic Left activists for emotional and moral support as well as material assistance with their families. They often spend time in Catholic Left communities after they are released in order to debrief and recover and to help with the post-prison transition. To get through the whole process of planning an action, dealing with their fears, preparing their trials, surviving prison, and continuing their resistance, U.S. activists must depend on others in the movement. After they have made these sacrifices, Plowshares activists often have a high degree of continuance commitment that gives them a greater stake in seeing the movement continue. Allowing it to collapse would minimize the significance of their sacrifices.[62]

In contrast, Swedish activists do not typically receive such harsh punishments. Among the twenty-three people who participated in Swedish Plowshares campaigns, the longest sentence was twelve months. Several activists did not receive any prison time but were ordered to pay restitution for the damage, which they refused to do. Others were sentenced to time served while awaiting trial. The average sentence for Swedish activists was slightly less than two months.[63] Among those who were incarcerated, many did not find the prison experience to be traumatizing. In fact, some joked that it was a chance to catch up on their reading and watch television. Because Swedish activists sacrificed less than U.S. Plowshares participants, they typically did not form the same degree of continuance commitment as their American counterparts did. In fact, Herngren noted that instead of being more committed to the movement, many dropped out after their prison sentences were completed, believing that they had done their part in the fight against militarism.[64]

While the severity of sanctions pulls American Plowshares activists together, the lighter punishments in Sweden meant that activists were less reliant on one another for survival. Swedish participants generally sacrificed less than their American counterparts; consequently, their stake in

---

[62] della Porta, Donatella. 1992. *Social Movements and Violence: Participation in Underground Organizations*. Greenwich, CT: JAI-Press; Kanter, Rosabeth Moss. 1968. "Commitment and Social Organization: A Study of Movement Mechanisms in Utopian Communities." *American Sociological Review* 33: 499–517.

[63] This information is derived from Arthur Laffin's book, *Swords Into Plowshares: A Chronology of Plowshares Disarmament Actions, 1980–2003*. Marion, SD: Rose Hill Books.

[64] Interview with Per Herngren, conducted by the author, December 5, 2002.

the movement's survival was weaker. Of course, there are some individuals who found prison traumatizing and others who gave up a great deal. In addition, many people invested a lot of time and energy into the cause. For those individuals, the demise of the movement was particularly painful and disappointing.

Conclusion

Although establishing a decision-making system and a movement infrastructure was challenging, Swedish Plowshares activists created a provisional system that was fragile, but sufficient for the movement to initially grow. But as it shifted into the expansion stage and activists altered their movement to encourage greater participation, the degree of heterogeneity among participants increased. Consequently, some began to seriously question and challenge the movement's structure. This generated internal tensions, which ultimately constituted the biggest obstacle to activist retention and movement persistence. While every movement experiences intragroup disputes, certain conditions can increase or decrease the significance of these differences for activists. In this case, a more favorable view of the government meant that the Swedish activists had greater freedom and latitude to address their internal problems. Additionally, lighter punishments led to less continuance commitment among the Swedes. Finally, a commitment to participatory democracy and consensus decision-making brought tensions to the surface over leadership issues in ways that the charismatic leadership model of the U.S. movement did not. The combined effect of these factors was detrimental to the Swedish movement, generating divisions that ultimately caused the movement to implode.

7

Witnessing or Winning?

THE BRITISH PLOWSHARES
MOVEMENT

To strengthen cross-continental movement ties, European activists sponsored the first global Plowshares gathering in Kiel, Germany, in May 1996.
The theme of the retreat was "Evaluating the Plowshares Movement: Building the Movement Worldwide." Twenty-seven people attended – four from
Great Britain, three from the U.S., twelve from Sweden, six from Germany,
one from the Netherlands, and one from Australia. During this gathering,
it became quickly apparent that regional distinctions and cultural variations
had evolved as the movement spread internationally. Stephen Hancock, an
English Plowshares activist, described some of the differences that were
evident at this trans-Atlantic gathering.

Perhaps the greatest tension within the gathering was between the U.S. and Swedish
Plowshares traditions.... The mainstays of the movement [in the U.S.] have been
the east coast Atlantic Life Community, Baltimore's Jonah House, ... and the more
radical houses of the Catholic Worker movement. They exercise a radical Christian
faith based on Bible study, political reflection, community living and worship, often
hospitality work and regular acts of nonviolent resistance.... The actions are seen
as a witness to God's intended order of comprehensive justice and peace, acts of solidarity with the poor, and calls to others to join resistance. Practically all the actions
have leaned towards symbolic levels of military property damage, the symbolic com-
municating that three or four people cannot achieve disarmament – the hands of
God and others are needed. Largely ignored by the media, the [U.S.] activists talk
of an essential value to the actions that does not depend on results....
    The [Swedish] Plowshares movement describes and views itself in very strategic
political terms, almost devoid of the religious language and images prevalent in the
U.S. movement. The movement is a fusion of radical liberalism and nonviolent
anarchism and understands the dynamic of Plowshares actions as acts of civil disobedience attempting to create dialogue and to reach a consensus of both morality
and action, especially around the issue of Swedish weapons exports.... Plowshares
groups often form openly and they publicly announce their intention to disarm. In

the wake of the 1993 "JAS into Plowshares" action, the movement was extensively covered by the media, such that it is now a household name. . . .

During the gathering, I came to see the significant differences of practice and ideology as being rooted in two very different histories and cultures. The Swedes act in a liberal, post-Christian culture, which takes civil disobedience seriously and seems to take up the invitation to dialogue, even to the extent of military personnel debating with Plowshares activists on television. Even though conspiracy laws exist within Sweden, they are rarely used and prison conditions are among the best in the world. However, in the U.S. movement there is no such sense of the authorities being open to reason or dialogue. The threat of conspiracy charges is high and the experience of financial, organizational, and emotional drain in such cases as the Harrisburg conspiracy trial . . . still feature strongly in the collective memory of the movement. There is a paramount concern among [U.S.] Plowshares activists that people not directly involved in action do not get drawn into charges, charges which could result in serious prison time. . . .

I sensed that people had been struggling with marked differences in language and outlook. . . . Framed between a strong identification with the poetic and prophetic image of beating swords into plowshares and a strong commitment to nonviolent resistance, most other aspects of the movement were up for question and argument and experimentation.[1]

Some of the same differences that Hancock observed between the Swedish and U.S. Plowshares movements would soon become even more pronounced in his own country of Great Britain. Although the Swedes made various cultural adaptations, they did not depart significantly from the general spirit of the originating movement in the United States. Some British activists, however, made more comprehensive changes that ultimately separated the movement into two segments. One faction, calling itself "orthodox," adhere to more traditional Plowshares methods; the other reflects a "reformed" approach that has a stronger utilitarian emphasis. To understand how this developed, I will give a brief history of the British Plowshares movement.

The Beginnings of the British Plowshares Movement

The British Plowshares movement evolved initially from the efforts of Stephen Hancock, who was active in the peace movement while studying at Oxford University during the 1980s. Eventually he left college to devote himself fully to peace work, and during this period he became captivated by

---

[1] Hancock, Stephen. 1996. "Ploughshares Activists Find Unity in their Vulnerability, Despite Trans-Atlantic Tension." *Peace News*, August/September, p. 6.

the American Catholic Left. A committed Anglican at that time, Hancock read about the Catholic Worker movement and the Berrigans with great interest. Intrigued by this combination of faith, anarchism, and radical war resistance, he eventually traveled to Jonah House in the United States to learn more.

On his return to the United Kingdom, Hancock began planning the first British Plowshares campaign. He met with groups such as Catholic Peace Action and the Fellowship of Reconciliation to discuss his idea and to recruit participants. Eventually, Mike Hutchinson, a Quaker, agreed to join him,[2] and the two decided to target the Upper Heyford United States Air Base that housed F-111 fighter planes. These planes had nuclear capabilities, along with low-level navigation and weapons delivery systems that made it possible to engage in night bombing, even in inclement weather. On March 21, 1990, Hancock and Hutchinson armed themselves with hammers and bottles of blood. They also wore Mickey Mouse ears to provide a non-threatening silhouette to any American soldiers they might encounter. They managed to enter the base and locate an F-111 without being detected. After smashing the outside of the fighter plane, they entered the cockpit, where they hammered and spilled blood on the nuclear weapons control panel. Finally they hung a banner with the message, "Isaiah was here!" The two were soon apprehended and arrested. About six months later, Hutchinson and Hancock were convicted of criminal damage and "possessing mallets and fluid with intent to damage property."[3] They were sentenced to fifteen months but were paroled after six months in prison.[4]

Chris Cole, who was part of Hancock and Hutchinson's support network, launched the second British Plowshares action on the liturgical feast of the Epiphany in January 1993. For several years, Cole had been working on the issue of weapons exports. To learn more about this topic, he had done a great deal of research, particularly on the arms produced at the British Aerospace (BAe) weapons factory. He recalled:

I had been campaigning and focusing on British Aerospace for about five years before I did my action and I gathered a lot of information. I wanted to disarm the nose cones for the European Fighter Aircraft and the Hawk Strike Attack Aircraft. I discovered the site where they were made and wrote to them [BAe] saying that I was

---

[2] Interview with Chris Cole, conducted by the author, July 4, 2003.

[3] Laffin, Arthur. 2003. *Swords Into Plowshares: A Chronology of Plowshares Disarmament Actions, 1980–2003*. Marion, SD: Rose Hill Books, p. 45.

[4] Laffin, Arthur. 2003. *Swords Into Plowshares: A Chronology of Plowshares Disarmament Actions, 1980–2003*. Marion, SD: Rose Hill Books, p. 45.

studying this, giving the impression that I was a student but not actually saying that. So they sent me lots of information, including a map with a sign showing which buildings were what. So that was obviously very useful. After a year of preparing, I broke in. Using the map, I pretty much found my way to where I wanted to be and I disarmed the nose cones. I also did some other damage. There were lots of computers and various things and I turned them off. Then I poured blood, the traditional thing really.... I was there for about two and a half hours before I was actually apprehended.[5]

Before he was arrested and removed from the site, Cole left a statement reading, "The Epiphany remembers when three men presented gifts to the infant Jesus. My gift of disarmament is for all the infants who are threatened with BAe weapons, from Northern Ireland to East Timor."[6]

Cole was charged with criminal damages amounting to approximately $700,000.[7] When he was brought to trial in the British Crown Court, he was allowed to introduce evidence about the illegal activities of British Aerospace. He told jury members that he had tried for years to appeal to BAe, but to no avail. After he concluded his defense, the judge instructed the jury to choose its verdict based on "conscience, common sense and common humanity."[8] Cole commented, "I was very lucky because I got one of the better judges. He had only just been appointed about a year beforehand.... He actually said, 'Mr. Cole, if what you say is true, this could amount to genocide, which is a crime against British and international law'."[9] After deliberating for hours, the jury could not reach a unanimous verdict, resulting in a hung jury. Cole was reassigned to a new judge, who was far less sympathetic. The second jury found him guilty and he was given an eight-month sentence.

The third British Plowshares campaign, known as the Seeds of Hope action, was carried out in 1996 by four women. One participant, Andrea Needham, had been connected to U.S. Plowshares activists for some time. Her first exposure to the movement occurred when she was living in Washington DC in the late 1980s. She stated:

---

[5] Interview with Chris Cole, conducted by the author, July 4, 2003.
[6] Laffin, Arthur. 2003. *Swords Into Plowshares: A Chronology of Plowshares Actions, 1980–2003.* Marion, SD: Rose Hill Books, p. 50.
[7] Laffin, Arthur. 2003. *Swords Into Plowshares: A Chronology of Plowshares Actions, 1980–2003.* Marion, SD: Rose Hill Books, p. 50.
[8] Laffin, Arthur. 2003. *Swords Into Plowshares: A Chronology of Plowshares Actions, 1980–2003.* Marion, SD: Rose Hill Books, p. 50.
[9] Interview with Chris Cole, conducted by the author, July 4, 2003.

The British Movement

I spent several years living in Washington D.C., firstly as a volunteer at the Community for Creative Nonviolence (CCNV), then at a Catholic Worker house. Before coming to D.C., I had had no involvement whatsoever in radical movements (my family was not at all political) and no experience of poverty in a first world country. I was utterly shocked by the poverty I saw in D.C. – people with absolutely nothing, living in the capital city of the world's richest country, and for the first time started questioning the way the world is organized to the benefit of the few of us lucky enough to be born into a privileged situation. I did a lot of reading and talking to people, and learned a lot about militarism and how such vast quantities of money are spent by the Pentagon on war whilst the U.S. is unwilling to spend even a relatively small amount of money to lift millions of its citizens out of desperate, grinding poverty. . . .

I spent two years at CCNV, where I took part in civil disobedience for the first time. In 1989 I moved to the Catholic Worker, where I stayed until 1991, and became more involved in the peace movement. . . . A number of people there had taken part in civil disobedience over the years, and many had been to prison, and Plowshares was something which was often talked about. At first I was just amazed that anyone would do something like that, potentially risking years in prison. Later, as I got to know more people who'd taken part in actions, I began to realize that they were not the "special" people I'd originally thought – that is, they were special only insofar as each one of us is special, but were otherwise no different to me (a rather uncomfortable realization – I could no longer pretend that this kind of action was not something that I'd ever be able to do because I wasn't one of those "special" people!).[10]

When Needham returned to Great Britain, she got involved in the Oxford Catholic Worker and began exploring the possibility of conducting a Plowshares action in her home country. Eventually, she found several co-conspirators including Joanna Wilson, Angie Zelter, and Lotta Kronlid. Kronlid, a Swede, had been active in the Swedish Plowshares movement, and she and Zelter had both attended several Hope and Resistance Retreats. Kronlid recalled:

The very first time I heard about the Plowshares movement was via the national media when Swedish activist Per Herngren had taken part in an action in the U.S. My reaction then was that people would find it ridiculous. I think it was the symbolism of it, the blood; it seemed like a ritual. That didn't appeal to me then. The second time was at a horticulture college where a fellow student had a partner who'd taken part in an action in Sweden. This time I was more positive. I thought . . . these people [are] seriously doing something right and constructive. The consequent nonviolence, the seriousness and the absolute rightness of it won my heart.[11]

[10] Needham provided this statement in reply to an open-ended question on my survey (2001).
[11] Kronlid provided this statement in reply to an open-ended question on my survey (2001).

When the four women started planning their action, they also chose to target British Aerospace because it had received a $750 million contract to produce twenty-four Hawk attack aircraft, which were to be sold to the Suharto dictatorship in Indonesia. In 1975, the Indonesian regime had illegally invaded the nation of East Timor, starting a genocidal occupation that killed over 200,000 people – approximately one-third of the entire population.[12] To maintain control of the region, the Indonesian military terrorized the Timorese, resulting in massive human rights abuses.[13] Because Suharto's armed forces had previously used planes like the Hawks to bomb East Timor, the Plowshares women believed that these fighter jets would cause more harm to innocent civilians. They decided to intervene in this killing by disarming the Hawk planes. Needham describes the process that led to their decision:

The action I took part in – disarming a Hawk attack plane being sold to Indonesia – came out of several years of "conventional" resistance to the deal with Indonesia. Together with thousands of others, I'd spent years doing all the usual stuff: letter writing, petitions, rallies, marches, public meetings, vigils, civil disobedience, meeting with the company (British Aerospace) which made the planes – all to no avail. At the point where we started planning the action (a year before the planes were due for delivery) we felt fairly sure that nothing short of disarmament would stop the planes being sent out as planned. However, during that year we continued to campaign against the sale, in the hope that it would be stopped in the meantime. The final decision to go ahead was made only at the last minute, when it was clear that the planes were about to leave the UK and we had to act immediately. For me, the strength of the action... was that we'd spent years doing all the other things, and this was the next logical step – it was part of a process, rather than us simply deciding we didn't like the planes, and descending out of the blue to disarm them. It was also a strong action because it was so clear: the planes were being sold to Indonesia, Indonesia would use them to kill people in illegally occupied East Timor (as they've done with previous planes).... Ultimately what drove me to do it was that I was so utterly outraged and disgusted with what my government was doing – selling weapons to a genocidal regime – that I felt I had to take action.[14]

On January 29, 1996, the women entered the British Aerospace factory in Warton, Lancashire. They found their way to the hangar where the Hawk aircraft were kept, already painted with the markings of the Indonesian

---

[12] "They Keep Us Slaves." Interview with Bishop Belo, *Der Spiegel*, October 14, 1996, p. 165.
[13] Aditjondro, George. 2000. "Ninjas, Nanggalas, Monuments, and Massad Manuals: An Anthropology of Indonesian State Terror in East Timor," pp. 158–188 in Jeffrey Sluka (ed.), *Death Squad: The Anthropology of State Terror*. Philadelphia: University of Pennsylvania Press.
[14] Needham provided this statement in reply to an open-ended question on my survey (2001).

military. Wielding hammers, they struck the control panel and the radar nose and placed photos of Timorese children on the aircraft's wings. Then they sang and danced in front of the security cameras. Returning to the hangar, they called their support network, asking them to release information about the action to the media. When the police arrived, the women were arrested and charged with conspiracy and criminal damage.

In their subsequent trial at the Liverpool Crown Court, the women were prepared to fight hard for an acquittal based on the "necessity" defense. Departing from the customary Plowshares method of defending themselves, Needham, Wilson, Kronlid, and Zelter secured an attorney who had an impressive record with political cases, including some notable victories with Irish Republican Army-related trials. The women also had the foresight to provide video documentation of their previous efforts to stop the shipment of weapons to East Timor. They brought this video along when they conducted their action at the British Aerospace factory, intentionally leaving it at the scene when they were arrested. When the police confiscated it, the video became part of the evidence that the jury was allowed to see.[15] This video was critical in demonstrating a key element of the necessity defense – that drastic measures were justified because the normal channels for addressing this concern had proven ineffective. The four activists also presented evidence that linked the use of British Aerospace weaponry to human rights abuses in East Timor, thereby supporting their claim that they were using reasonable force to prevent a greater crime. On the stand, Joanna Wilson stated that their situation paralleled a recent shooting spree that had occurred at a school in Scotland. She argued that if someone had tried to stop the gunman by taking away his weapon, that individual would have been honored, not prosecuted. Wilson said that she and her co-defendants were simply trying to stop a similar slaughter of children in East Timor. When the defense finally rested its case, the women waited for a verdict. Needham recalled:

The jury was sent out at 11:45 and we were whisked back down to the cells to await the verdict. The next few hours were nerve-racking; we thought if the jury came back very soon, it would almost certainly mean a guilty verdict, so every time a jailer came near our cell we all held our breath, hoping they weren't coming for us.... The jury was out for five hours in all. After four hours they reported that they couldn't reach a verdict so the judge sent them out again with a majority direction. An hour later they

---

[15] Information provided by Stellan Vinthagen in personal correspondence with the author, September 1, 2005.

were back with a verdict. . . . We sat in court, holding hands tightly as the foreman stood up to deliver the verdicts. There were seven in all – three counts of criminal damage and four of conspiracy. At the first "not guilty" there was a collective gasp which echoed around the courtroom, and the judge turned to the public gallery and yelled for silence. We hardly dared breathe as the other six verdicts were read out. Over and over again came the words. "Not guilty." "Not guilty." "Not guilty." Finally they were all read out, we breathed again and people all over the courtroom burst into tears. . . . Ten minutes later we were walking out of the front door of the court – we'd only ever come in through the basement, in handcuffs, before – to be greeted by a cheering crowd.[16]

This was the first full acquittal in the history of the Plowshares movement. Not only were the women elated with the outcome, but they were also delighted to receive a message from Timorese leader Jose Ramos Horta. Horta supported the armed resistance in his homeland, but he had also been working with the United Nations for a diplomatic resolution to the conflict. He wrote to the four women; "In 20 years of resistance, we were never able to shoot down an aircraft. You did it without firing a single shot and without hurting the pilot. Keep up your courage."[17]

The Reformed Approach: The Trident Plowshares Campaign

When the Seeds of Hope defendants convinced a jury that physically intervening in the weapons trade is permissible under international law, some British activists began contemplating a politically instrumental approach to Plowshares activism. This impulse grew stronger when the International Court of Justice in The Hague, Netherlands released a document in 1996 known as the "Advisory Opinion on the Legality of the Threat or Use of Nuclear Weapons." In this document, World Court advisors stated that humanitarian law prohibits preparation for genocide and forbids any military practice that causes unnecessary suffering. Because nuclear missiles are weapons of *mass* destruction that do not distinguish between military targets and civilians, court advisors argued that the use or threatened use of nuclear weapons contradicts international law. Hence they called upon all nuclear nations to work toward disarmament. They also confirmed the Nuremberg

---

[16] Needham, Andrea. 1996. "Views of the Verdict: The Defendant." From the DePaul University Archives, Berrigan-McAlister Collection.

[17] As quoted in Claron O'Reilly's article, "For Swords into Plowshares, the Hammer Has to Fall!" *Mutual Aid: Newsletter of the West End Catholic Worker* (1996). Issue 43: 3.

Charter, which emphasizes that citizens must uphold international law even when their governments violate it.[18]

Convinced that the Advisory Opinion provided a strong basis for challenging British military policies, Angie Zelter began planning an alternative type of Plowshares movement that would go beyond prophetic acts of moral witness. She envisioned a popular uprising whereby activists would become a true political force, effectively demanding compliance with these international mandates. This "reformed" Plowshares movement, however, required a critical mass, and at the time, there were only a handful of Plowshares activists in Great Britain. Believing that the long prison sentences associated with the movement deterred prospective participants, Zelter redesigned the British movement to incorporate lower-cost forms of protest alongside high-risk actions. Then, using a technique from the 1960s known as the "Committee of 100," she planned to get at least 100 people to commit themselves to a direct action campaign. She hoped that eventually thousands would mobilize against the United Kingdom's nuclear weapons – especially the Trident nuclear submarines located at the Faslane Royal Naval base in Scotland.

Zelter discussed her proposal with experienced peace activists, and finally six people became the architects of the Trident Plowshares campaign. They drafted a handbook that spelled out the movement structure and participation rules; they also established a time line to recruit and train activists from October 1997 to April 1998. In May of 1998, they intended to send a letter to British political leaders, asking them to negotiate a plan for disarmament. If the leaders refused, the activists would then present a "Conspiracy to Prevent Crime" document stating that Trident nuclear submarines violated international law. This document would contain the signatures of the 100 or more individuals who pledged to resist the government's illegal possession of nuclear weapons. After that, Trident Plowshares participants would inaugurate a series of lower-risk actions, calling for a nuclear-free world by 2000.[19]

With a plan in place, the activists began the mobilization process. Although they were operating within a short time frame, they launched the campaign successfully. By August 1998, several hundred people gathered at

---

[18] Zelter, Angie. 2001. *Trident on Trial: The Case for People's Disarmament*. Edinburgh: Luath Press Limited.

[19] *Tri-denting It Handbook: An Open Guide to Trident Ploughshares 2000*. From DePaul University Archives, Berrigan-McAlister Collection, Box 15.

the Faslane Royal Navy base for a two-week long disarmament camp that culminated in more than 100 arrests.[20] Over the next few years, the actions expanded, so that by the end of 2004, approximately 2,200 arrests had occurred.[21] The "reformed" Plowshares initiative flourished, successfully shifting into the expansion stage, so that campaigns at Faslane and other military bases in Great Britain are now routinely held four times a year.[22]

This movement's ability to expand is partly due to the fact that organizers effectively surmounted the various developmental challenges that burgeoning movements face. In the next section, I discuss how Angie Zelter and her colleagues made cultural adaptations to the British context, gained legitimacy of means, and carefully designed the reformed movement's infrastructure and leadership.

Cultural Adaptations

Trident Plowshares organizers recruited more participants than orthodox Plowshares activists partly because they implemented changes that made the reformed approach more compatible with the British context. Specifically, reformist leaders tempered the heavily religious language and rituals, setting a more secular tone. For example, while Hancock, Hutchinson, and Cole used blood in their orthodox acts of disarmament, the Trident Plowshares campaigns do not since they maintain that the theological significance will not resonate with the broader population. Similarly, Trident organizers emphasize that while their campaign is inspired by the American Catholic Left, it is not explicitly faith-based. The minimization of the movement's Catholic roots is evident in the Trident Plowshares handbook:

The Plowshares movement originated in the North American faith-based peace movement. Many priests and nuns in the 1970s began to resist the Vietnam War, thereby connecting with the radical political secular movements. When the war ended, the arms race and nuclear weapons became the focus of resistance.... The first Plowshares action was carried out in 1980. On September 9th the "Plowshares Eight" entered a General Electric plant in King of Prussia, Pennsylvania, USA, where the nose cones for the Mark 12A nuclear warheads were manufactured.

---

[20] *Tri-denting It Handbook: An Open Guide to Trident Ploughshares 2000.* From DePaul University Archives, Berrigan-McAlister Collection, Box 15. Third edition (2001) available online at www.tridentploughshares.org.

[21] From the Trident Plowshares movement website: www.tridentploughshares.org.

[22] *Tri-denting It Handbook: An Open Guide to Trident Ploughshares.* 2001 (3rd edition). Section 1.4 "Timetable for Actions." Available at www.tridentploughshares.org.

Enacting the Biblical prophecies of Isaiah (2:4) and Micah (4:3) that people should "beat swords into plowshares," they hammered on two of the nose cones and poured blood on documents....

Although the name comes from the Hebrew scripture, the Plowshares movement is not a Christian or Jewish movement. It includes people of different faiths and philosophies. Actually, in most Plowshares groups the members adhere to a range of different faiths or philosophies. Some people have seen their action arising out of the Biblical prophecy of Isaiah and as witnessing to the kingdom of God. Others, coming from a secular perspective, have viewed their action as being primarily motivated by a humanist or deeply held conscience commitment to nonviolence and solidarity with poor. Then again there have been other people with a range of religious, moral or political convictions. What they all have in common is a striving to abolish war, an engagement in constructive conversion of arms and military related industry into life affirming production, and the development of nonviolent methods for resolving conflicts.[23]

The orthodox wing of the British movement still maintains its religious character, but the number of practicing Catholics in the United Kingdom has dwindled significantly. By establishing a more inclusive tone, Trident Plowshares organizers appealed to a wider segment of the British population. One woman underscored the importance of that choice: "I do think that in our society ... there is quite a lot of prejudice towards the Christian church and discomfort with spirituality generally.... I think there are a lot of people like me who are sort of spiritual vagrants as it were ... [since this] is a bit of a spiritual wasteland that we find ourselves in."[24]

Gaining Legitimacy of Means

Trident Plowshares organizers also departed from the orthodox tradition by offering recruits a choice between high- and low-risk forms of action, which they refer to as "minimum" and "maximum" acts of disarmament. Convinced that few people are willing to undergo lengthy preparations and serve serious prison sentences, reformist leaders provide opportunities for recruits to participate in low-risk actions after a two-day training session. This typically involves blocking the entrance to the Faslane naval base or trespassing onto military compounds in an attempt to hammer on the submarines. Since these actions are done openly and the police are informed in

[23] *Tri-denting It Handbook: An Open Guide to Trident Ploughshares.* 2001 (3rd edition). Section 1.6 "Background History and Philosophy of the Ploughshares Movement to Date." Available at www.tridentploughshares.org.

[24] Interview with Rowan Tilly, conducted by the author, October 17, 2003.

advance, few actually reach their target. Fredrik Ivarsson, a Swedish citizen who took part in this type of minimum disarmament action, stated: "Hundreds of people show up at Faslane, try to cut the fence, and get to the submarines to do some damage. Most don't succeed, however, because the guards are there, ready to arrest them."[25] Although these tactics are less likely to cause damage to the weapons than orthodox Plowshares campaigns, reformist leaders argue that the sheer number of people willing to participate can have an important effect. One leader stated:

Several hundred is a good enough number to be able to exert a considerable political impact.... As this project is open and the "authorities" will know who we are and the dates for our attempt, it will be very hard to get near the Trident submarine. Even if we are arrested before we get near the bases or whilst we are attempting to cut through the fences, we will not have failed because this project is also about disarming the public mind and persuading the Government to respond to popular opinion.... Maybe hundreds of us, committed to disarming Trident ourselves, will persuade the British Government to do the disarmament themselves.[26]

These minimum disarmament actions therefore provide people with a way to feel as though they are having a real effect without making costly personal sacrifices. In most cases, activists are quickly released from jail and receive only modest sanctions. Ivarsson, for example, received a fine of fifty British pounds – about the same as a speeding ticket in United Kingdom.[27]

The shift to blockading and trespassing also made it easier for the Trident Plowshares group to establish legitimacy of means since these forms of protest are a familiar, long-standing part of the British peace movement's tactical repertoire. For example, as early as 1961, 5,000 British citizens conducted a sit-in at the Ministry of Defence to express their opposition to their government's nuclear policies. In the 1980s, dozens of blockades and trespassing actions occurred at the Greenham base. It was also during this time that the Snowball Campaign began in which 3,000 people cut strands of wire from various nuclear bases and then submitted to arrest.[28] Because minimum disarmament actions seldom entail destruction of weaponry, and

---

[25] Interview with Fredrik Ivarsson, conducted by the author, June 23, 2003.

[26] Boyes, Sylvia, Tracy Hart, Ellen Moxley, Jen Parker, Brian Quail, Helen Steven, and Angie Zelter. 1997, pp. 3–4 in "An Invitation to Join Trident Ploughshares 2000." DePaul University Archives, Berrigan-McAlister Collection, unmarked.

[27] Interview with Fredrik Ivarsson, conducted by the author, June 23, 2003.

[28] *Tri-denting It Handbook: An Open Guide to Trident Ploughshares.* 2001 (3rd edition). Section 1.7 "Chronology and Succinct Summary of the Anti-nuclear Weapons Campaign to Date." Available at www.tridentploughshares.org.

because Trident Plowshares activists never pour blood, the most controversial aspects of the orthodox movement are not present. Consequently, the reformed British movement has not faced the same challenges in establishing legitimacy of means.

There were a few maximum disarmament campaigns within the Trident Plowshares movement that might have provoked a demand for tactical justification. The first occurred in November 1998 when two activists swam with hand tools toward the HMS *Vengeance* Trident submarine at the Barrow shipyard in Northern England. Before they reached their destination, they were arrested by security guards and charged with conspiracy to commit criminal damage. During their trial, the two presented evidence that Trident submarines are not defensive weapons and therefore violate international law. They were acquitted.

The next effort to disarm this submarine took place in February 1999, when Rosie James and Rachel Wenham swam in freezing conditions, armed with hammers, chisels, crowbars, screwdrivers, and spray paint. They managed to climb aboard the submarine and destroy radio equipment. During their trial, the women pled "not guilty," claiming the legal right to commit criminal damage if the goal were to protect life in a situation of duress. The jury could not reach a verdict, and a new trial was ordered. The second jury also failed to convict the women, and the Crown court prosecutors dropped the case.[29]

In June 1999, a third group used an inflatable raft to gain access to the *Maytime* – a floating laboratory run by the Defense Evaluation and Research Agency. This barge provides a critical function to the British nuclear system since it ensures that Trident submarines are successfully equipped to evade sonar detection.[30] Undetected by the Ministry of Defense police, Angie Zelter, Ellen Moxley, and Ulla Roder floated out to the barge, tied up their raft, and found an unlocked window. The window opened right into the main research facility, filled with computers and other types of equipment. Zelter recalled:

As I looked around, I realized that it made no sense to smash them up where they were – the cleanest, safest and quickest way to disarm this laboratory was to throw everything into the loch. I unplugged a computer and lugged it over to a larger

---

[29] Laffin, Arthur. 2003. *Swords Into Plowshares: A Chronology of Plowshares Disarmament Actions, 1980–2003*. Marion, SD: Rose Hill Books, pp. 68–69.

[30] Zelter, Angie. 2001. *Trident on Trial: The Case for People's Disarmament*. Edinburgh: Luath Press Limited, p. 40.

window, which I was able to open from the inside. Meanwhile, Ulla had joined me. We decided that Ellen should stay on the outside so we could hand the equipment to her through the window – she had the joyous task of throwing everything into the water.[31]

The activists damaged twenty computers and circuit boxes, cut an antenna, jammed other types of machinery, and tossed files overboard.[32] After they were arrested, the women were held in custody for approximately four months. When they went to trial, they argued that they were acting within the parameters of international law. The presiding judge concurred, and they were acquitted.

Although these acts of maximum damage could have brought the movement's tactics into question, the need to establish legitimacy of means was tempered by the fact that the activists were acquitted of all criminal charges. In other words, British courts provided justification for the movement by determining that its actions were legal. Although some may question whether this is the best way to actually eliminate nuclear weapons from Great Britain, the movement's methods are not generally perceived as beyond the parameters of acceptability.

Establishing a Movement Infrastructure and Workable Form of Leadership

In addition to making cultural adaptations and establishing legitimacy of means, Trident Plowshares organizers also successfully built a movement infrastructure. Anticipating that thousands would join their campaign, reformist leaders recognized the need for some administrative capacity, so they set forth the following operating system. First, recruits are asked to become "individual pledgers," committing themselves to the prevention of nuclear crimes and adherence to non-violent principles. Second, each pledge must then join a Trident Plowshares affinity group – an organizing cell of three to fifteen people who serve as a support system. Individuals may be assigned to an affinity group, but they are also encouraged to independently form their own group around a particular identity, such as grandmothers, war veterans, and so forth. The affinity group members then register with the "core group," which handles the practical and

---

[31] Zelter, Angie. 2001. *Trident on Trial: The Case for People's Disarmament*. Edinburgh: Luath Press Limited, p. 41.

[32] Laffin, Arthur. 2003. *Swords Into Plowshares: A Chronology of Plowshares Actions, 1980–2003*. Marion, SD: Rose Hill Books, p. 71.

administrative aspects of the movement. Early in the Trident Plowshares campaign, core members were also responsible for working with the press, supplying food during actions, and providing legal support. Eventually, they delegated these responsibilities, forming separate legal teams, prison support groups, and a media committee. Overall, the core group guides and coordinates the Trident Plowshares movement.

Although the core group wields significant power, organizers did not want an authoritarian form of leadership. To ensure a non-hierarchical, democratic movement, new members periodically join the core group as others cycle out. This system of shared leadership is also designed to address concerns about repression. The organizers note: "State Authorities [may] try to prevent the success of a campaign by 'taking out' those whom they consider to be leaders.... Often in such campaigns information is held by a few individuals. One danger is that if certain key people are 'removed'... important information necessary for the campaign is lost."[33] Consequently, the core group members hold a "Representatives Meeting" every six months to discuss movement policies and strategies. Each affinity group sends one or two members to this meeting, where all decisions are made by consensus.

Because this structure was firmly established from the beginning, few people challenged or contested it as they did in Sweden, where organizers tried to collaboratively build an infrastructure with recruits. In fact, the initial six organizers state in their campaign handbook that the movement structure is not open to debate. They write: "People who subsequently came into Trident Ploughshares were presented with a coherent and fairly well-thought out project. Many of the major decisions had already been made and were not negotiable."[34] This stable, uncontested infrastructure provided a solid foundation for the expansion of the Trident Plowshares movement.

Media Work

In line with their instrumental strategy that emphasizes winning over witnessing, the reformed Plowshares movement also places greater emphasis on media work than do those in the U.S. movement. They maintain that

---

[33] *Tri-denting It Handbook: An Open Guide to Trident Ploughshares.* 2001 (3rd edition). Section 2.4 "Joint Responsibility." Available at www.tridentploughshares.org.
[34] *Tri-denting It Handbook: An Open Guide to Trident Ploughshares.* 2001 (3rd edition). Section 2.1 "Overall Structure." Available at www.tridentploughshares.org.

coverage of their campaigns is important because it enables activists to get their views on nuclear weapons and international law into the public discourse, expanding awareness of the issues. In addition, the reformers hope that it will help mobilize sympathizers, thereby increasing the pressure on politicians to respond to their constituents' demands. Although Trident Plowshares activists are aware of the problems with mainstream media coverage, they believe that the potential benefits make it worthwhile. David Mackenzie stated:

The conventional media is a complex and diverse phenomenon and its negative features have been well catalogued. Suffice it to say that in TP [Trident Plowshares] we are familiar with its deficiencies, the sloppy cliché-ridden outputs, the editorial dead-hands, the bias towards the state, the inability to relate to longitudinal stories, the concentration of ownership, the ignorance, the automatic collusion with the 'Culture of Contentment,' etc. But we have also come across a number of positive features. There are lots of genuine journalists out there who want to do a good professional job, to chase a good story, report it accurately and set it in some kind of understandable context. Developing partnerships with individual journalists pays dividends. It also pays to build a reputation as a reliable source. If you devise a statement of reasonable length to accompany an event, usually the text agencies will pass it on unchanged.... There is another element. Nonviolent activism aims to communicate, to engage, to provoke dialogue. Consistency would mean that we do that with every kind of encounter in the process, including the media.[35]

The Trident Plowshares attitude toward the media differs from the U.S. movement for two reasons. First, the prophetic orientation of the U.S. movement means that activists are not too concerned about media coverage because they believe that the effects of their actions are in God's hands. But the reformed British movement emphasizes political gains, not just moral witness. If news coverage can help the movement achieve disarmament, then Trident Plowshares activists are willing to collaborate with journalists, despite the challenges and frustrations it involves. Second, the U.S. Plowshares movement has had to do more work to establish legitimacy of means for its tactics of property destruction and blood-pouring. Coverage by conventional media sources tends to de-legitimize these tactics by portraying Plowshares activists as fanatics and deviants. In contrast, the reformed British movement has been less concerned about establishing legitimacy of means since most of their participants engage in "minimum" acts of disarmament (low-risk actions) that are part of the established (and mostly accepted) tactical repertoire of British peace movements. Even those

[35] Mackenzie, David, personal correspondence with the author, January 30, 2007.

engaged in "maximum" disarmament actions have been acquitted in court, thereby establishing a degree of tactical justification. Consequently, reformers may not incur the same risk of potentially undermining their legitimacy of means by working with reporters who might portray them negatively.

In short, the reformed Trident Plowshares movement emerged and quickly expanded as a result of key decisions made by organizers at the micro-level. These decisions – to adapt the movement to suit a more secular culture, to include more low-risk forms of participation that created legitimacy of means, and to establish an infrastructure that was non-negotiable – all contributed to a trajectory of growth. This growth caught the attention of reporters, whose coverage has fueled the movement even further. Naturally, political opportunities – particularly the International Court of Justice's ruling on nuclear weapons – aided this process. However, this ruling was not sufficient to sustain Plowshares groups in other nations, and we must therefore recognize that while political opportunities may contribute to a movement's growth and success, micro-level decisions also have a strong influence on its trajectory.

The Orthodox Plowshares Movement

As the reformed Plowshares movement grew, the orthodox wing of the British movement struggled. Orthodox organizers still adhered to the prophetic spirit of the American Catholic Left, trying to implement it in a British context. They also continued to employ a similar movement infrastructure rooted in faith-based communities of resistance. The problem, however, is that such communities are quite rare in the United Kingdom, and those that do exist are often small and fledgling. For example, while doing support work for the Seeds of Hope activists, Ciaron O'Reilly started a Catholic Worker in Liverpool, but it collapsed after a couple of years because of government infiltration and internal conflict.[36] The London Catholic Worker is also limited in the type of practical support it can give Plowshares activists because it is primarily a reflection and non-violent action group, not a house of hospitality.[37] Thus it cannot provide the same forms of assistance that Jonah House and other Catholic Worker communities in the United States offer, such as child care and housing. This limits the movement's capacity to expand.

[36] Interview with Ciaron O'Reilly, conducted by the author, July 27, 2003.
[37] Field notes taken from my visit to the London Catholic Worker, July 3, 2003.

Despite this weak infrastructure, the broader European Catholic Worker network did facilitate the Jubilee 2000 Plowshares action. The idea for this campaign began at a Catholic Worker retreat where Susan van der Hijden met English priest Martin Newell. Van der Hijden had previously tried to organize a Dutch action, but was unsuccessful. As she spoke to Father Newell, he indicated a desire to participate in a Plowshares campaign. They decided to act together, targeting the Wittering Air Force base in southern England, where trucks are loaded with the nuclear weapons that are subsequently transported to the Faslane Royal Naval base. The two prepared for an entire year before they put their plans into action. Van der Hijden described what happened when they entered the Wittering base:

We didn't know exactly which building the truck would be in so we tried all the doors. Then we opened one of the easier doors with a crow bar ... and looked around a bit. Martin looked inside some of the cars there and he bumped the horn of one accidentally ... but nobody came so we went to the next building. ... We found the door was open; we were sure we had checked it before but now it was open. There were lights on and there was the truck. It was the Holy Spirit. It's too much of a coincidence. ... So first we did silent things, like hanging up banners, and then we started hammering. I was pretty quickly fed up but Martin ... wanted to get into the cockpit of the truck and hammer on the instruments there. He was hammering on the glass and then he hammered on the lock [on the outside of the truck] and bing, the door opened.[38]

Before Newell and van der Hijden left the damaged truck to turn themselves in to the security guards, the two left a statement declaring, "Through the Jubilee 2000 campaign, the church has committed herself to working for justice for the poor and oppressed. British nuclear weapons are a central part of the chains of oppression. As Christians we have taken responsibility and acted in solidarity with the least of the world."[39]

This orthodox Plowshares action occurred at the same time as the reformed Trident Plowshares campaign was under way. The two factions of the movement supported one another, and in fact Newell and van der Hijden had initially hoped to conduct their campaign as a "maximum disarmament action" in conjunction with others who identified more strongly with the reformed tradition. However, the differences between the two groups made direct collaboration a challenge. Van der Hijden recalled:

[38] Interview with Susan van der Hijden, conducted by the author, June 24, 2003.
[39] Laffin, Arthur. 2003. *Swords Into Plowshares: A Chronology of Plowshares Actions, 1980–2003.* Marion, SD: Rose Hill Books, p. 78.

The British Movement

We started with a group [of reformed Plowshares activists] but after a while we split up. There was a cultural issue there because Martin and I are really inspired by the traditional Plowshares, the American movement. The "orthodox Plowshares" – that's what we call ourselves. The others were inspired by the Trident campaign in England. They don't do that much disarmament really; they are much more into blockading, campaigning and protesting.... What actually split us up in the end is that one of [the reformists] felt that Martin wasn't ready to go to prison and he didn't want to be responsible for Martin suffering in prison. It was really strange. But it might also be that we were quite radical, going too fast for them. Being inspired by the American Plowshares movement, we were thinking 5–10 years in prison easily. They were more from this English tradition and they were thinking that three months is a lot. So there was an imbalance in that. Also, we were much stronger Catholics, although we were excited about working together with other people. I think [the Catholic identity] made us more accepting of sacrifices or the idea of suffering for your beliefs. It was normal for us. It was kind of horrifying to them.[40]

The experience of the Jubilee 2000 Plowshares campaign also revealed another difference between the reformist and orthodox groups. Because the reformist wing is oriented toward political efficacy, its members view prison sentences as nothing more than a consequence that they must accept. They typically post bail so that the member can be released from jail as quickly as possible. They fight for acquittals or minimal sentences. In contrast, members of the orthodox wing view prison as a central part of their witness, just as U.S. Plowshares activists do. They refuse to post bond, out of solidarity with the poor who cannot afford bail, and as a means of keeping the public engaged. Father Martin Newell explained:

About the whole going to jail thing, I certainly believe that if we had accepted bail – conditions and all – we would have had no impact beyond the converted.... I realize how much it would cut down the witness of what this is about – its power of the Spirit to make people question, and be inspired and converted.... "Peace people" seem to have two views of prison: either it is the only time they experience a life shared with the poorest and most oppressed of our society and so they find it an inspiration, a challenging and positive time outside of usual experience. Or they see it as a campaign tool, something that has to be endured. I think for myself... we can learn from it and apply the lessons we do learn to our daily life outside afterwards. And not just to peace work, or nonviolent action, or our general philosophy of life, but being able to accept and express and live in solidarity with the poor all the way. If we can join in with their "community of destiny," we may be less tempted to give

---

[40] Interview with Susan van der Hijden, conducted by the author, June 24, 2003.

up the struggle. Because if you associate too much with those who are comfortable, we can begin to yearn for that.[41]

Although the two factions of the British Plowshares movement are on amicable terms and share the goal of abolishing nuclear weapons, their differences are significant. The orthodox are directly inspired by the U.S. Catholic Left and its spirituality, whereas the reformed have only a nominal connection to it. The orthodox continue to emphasize the importance of symbolic actions, whereas the Trident Plowshares participants seek to become a viable political force that can hold the British government accountable to international law. Prison witness is essential to one wing of the movement but not the other. The orthodox see themselves as a prophetic minority whose greatest obligation is to be faithful to God's will; the reformists seek allies in order to build their base of power so that they can realistically influence Great Britain's military policies. Those who are drawn to the orthodox tradition seek political changes, but they also aim for a spiritual transformation of the church and society. Father Newell observed:

The World Court judgment has been a significant motivator for me. . . . I wanted to see it enforced and . . . it seems like the most likely way to get rid of British Trident and bring about nuclear de-escalation *if* courts and public opinion can be brought behind it. However, that would not be enough of a reason to do a plowshares action for me. I want to emphasize the spiritual dimension. It is the planting of those seeds that ultimately bear fruit. As Bernard Häring said, it is about the healing power of nonviolence. Doing away with nukes is good, but something else will replace them if the spirit of violence is not exorcised. "Cast out one devil and seven worse ones will replace it."[42]

Conclusion

As movements spread across national borders, organizers must make various cultural adaptations. Trident Plowshares organizers recognized this, noting that the heavily Catholic form of high-risk activism in the U.S. movement would have limited appeal to secular British peace activists. Consequently, within the reformed British Trident campaign, one rarely finds the scriptural references and Catholic rituals that are so characteristic of the U.S.

---

[41] Letter from Martin Newell to Susan van der Hijden, written December 20, 2000, provided to the author by Susan van der Hijden.

[42] Letter from Martin Newell to Susan van der Hijden, written August 12, 2000, provided to the author by Susan van der Hijden.

Plowshares movement. Similarly, the majority of Trident participants do not see themselves as prophets but rather as a political force. Thus the cultural adaptations implemented by reformist leaders are so far-reaching that this spin-off movement barely resembles the original one.

Yet these changes have helped the Trident Plowshares movement grow and expand. And even though they have not yet accomplished their goal of abolishing Great Britain's nuclear arsenal, Trident Plowshares organizers have achieved some notable gains. First, by successfully addressing these micro-foundational developmental tasks, reformed leaders have been able to recruit greater numbers of participants and sponsor multiple actions each year. This has helped to keep the issue of nuclear weapons alive in British political discourse and debate. Second, the reformed Plowshares movement also appears to be having some real influence on public opinion. A 2001 poll indicated that 51 percent of Scottish people held favorable attitudes toward a scheduled Trident protest, whereas only 24 percent opposed it.[43]

It is too early to predict what the reformed Plowshares movement's long-term trajectory will be. Certainly, if Trident organizers hope to sustain resistance over time, they will have to deal with the issue of activist retention. They will have to find strategies for reinforcing commitment and countering the factors, such as burn-out and growing life responsibilities, that can undermine long-term participation. In addition, because the Trident Plowshares movement is more oriented toward winning than witnessing, it must also develop an ideology – distinct from the U.S. Plowshares theology of resistance – that compels activists to persistently resist even if they see no progress toward their goals. If they fail to address these tasks, the movement will likely terminate or shift into abeyance.

The orthodox Plowshares movement in Great Britain faces its own challenges as well. With just four actions – occurring in 1990, 1993, 1996, and 2000 – this segment of the movement has had a trajectory of intermittent resistance that parallels the movements in Germany, the Netherlands, and Australia. Similar to those cases, the orthodox movement's path has been shaped by the lack of a stable infrastructure and clear leadership. Moreover, because orthodox activists did not make many cultural adaptations – using the same tactics, symbols, and Biblical justifications as their American counterparts – they have had little success in establishing legitimacy of means. The strongly religious character of the movement simply does

---

[43] Laffin, Arthur. 2003. *Swords Into Plowshares: A Chronology of Plowshares Actions, 1980–2003.* Marion, SD: Rose Hill Books, p. 72.

not resonate in a secular British context. If the orthodox movement is to expand and grow, it will have to address these micro-foundational tasks. However, given the emphasis on faithfulness and moral witness, orthodox activists may decide that expanding the movement is not a priority. They may be content to continue their sporadic acts of resistance, knowing that they are fulfilling their religious and moral obligations.

Conclusion

FROM FAILED ATTEMPTS TO PERSISTENT RESISTANCE – UNDERSTANDING DIVERGENT MOVEMENT TRAJECTORIES

Since 1980, Plowshares activists throughout the world have been breaking into military bases and weapons production sites to call for disarmament and the abolition of war. During this time, the world has changed dramatically. The first Plowshares action at General Electric occurred when the arms race was escalating and the rapid proliferation of nuclear weapons generated great public concern. Then the Berlin Wall fell, the Soviet Union collapsed, and the Cold War ended. Political leaders were signing disarmament agreements and peace appeared to be breaking out all over. The sense of international tranquility did not last long, however, as the al Qaeda attacks on September 11, 2001 – along with subsequent terrorist acts and the ensuing U.S. wars in Afghanistan and Iraq – created a new set of hostile geopolitical dynamics. Bellicose attitudes and heightened security concerns constituted another shift in the political environment at the start of the twenty-first century.

Remarkably, these changing circumstances and fluctuating political conditions have not had a strong influence on the trajectories of the Plowshares movement. Its activists have organized under a variety of conditions – some favorable, some not. The U.S. movement has faced significant repression but has persisted steadily for decades, continuously drawing attention to the fact that nuclear weapons still exist and pose a threat to all humanity. Some of the international branches, such as the British, Dutch, and Swedish Plowshares movements, began mobilization efforts in the late 1980s and early 1990s when most other peace movements were on the decline due to the lack of political opportunities and the perceived belief that nuclear weapons were no longer a serious concern. German Plowshares organizers initially appeared to have the best timing and the most advantageous conditions. The German movement started in 1983 – a time when the peace movement was strong and thousands of Germans were opposed to the deployment of nuclear missiles on their soil. At that time, one poll found that 50 percent of West Germans were generally sympathetic to the peace movement's goals.[1] Moreover, German Plowshares activists had more political allies and encountered fewer sanctions than their U.S. counterparts, yet they only managed to launch two actions, never materializing into a full-fledged movement.

These Plowshares movements challenge the assumption that changes in the social environment and political climate determine when movements emerge and decline. It is clear that the movement branches' divergent trajectories – ranging from intermittent resistance to limited expansion to successful mobilization and persistence – cannot be fully explained by macro factors such as shifting political opportunities, accessibility of resources, or the degree of repression. Although such structural factors do matter, they are only part of the story. To complete the picture, we must shift our focus to the micro-foundations of movements, where activists make strategic decisions about how they will respond to these macro conditions and how they will handle the challenges that arise with movement development. As illustrated in Table C.1, I argue that four issues were particularly important in shaping the course of Plowshares groups' trajectories. These include decisions about (1) the type of infrastructure and leadership to create; (2) the methods used to establish legitimacy of means; (3) appropriate cultural adaptations (for the international movement branches); and (4) techniques for activist retention. A broader comparison of these four issues will illustrate the importance of these micro-foundational tasks and reveal other factors that may influence a movement's ability to mobilize, expand, and persist over time.

Movement Infrastructure and Leadership

For any new movement to take root and grow, some type of infrastructure and decision-making capacity is needed. Yet despite many years of research, there is no consensus about the type of administrative system or leadership form that is most effective. Some studies indicate that formalized

---

[1] Wittner, Lawrence S. 2003. *Toward Nuclear Abolition: A History of the World Nuclear Disarmament Movement, 1971 to the Present*. Stanford: Stanford University Press, p. 149.

Table C.1. *Overview of Micro-Foundational Tasks and Movement Trajectories by Country*

| | Trajectories | | | | | | |
| | Intermittent activity | | | Orthodox | Limited expansion | Persistence | Undetermined |
Tasks	West Germany	Netherlands	Australia	UK	Sweden	United States	Reformed UK (Trident Plowshares)
1. Established operational form of leadership and stable infrastructure	—	—	●	●	●	+	+
2. Established legitimacy of means	—	—	—	—	+	+	+
3. Made suitable cultural adaptations	—	—	—	—	+	n/a	+
4. Implemented activist retention techniques	n/a	n/a	n/a	n/a	—	+	?

+ = accomplished
— = did not accomplish
● = partially accomplished
n/a = not applicable
? = not yet determined

organizations have a greater likelihood of obtaining their goals and persisting,[2] whereas others argue that they blunt militancy and divert energy toward organizational preservation rather than toward protest.[3] Similarly, research on movement leadership reveals that each type possesses both strengths and weaknesses.[4] In reality, movement participants are likely to make choices in this developmental task based on their goals, preferences, and ideological and cultural inclinations, as well as on practical considerations. Yet what can we learn about how these infrastructural and leadership decisions shape a movement's ability to expand and sustain itself?

In comparing the various Plowshares movements, it appears that the form of leadership and infrastructure did not make a difference. The two branches that successfully moved into the expansion stage and have sustained continuous actions – the U.S. movement and the Trident Plowshares movement in Great Britain – made distinct choices on this issue. The U.S. movement coalesced around a set of charismatic leaders who provided guidance to a loosely coordinated network of intentional communities. The Berrigans and McAlister intentionally rejected the idea of a formal Plowshares movement organization, fearing that it would make participants vulnerable to state repression. In contrast, the British Trident Plowshares leaders established a more formal organization whereby all participants are registered with the coordinating body of the movement known as the "core group." This group coordinates and directs the movement but, unlike its American counterparts, leadership responsibility rotates as different people join the core group and others leave after serving in that capacity for several years. Although the U.S. and the reformed British movement have different infrastructures, each has managed to mobilize and expand.

The Swedish case provides an interesting counterpoint. In addressing this developmental task, Swedish Plowshares activists first adopted the American model of grassroots resistance communities. When it failed, they switched to an infrastructural style that more closely resembled the

---

[2] Gamson, William A. 1975. *The Strategy of Social Protest*. Homewood, IL: Dorsey; Staggenborg, Suzanne. 1989. "Stability and Innovation in the Women's Movement: A Comparison of Two Movement Organizations." *Social Problems* 36: 75–92; Taylor, Verta. 1989. "Social Movement Continuity: The Women's Movement in Abeyance." *American Sociological Review* 54: 761–775.

[3] Piven, Francis Fox and Richard Cloward. 1977. *Poor People's Movements*. New York: Random House.

[4] Klandermans, Bert. 1989. "Introduction: Leadership in Decision Making." *International Social Movements Research* 2: 215–224; Polletta, Francesca. 2002. *Freedom Is an Endless Meeting: Democracy in American Social Movements*. Chicago: University of Chicago Press.

reformed British model. Yet neither structure provided the Swedes with the foundational stability they needed to expand their movement. This indicates that it may not be so much the type of infrastructure and leadership that matters but how the decision is made and by whom.

The *process* of handling this developmental task varied notably in the Swedish case, on the one hand, and in the U.S. and reformed British movements, on the other hand. In the U.S. context, Plowshares activists inherited a pre-existing stable infrastructure from earlier Catholic movements, thereby eliminating the need to create a new one. In addition, the leadership of the U.S. Plowshares movement was never seriously contested because the charisma of the Berrigans, established during the Vietnam War draft raids, inspired many individuals to join. In fact, the Berrigans did not initially intend to create a movement when they entered the General Electric plant in 1980, but others soon followed their example, causing a movement to emerge around them. In Great Britain, Trident Plowshares organizers did not have a pre-existing infrastructure to build upon and thus they had to create their organization from the ground up. Yet the task was not burdensome because organizers used earlier peace organizations as a model, and they chose an infrastructure that is bureaucratically light. Their administrative system requires only minimal contact with the core group and little investment of time, as opposed to intentional communities that require a lot of time and encompass virtually every aspect of life. Moreover, Trident Plowshares organizers established their infrastructure and decision-making process and then declared that it was not open to negotiation. Anyone interested in joining the campaign was informed about the operational mechanisms of the movement and were told that they would have to accept them as they were. Therefore, in both the U.S. and reformed British movements, leadership and infrastructure were determined before activist ranks began to fill and the movement expanded. In all likelihood, those who had serious issues with these systems did not join, thereby minimizing any conflict on this matter.

In contrast, Swedish organizers placed a strong emphasis on democracy and egalitarianism and therefore tried to collectively build an infrastructure with recruits. This meant that every aspect of the movement was open to discussion and debate. Negotiating the infrastructure was further complicated by an additional factor – the degree of heterogeneity within the movement. There were many ideas about the type of organization Swedes should build and the type of authority that is legitimate. Therefore the process of addressing this developmental task was highly contentious, resulting in various internal tensions and disputes that ultimately contributed to the movement's demise.

Yet is a working infrastructure and decision-making process really essential for social movement expansion and persistence? In this case, it was one of the most decisive factors. For those Plowshares groups that failed to establish a stable form of leadership and organization, recruiting people to this type of high-risk activism was difficult. Without reassurance that a community would provide assistance with family obligations and financial needs, prospective recruits had to consider the effects on their families and futures. This was certainly an obstacle that German Plowshares organizers encountered as they sought to enlist participants. This was also an issue for the British orthodox movement. It is not surprising, therefore, that most of those who participated in orthodox British Plowshares actions were neither married nor had children at the time. Moreover, many of them had given up careers to do full-time peace work and were therefore not concerned about losing their jobs or jeopardizing indispensable sources of income. But such individuals are quite rare, and thus the number of recruits remained small.

Those Plowshares groups that did not have a secure infrastructure were also more heavily influenced by the effects of burn-out, repression, internal conflicts, and shifting political opportunities. In Australia, for example, activists became exhausted from this intense way of life; when they decided to take a break, the movement collapsed because their communities were small and fragile. In contrast, U.S. Plowshares activists periodically go to monasteries or other religious communities for a period of reflection and renewal after a prison sentence.[5] The stable network of Catholic resistance communities enables the movement to continue even as some individuals take a temporary reprieve. The lack of a secure infrastructure can also make it difficult for groups to weather state-sponsored repression. Dutch activists did not devote themselves to the task of establishing an infrastructure; instead, they used a pre-existing, twelve-person affinity group for support. The precarious nature of this foundational base became evident when a government agent infiltrated the circle of activists, causing the group to collapse. Subsequently, another Plowshares action did not take place in the Netherlands for more than a decade. And in the Swedish case, Hasse Leander recognized that the lack of a secure organizational basis made it harder for the group to survive its internal conflicts. He observed: "It's difficult when you're not a large group; you're really vulnerable to

---

[5] Interview with John Schuchardt, conducted by the author, July 22, 2003.

personality issues and our newly formed organization was very, very fragile. Otherwise, in an organization like the church, you could have a conflict but you have the back-up of the organization's structure. We didn't have that back-up here."[6] Of course, some movements with a durable infrastructure are still undermined by these problems; however, the likelihood of surviving repression, internal conflicts, and fluctuating political conditions is greater when there is a secure foundation.

Establishing Legitimacy of Means

Although a stable infrastructure and a workable form of leadership are important, they are not the only factors that determine whether activists can transform initial outbursts of protest into a movement. Movement leaders must also convince others that their tactics and strategies are a valid way to achieve their stated goals. For many groups that use standard, accepted methods drawn from a pre-existing tactical repertoire, little to no attention may be given to this developmental task. Yet when groups engage in tactical innovation or use highly controversial techniques, they are often forced to justify their methods of protest. If they fail to establish legitimacy of means, recruitment will be difficult, if not impossible.

As the tactical innovators of the Plowshares movement, Philip and Daniel Berrigan and their supporters were initially responsible for this developmental task. With their religious training and biblical knowledge, the Berrigans and others have argued that civil disobedience and confrontational acts are completely consistent with scriptural mandates and the example that Jesus set. Their theology of resistance has not persuaded large numbers of Catholics to join them, and probably never will, but building a mass movement is not important to U.S. Plowshares activists. Since their tactical justification is rooted in the prophetic biblical tradition, they assume that they will be not be widely accepted, just as prophets throughout Judeo-Christian history have been marginalized and ignored. But they have convinced enough people that such acts of prophetic provocation are necessary and an essential part of Christian faith so that a small but steady stream of activists have participated in Plowshares campaigns, perpetuating the movement over several decades.

Organizers of Plowshares actions overseas also found that tactical justification was a critical task. Those who managed to establish a movement

[6] Interview with Hasse Leander, conducted by author, June 27, 2003.

did not simply adopt the religious arguments and scriptural references of U.S. Plowshares leaders. The Swedes emphasized that their tactics challenged the mentality of obedience within the population and demonstrated the power that citizens have to take responsibility for disarmament. They argued that these tactics strengthen democracy, generating greater citizen participation in military policies rather than acquiescing to the decisions of government officials. The reformed British Plowshares movement took a two-pronged approach to establishing legitimacy of means. First, it shifted the predominant rationale from a theological argument to a legal one, building from the 1996 World Court document that stated that it is illegal for a nation to threaten other countries with nuclear weapons. As international law requires citizens to intervene when their government is committing a crime, the Trident Plowshares organizers claimed that their tactics were justified because they were preventing more serious crimes against humanity. Second, Trident organizers changed the movement's methods, primarily using familiar and accepted forms of protest such as blockades and trespassing. This enabled them to recruit enough people to facilitate the movement's transition to the expansion stage.

Organizers in West Germany and Australia attempted to gain legitimacy of means mainly by employing the religious justifications of the American Plowshares movement. This was largely ineffective because German and Australian societies are much more secular than the United States. According to one recent survey, 44 percent of U.S. citizens attend church on a regular basis, but only 27 percent of British, 16 percent of Australian, 14 percent of German, and 4 percent of Swedish citizens do so.[7] Christian references and scriptural teachings thus had far less cultural resonance in these nations. Although Swedish and reformed British organizers recognized this and made appropriate changes, German and Australian leaders did not, resulting in less acceptance of these tactics and little response to recruitment appeals.

Dutch Plowshares organizers also failed at this task, but for a different reason: they never seriously attempted to establish legitimacy of means. Dutch activists wanted to carry out campaigns, not build a movement. They were therefore not concerned about persuading others that these controversial tactics were acceptable. As a result, they seldom articulated

---

[7] Swanbrow, Diane. 1997. "Study of Worldwide Rates of Religiosity, Church Attendance." University of Michigan news release available at http://www.umich.edu/~newsinfo/Releases/1997.

an ideological or theological justification for their actions. Given that the survey cited earlier indicates that 35 percent of people in the Netherlands attend church regularly,[8] and the fact that the mass demonstrations against nuclear weapons in the early 1980s were sponsored by Christian groups (including the Catholic peace organization Pax Christi), the theology of resistance and the religious references of the U.S. movement might have elicited some response. Moreover, those who conducted Plowshares actions in the Netherlands felt justified by international law, but their arguments were usually confined to the courtroom. And even if Plowshares activists in the Netherlands had publicly promoted these scriptural and legal justifications, their tactics still may not have been granted much legitimacy by Dutch citizens. Theologian and activist Heleen Ransijn reflected: "Perhaps it doesn't fit with our Dutch character. I don't know to what extent you could actually speak of the character of a whole nation... but I do think in general that Dutch people tend to be rather matter of fact about things. So we don't easily resort to pouring our own blood. That would be just a bit too dramatic... I think it has something to do with a trait you find in a lot of Dutch people; we don't like to be dramatic."[9] In short, because Dutch activists were more interested in destroying weaponry than justifying their tactics, their ability to attract new participants was limited and their capacity to grow was restricted.

Comparing all Plowshares group trajectories in Table C.1, we can see that the four groups that failed to establish legitimacy of means (the German, Dutch, Australian, and orthodox British groups) never fully mobilized. The other three groups successfully resolved this task, but did so in different ways. The legal justifications of the reformed British movement, the Swedes' appeal for greater democracy, and the U.S. movement's theology of resistance enabled these groups to establish some degree of tactical legitimacy. However, their preferred strategies for accomplishing legitimacy may have different long-term implications since not all ideological justifications are equal in their ability to sustain collective action over time.

In part, the U.S Plowshares movement has endured for so long because it is rooted in a theology that emphasizes fidelity over efficacy. Smashing idols, confronting unjust institutions, making personal sacrifices for the

---

[8] Swanbrow, Diane. 1997. "Study of Worldwide Rates of Religiosity, Church Attendance." University of Michigan news release available at http://www.umich.edu/~newsinfo/Releases/1997.

[9] Interview with Heleen Ransijn, conducted by the author, June 20, 2003.

cause, and denouncing war are all seen as inherently valuable expressions of Christian commitment, regardless of the results. This view – that faithful actions are more important than measurable progress – has powerfully sustained Plowshares activism long after the momentum of the broader peace movement had subsided. This does not imply that U.S. Plowshares activists have no interest in winning.[10] They do, in fact, aim to prove in court that nuclear weapons violate international law and must therefore be abolished. Toward that end, they have developed noteworthy legal strategies and put together teams of internationally renowned expert witnesses. Moreover, they do indeed hope to impair their government's war-making capacity by damaging weapons enough to render them useless, even if only temporarily. Philip Berrigan wrote: "[O]ur actions are meant to be more than symbolic. We pound on bombers and submarines with hammers, intending to damage, and if able, literally to disarm them."[11] Yet their failure to win in court, to actually abolish weapons of mass destruction, or even to seriously mar the weaponry of the U.S. military has not undermined their commitment. U.S. Plowshares activists are not discouraged by this lack of results, because their theology holds that prophets will be ignored by the population but their duty is to faithfully carry out God's will nonetheless.[12]

When visible measures of success are not the primary motivating force for activists, then the failure to obtain goals is less likely to contribute to movement decline. But what implications does this have for the reformed British movement, which is not driven by a belief that it is maintaining a biblical prophetic tradition? While we have yet to see how well the Trident

---

[10] In her book *Freedom Is an Endless Meeting: Democracy in American Social Movements*, Francesca Polletta has persuasively argued that the division between expressive and instrumental movements is not as clear cut as we often assume, because many expressive groups are indeed interested in winning. I concur with Polletta, but note that most movements will often place greater emphasis on one type of strategy over the other, even as they value both. In the U.S. Plowshares movement, activists do, in fact, want to attain their goal of a world free from war and weapons of mass destruction. However, their concern with biblical fidelity is more important than actually achieving their goals.

[11] Berrigan, Philip. 1996. *Fighting the Lamb's War: Skirmishes with the American Empire.* Monroe, ME: Common Courage Press, p. 191.

[12] The capacity of religious or moral ideologies to sustain activists – even in high-risk situations and when they are unlikely to achieve their goals – is also seen in Elisabeth Jean Wood's study of insurgency in El Salvador. She notes that liberation theology meant that many poor Salvadorans found that participation in the struggle was valuable in itself because it contributed to the reign of God and gave meaning and value to life. Moreover, defying injustice brought dignity to activists, regardless of whether they achieved their goals or not. For further information on Wood's findings, see Wood, Elisabeth Jean. 2003. *Insurgent Collective Action and Civil War in El Salvador.* New York: Cambridge University Press.

Conclusion: Understanding Divergent Movement Trajectories

Plowshares movement will persist over the long run, it is likely that it will need to make consistent gains in order to sustain the movement. After refashioning themselves to be more politically influential than orthodox Plowshares groups, reformed Plowshares activists want to see evidence of change. The successes they have achieved – mainly court acquittals that reinforce the group's view of international law – have undoubtedly contributed to the reformed movement's expansion, as activists have come to believe that they can win. But when a movement depends on victories to create a sense of efficacy, those victories must continue, or momentum will slow, causing the movement to decline or go into abeyance.

Cultural Adaptations

In this study of the Plowshares movement, we have also examined how movements change as they spread across national borders. Such changes are probably inevitable as organizers work to resolve these developmental tasks in a manner that resonates with the local culture. In this case, we can see that some Plowshares organizers made cultural adaptations in several key areas: tactics, operational policies, and strategy.

In terms of tactics, all of the Plowshares movement branches have continued the U.S. tradition of property destruction, using hammers to "beat swords into plowshares and spears into pruning hooks." Although the tools range from household hammers to sledgehammers and jackhammers, the symbolism has remained intact. The tactic of spilling blood, however, has been eliminated in many European campaigns. Susan van der Hijden stated: "I'd like to [spill blood] but I've never been in a group with people who would agree. They say it's a very Catholic thing and Europe is very secular. People won't understand that symbolism.... Europeans just associate it with something very unsanitary."[13] Ciaron O'Reilly concurred: "What we do is very liturgical.... It's pretty Catholic [where the]...emphasis is on sacrament, on ritual, on symbol."[14] Recognizing that this tactic has greater potential to alienate than to communicate, most European activists have chosen not to adopt this practice.

Operational policies also shifted as the movement spread to other continents. These changes reflect the distinct values and micro-level choices of groups. Specifically, German and Swedish Plowshares activists departed

[13] Interview with Susan van der Hijden, conducted by the author, June 24, 2003.
[14] Interview with Ciaron O'Reilly, conducted by the author, July 27, 2003.

from the U.S. tradition of operating in secret. They organized openly, informing the police and factory representatives of their plans in advance. The only information they kept secret was the exact date and time that the disarmament campaign would be launched. Per Herngren, one of the founders of the Swedish Plowshares movement, strongly advocated greater openness. His position was not only shaped by the fact that the Swedish government seldom charges activists with conspiracy, it also reflected an intentional choice that he made after an experience of infiltration during his Plowshares action in Florida. He explained:

Orlando's Freeze, a group in Florida that functioned as our support group at the Plowshares action in 1984, was subjected to at least three infiltrators. Bruce Gagnon, a member of the group who exposed two of the infiltrators, wrote an open letter to the police asking them to call instead when they wanted to know something. . . . Now and then the FBI had sent in infiltrators. Some of my friends told me that they were able to point out several of them. This is where the problem is. The feeling of suspicion caused everybody to brand people who acted a little strange as infiltrators. Several of us realized that the only solution was to keep acting out in the open. . . . Others thought that we should . . . be more careful about what we said and who we said it to. These attitudes lead to two completely different movements. Openness is a condition for democracy. . . . A secret organization has trouble maintaining its democratic dynamics, and it also becomes difficult for the group to gain wide support. It is therefore important to resist attempts to make an organization more sectarian and secret. Suspicion helps only those who want to control the movement.[15]

We also see that some groups altered the movements' underlying strategy. This occurred to some extent in Sweden, but is more evident in Great Britain, where the orthodox wing of the movement continues to use the U.S. Plowshares strategy of prophetic witness, whereas the reformed wing places greater emphasis on winning by becoming a viable political force. This altered strategy had numerous repercussions. It required a greater emphasis on recruitment in order to expand activist ranks. This, in turn, led to the incorporation of lower-risk tactics, because it was hard to convince large numbers of people to take an action that may put them behind bars for years. Moreover, this type of instrumental approach often leads activists to build alliances with other groups. This, too, can shift the dynamic from prophetic groups that can speak and act freely (albeit on the margins of

---

[15] Herngren, Per. 1993. *Path of Resistance: The Practice of Civil Disobedience*. Philadelphia: New Society Publishers, pp. 42–43.

society) to those that may not want to alienate potential allies. Thus cultural adaptations that include strategic changes, like those implemented by Trident Plowshares organizers in Great Britain, may transform the character of the movement more comprehensively than alterations in operational policies and practices. In fact, one Swedish Plowshares organizer questioned whether or not the Trident Plowshares movement should even be considered part of the Plowshares movement. He stated: "The Trident Plowshares [movement] is not expanding Plowshares, they are expanding civil disobedience and nonviolent direct action.... They are an interesting and inspiring case... but should not count as an expanding Plowshares movement comparable to the U.S. Plowshares [movement]."[16]

To varying degrees, these international spin-off groups implemented cultural adaptations as they sought to build a Plowshares movement in their home countries. In the process, a new set of questions arose for activists: How closely did they want to reflect the originating movement? How many changes could be implemented before the new movement lost its connection to the spirit and practice of the initial one? While some adaptations are necessary for a foreign movement to take hold in a new context, activists will likely hold differing opinions on the extent of changes that they want to enact.

Activist Retention

The ability of Plowshares groups to establish a movement and grow was largely shaped by whether they effectively addressed the first three developmental challenges – establishing an infrastructure, gaining legitimacy of means, and making appropriate cultural adaptations. As Table C.1 indicates, Plowshares groups that have had intermittent campaigns but never fully mobilized (Germany, the Netherlands, Australia, and the orthodox British movement) did not successfully complete any of these tasks. Swedish Plowshares activists did manage to launch a movement, but their ability to expand was limited by their internal conflicts over infrastructure and leadership. These tensions caused many individuals to drop out, and ultimately led to an infrastructural collapse. The two movements that did expand – the

---

[16] Quotation from Stellan Vinthagen, in personal communication with the author, September 1, 2005.

U.S. and reformed British Plowshares groups – dealt productively with all these issues.

But the U.S. movement is the only Plowshares group that has demonstrated the capacity to persist over the long run, even in unfavorable conditions. Its trajectory of sustained resistance is due in no small part to the movement's ability to retain activists. This has been a significant challenge, because the risks and costs involved in ongoing Plowshares activism can be severe. In fact, judges in the U.S. intentionally began imposing longer sentences on Plowshares activists in the mid-1980s in order to raise the stakes of movement participation. The belief was that many activists would be unwilling to pay the price and thus drop out while new recruits would be deterred from joining. However, heavy sanctions can sometimes have the reverse effect, deepening participants' commitment to the cause and intensifying activist identities.[17] This indicates that repression does not automatically cause movement decline. Rather, it is how activists respond to repression that determines the effect of sanctions on a movement's trajectory. In the words of one Plowshares activist: "It is our *attitude* toward punishment that decides its effectiveness."[18]

To understand how U.S. Plowshares organizers have retained activists, we must examine their micro-level efforts to sustain participation in the face of harsh sanctions. First, Plowshares leaders have called on others to make a conscious decision to not allow serious punishments to deter them. Philip Berrigan repeatedly discouraged people from calculating the costs of actions, encouraging them to focus instead on the moral imperative of resisting war.[19] Even when two individuals were sentenced to eighteen years in prison for their part in the Silo Pruning Hooks action, many activists maintained their resolve. Naturally, this commitment to persist despite all costs must be regularly reinforced. This occurs through various

---

[17] Flacks, Richard and J. Whalen. 1989. *Beyond the Barricades*. Philadelphia: Temple University Press; Francisco, Ronald A. 2004. "After the Massacre: Mobilization in the Wake of Harsh Repression." *Mobilization* 9(2): 107–126; Gitlin, Todd. 1987. *The Sixties*. New York: Bantam; McAdam, Doug. 1988. *Freedom Summer*. New York: Oxford University Press; Zwerman, Gilda, and Patricia Steinhoff. 2005. "When Activists Ask for Trouble: State-Dissident Interactions and the New Left Cycle of Resistance in the United States and Japan," pp. 85–107 in Christian Davenport, Hank Johnston, and Carol Mueller (eds.), *Repression and Mobilization*. Minneapolis: University of Minnesota Press.

[18] Herngren, Per. 1993. *Path of Resistance: The Practice of Civil Disobedience*. Philadelphia: New Society Publishers, p. 135.

[19] Informal conversations with Plowshares activist, author's field notes, May 23, 2001.

216

Conclusion: Understanding Divergent Movement Trajectories

communal practices, such as retreats, rituals, and Bible study. It is also constantly reiterated by the movement's charismatic leaders. Indeed, the need for ongoing resistance was one of the main points that Philip Berrigan emphasized throughout his thirty-five years of anti-war activism. His oldest daughter Frida recalled one of his final public speeches:

On April 20, 2002 there was a huge peace march in Washington D.C. and Dad was asked to speak at it.... We brought a folding chair because Dad was due for hip surgery and it was hard for him to stand.... He was so energized to see how many thousands had turned out to protest how the attack of September 11th had been used as an excuse to wage war. When it was his turn to speak, he got up on the stage and saw for the first time how huge the crowd was. He was silent for a second, and mustered up new energy to be heard. He started off by saying, "You are the answer. You are the answer. Don't get tired. Don't get tired."

I was sitting on the side of the stage watching him. I had helped him up the stairs, and I knew he was in a lot of pain, that bone on bone grind of his hip and socket. I knew he was tired. Tired of pain, but mostly tired of bullshit and half-heartedness. And in front of all those thousands, that tired was melting away, being replaced by the energy and hope of tens of thousands. His "don't get tired," was an injunction, an order, but it was also a plea.... He only had a few minutes to speak. And with the deftness and simplicity of a haiku master, he laid out all the challenges facing the peace movement, all the war, injustice, pain and wrong. He ended by saying: "What can we do about this can of worms?

1. Love God, love our neighbors, love our enemies.
2. Stay loving, just, strong, nonviolent.
3. Don't mourn, organize.
4. Non-cooperate now; don't run the rotten system for the bosses and billionaires.
5. Oppose any and all wars. There has never been a just war.
6. Be clear: 'The killing stops here with each of us!' We will prevent others from killing. When we do that, marvelous things will happen.
7. Don't get tired.

God bless you."

I hear his voice in my head all the time, saying "Don't get tired."... That was his gift, his challenge to the peace movement – to good people in general. Don't get tired. Don't give up. It's a luxury that we cannot afford.[20]

---

[20] Berrigan, Frida. 2004. "Frida Berrigan Speaks at Greenham Common at the Unveiling of a Monument Celebrating the Life of Philip Berrigan," pp. 5–6 at www.jonahhouse.org/frida1004.htm.

Second, U.S. Plowshares organizers have used another micro-level strategy for countering the effects of repression: offering practical forms of material and emotional support to those facing incarceration. This has been critical because many activists have families. Although separation from friends and loved ones is never easy, serving a prison sentence is less daunting when activists are reassured that they will have a place to live when they are released and that in the meantime their families are being cared for in a committed, loving community. Members of these Catholic Left groups are also dedicated to visiting their comrades in prison to sustain their morale and spirits. In fact, many Plowshares activists stated that they received dozens of letters each day from supporters all over the world. Early on, the U.S. Plowshares movement understood that this type of support was critical for retention, which is why they have placed great emphasis on building community. Philip Berrigan reflected:

That's why we invested so much time, effort, and money into starting Jonah House. We wanted a place where people could share meals and ideas, study scripture together, and support one another through the long haul. When friends went to prison, we would care for their children. When they left jail, we would welcome them home. If someone was upset or depressed, we would listen to their problems... let them know we loved them. We tried to be a loving family, committed to the spirit and the reality of nonviolent resistance.[21]

Through these techniques, the U.S. Plowshares movement has managed to sustain activist commitment and counter the negative effects of repression. It has even experienced several unintended benefits from these sanctions. For instance, long prison sentences have forced activists to rely on one another, thereby strengthening interpersonal ties. This is important, because weakening relationships to movement organizations and other participants is strongly correlated with dropping out.[22] In addition, harsh punishments verify activists' view that the U.S. government is heartless and oppressive. When activists suffer under a common opponent or system, the group's shared identity grows stronger. Moreover, these types of external threats have contributed to internal cohesion, helping activists overlook internal disputes and differences.[23] Finally, the significant costs of

---

[21] Berrigan, Philip. 1996. *Fighting the Lamb's War: Skirmishes with the American Empire.* Monroe, ME: Common Courage Press, p. 167.

[22] Aho, James. 1994. *This Thing of Darkness: A Sociology of the Enemy.* Seattle: University of Washington Press.

[23] Coser, Lewis. 1956. *The Functions of Social Conflict.* New York: Free Press.

participation in the American movement translate into greater continuance commitment. Because U.S. Plowshares activists sacrifice a great deal for their cause, they are more likely to remain devoted as the significance of their sacrifice may be undermined if the movement dies.

Of course, members of the U.S. Plowshares movement do not actively seek repression in order to enhance group cohesion, strengthen activist identity, or deepen commitment. Rather, they persistently resist because of their deeply held belief that they must convey the prophetic message regardless of the consequences. This spiritual conviction is accompanied by practical experience and skilfull organizing. Plowshares activists have first-hand knowledge of what is needed to survive tough conditions, and have employed various practices to give their people the strength to continue. Thus severe sanctions have not shortened the movement's trajectory.

Activist retention will likely become one of the defining issues in the British Trident Plowshares movement. Whether it continues or declines will be determined by the extent to which Trident organizers can convince activists to persist over time, even when conditions are unfavorable. The future of the movement will depend on leaders' ability to reinforce normative commitment, strengthen relational ties to the movement, and implement practices that will counter exiting influences such as burn-out, opposition from others, and growing life responsibilities.

Conclusion

Social movement trajectories are influenced by macro forces – such as escalating levels of repression, shifting public opinion, changing political alliances, and world events – but they are not determined by them. Although activists may not be able to control the structural conditions in which they operate, they always have a choice in how they will respond to them and those decisions affect movement longevity. In this book, I have focused intentionally on the micro-level choices and activities of Plowshares groups in order to show that structural factors are not always more influential than human agency. But I do not wish to portray micro and macro factors as separate or isolated variables; a far more fruitful approach is to examine the dynamic interplay between them. For example, this study indicates that activists may make decisions that increase or decrease their vulnerability to repression and shifting political opportunities. Dutch Plowshares activists, who intentionally chose not to build a movement infrastructure, found that their group was more easily disrupted by government infiltrators than were other Plowshares groups. Similarly, Plowshares organizers in Germany did not develop a plan to provide material and family assistance to would-be activists. In this situation, the possibility of long prison sentences had a greater deterrence effect than it did in the U.S. movement. Moreover, Plowshares groups that choose a politically instrumental orientation, such as the reformed British movement, will likely be dependent on visible measures of success to sustain a sense of efficacy that will retain activists. If political conditions change – for example, if the World Court alters its stance on nuclear weapons, or a new set of British judges are appointed who dismiss appeals to international law – activists are likely to drop out of the movement, and this may cause movement decline. In contrast, groups who choose to see themselves as part of an expressive prophetic tradition are less likely to be affected by such shifting political opportunities. Thus structural changes do matter for movements, but it is activist choices that determine the extent to which these shifts will positively or negatively affect their ability to mobilize.

The choices that social movement organizers face are numerous and ongoing. Certainly there are other developmental tasks and challenges that influence movement trajectories aside from the four that I have examined here. One scholar, in fact, has listed twenty-five dilemmas that activists routinely encounter, and future research will undoubtedly uncover more.[24] Furthermore, the resolution of these challenges is not necessarily a one-time process. Activists may find that as the social and political environment changes, they may need to modify their infrastructure or create new tactical justifications. Similarly, internal movement developments may cause previously settled issues to resurface. This is the situation that U.S. Plowshares activists face at present. Although they had stable leadership for decades, they must revisit this issue now that Philip Berrigan has passed away and Daniel Berrigan has become an octogenarian.

By giving serious attention to activists' decisions and micro-level activities, we gain a better theoretical understanding of why some movements successfully mobilize, expand, and persist, while others struggle, fail, decline, or go into abeyance. We also develop insight into the question of how activists can overcome repression and opposition, and why some

---

[24] Jasper, James. 2004. "A Strategic Approach to Collective Action: Looking for Agency in Social Movement Choices." *Mobilization* 9 (1): 1–16.

Conclusion: Understanding Divergent Movement Trajectories

individuals make significant sacrifices, even when the conditions for organizing are abysmal and the movement's estimated chances for success are small. Indeed, it is only when we look at the micro level of the Plowshares movement that we see how its participants are able to resist the totality of war by offering the totality of their lives for peace.

Appendix A

A. Which of the following best describes your beliefs in God?
   1. I don't believe in God now and I never have
   2. I don't believe in God now, but I used to
   3. I believe in God now but I *didn't used* to
   4. I believe in God now and I always have

B. If you believe in God, what type of image are you most likely to associate with God? On a scale of 1–7, please circle the number on the spectrum that most closely approximates your position between the two images listed.

1. Mother   Father

| 1 | 2 | 3 | 4 | 5 | 6 | 7 |

2. Redeemer   Liberator

| 1 | 2 | 3 | 4 | 5 | 6 | 7 |

3. Judge   Lover

| 1 | 2 | 3 | 4 | 5 | 6 | 7 |

4. Friend   King

| 1 | 2 | 3 | 4 | 5 | 6 | 7 |

5. Master   Spouse

| 1 | 2 | 3 | 4 | 5 | 6 | 7 |

6. Creator   Healer

| 1 | 2 | 3 | 4 | 5 | 6 | 7 |

C. How often do you currently attend church services?
   1. Once or twice a year
   2. 3–4 times a year
   3. Once a month
   4. 2–3 times a month
   5. Once a week
   6. 2 or more times a week
   7. Never

D. In your opinion, how important should the following be for a Christian? Please rate on a scale of 1–5 in which:
   1 = extremely important
   2 = very important
   3 = moderately important
   4 = somewhat important
   5 = not very important
   ——— Proselytizing/evangelism
   ——— Works of mercy (feeding the poor, visiting the sick, etc.)
   ——— Reconstructing the social order
   ——— Regularly attending services at church
   ——— Resisting injustice
   ——— Upholding theological orthodoxy
   ——— Simple lifestyle
   ——— Giving money to charitable contributions
   ——— Protecting the environment
   ——— Maintaining sexual purity
   ——— Voting in political elections
   ——— Fighting for the rights of the poor and oppressed
   ——— Missions to foreign countries
   ——— Prayer
   ——— Following one's conscience even if it means going against what churches say and do
   ——— Creating gender equality in the church
   ——— Believing in God without question or doubt
   ——— Withdrawing from the capitalist system as much as possible
   ——— Biblical study and reflection
   ——— Resisting militarization and war
   ——— Supporting fair labor practices

Survey Questionnaire

E. To what degree have the following people shaped your beliefs, faith, and values? Please rate on a scale in which:

1 = very influential
2 = somewhat influential
3 = a little influential
4 = not influential at all
—— St. Francis of Assisi
—— Dorothy Day
—— Thomas Merton
—— Pope John XXIII
—— Mohandas Gandhi
—— Martin Luther King, Jr.
—— Augustine
—— Archbishop Oscar Romero
—— Pope John Paul II

F. What is your religious affiliation (e.g. Roman Catholic, Presbyterian, Baptist, Quaker, etc.)? Please write your affiliation or denominational membership:

G. Are you, or have you ever been, a member of a religious order?

H. To what degree have the following communities helped sustain your faith and activism? Please rank them on a scale from 1–5 in which:

1 = extremely important
2 = very important
3 = somewhat important
4 = not very important
5 = not at all
—— Catholic Worker
—— Jonah House
—— Atlantic Life Community
—— Local faith community or religious group
—— Other (please list):

I. Have you ever worked or volunteered at a Catholic Worker house?
—— Yes
—— No
If yes, for how long?

J. Have you ever attended an Atlantic Life Community gathering?
    —— Yes
    —— No
If yes, approximately how many have you attended?
    —— 1–3
    —— 4–7
    —— 8–14
    —— 15 or more

K. Have you ever visited or lived at Jonah House?
    —— Yes
    —— No
If yes, approximately how many times did you visit or how long did you live at Jonah House?

L. At the time of your participation in a Plowshares action:
    1. What was your marital status?
       —— Single
       —— Married
       —— Divorced
       —— Widowed
       —— Separated
    2. Did you have children? If so, what ages were they?
    3. What was your employment status?
       —— Full-time
       —— Part-time
       —— Unemployed
       —— Full-time volunteer/activist without pay
       —— Student
       —— Full-time homemaker
       —— Other
    4. If you were employed outside the home, what was your occupation? Please list:
    5. How old were you?

M. Did you face disapproval or opposition from family, friends, or co-workers?
    1. If so, from whom? (Check all that apply)
       —— Spouse
       —— Parents

—— Children
—— Extended family (cousins, aunts, uncles, in-laws, etc.)
—— Friends
—— Co-workers
—— Church or religious community
—— Other (please list):

2. To what degree? Please rank on a scale of 1 to 5 in which:
1 = very strong disapproval
2 = strong
3 = moderate
4 = minor
5 = very little
—— Spouse
—— Parents
—— Children
—— Extended family (cousins, aunts, uncles, in-laws, etc.)
—— Friends
—— Co-workers
—— Church or religious community
—— Other (please list):

N. Did you receive support from people who believed in your action?
1. If so, from whom? (Check all that apply)
—— Spouse
—— Parents
—— Children
—— Extended family (cousins, aunts, uncles, in-laws, etc.)
—— Friends
—— Co-workers
—— Church or religious community
—— Other (please list):

2. To what degree? Please rank on a scale of 1 to 5 in which:
1 = very strong disapproval
2 = strong
3 = moderate
4 = minor
5 = very little
—— Spouse
—— Parents

—— Children
—— Extended family (cousins, aunts, uncles, in-laws, etc.)
—— Friends
—— Co-workers
—— Church or religious community
—— Other (please list):

O. As you were preparing for or undertaking your action, what emotions did you experience? Rank them, listing the most salient or strongest emotion 1, the next strongest 2, etc. If you did feel not an emotion listed below, leave it blank.
—— Fear
—— Hope
—— Joy
—— Anger
—— Guilt/shame
—— Sadness
—— Other (please list):

P. During your time in prison, what emotions did you encounter, Again, rank them with 1 being the strongest emotion, 2 being the second strongest, etc.
—— Happiness
—— Boredom
—— Guilt/shame
—— Depression
—— Hope
—— Anxiety or fear
—— Anger
—— Sadness
—— Other (please list):

Q. As a result of your Plowshares activism, have you experienced the following (check all that apply)?
—— Loss of employment
—— Inability to obtain student loans or mortgages
—— Loss of friendship
—— Discrimination in applying for jobs
—— Harassment or repression
—— Loss of the right to vote

Survey Questionnaire

—— Strain on marriage or family
—— Other (please list):

R. How many Plowshares actions have you participated in?

S. What was your sentence? How much time did you serve? If you participated in more than one action, please list your sentence and the amount of time served for each instance.

T. How likely do you think the following situations will occur in the next 10 years?
   1. We will have an all-out nuclear war.

Won't happen				Certain to happen		
1	2	3	4	5	6	7

   2. We will have a conventional ground war involving thousands of troops.

Won't happen				Certain to happen		
1	2	3	4	5	6	7

   3. There will be some type of nuclear accident with serious consequences.

Won't happen				Certain to happen		
1	2	3	4	5	6	7

   There will an elimination of atomic weapons by both the U.S. and Russia.

Won't happen				Certain to happen		
1	2	3	4	5	6	7

   There will be repeated guerrilla wars against left-wing rebels.

Won't happen				Certain to happen		
1	2	3	4	5	6	7

U. Have you ever been involved in the following movements?
   —— Labor
   —— Civil rights
   —— Anti-Vietnam War
   —— United Farm Workers

—— Gay and lesbian movement
—— Central America/Sanctuary/School of the Americas Watch
—— Animal rights
—— Women's movement
—— Environmental movement
—— Other (please list):

V. Are you currently involved in any social movements? If so, please list:

W. What is your sex?
—— Male
—— Female

X. What year were you born?

Y. What is the highest level of education that you completed?
—— Some high school
—— High school graduate or equivalent (GED)
—— Some college
—— College graduate
—— Masters or professional degree (e.g. J.D. or M.Div)
—— Ph.D. or M.D.

Z. What is your total household income before taxes?
—— Less than $10,000
—— Between $10,000 and $20,000
—— Between $20,000 and $30,000
—— Between $30,000 and $40,000
—— Between $40,000 and $50,000
—— Between $50,000 and $75,000
—— Between $75,000 and $100,000
—— More than $100,000

AA. Would you be willing to participate in a face-to-face or telephone interview? The purpose of such an interview would be to allow you to expand on your answers in your own words, and to clarify any remaining questions. If you choose, your identity can be kept completely confidential.
—— Yes
—— No

Appendix B

LIST OF INTERVIEWS BY AUTHOR

1. Greg Boertje-Obed, October 21, 2000
2. Michelle Naar-Obed, October 21, 2000
3. Anonymous interview, October 21, 2000
4. Molly Rush, March 26, 2001
5. Father Carl Kabat, April 6, 2001
6. Karl Smith, May 5, 2001
7. Al Zook, July 22, 2001
8. Anonymous interview, July 23, 2001
9. Per Herngren, December 5, 2002
10. Macy Morse, May 27, 2003
11. Mary Sprunger-Froese, May 29, 2003
12. Kathleen Rumpf, May 29, 2003
13. Jean Grosbach, June 11, 2003
14. Father John Dear, June 11, 2003
15. Lin Romano, June 16, 2003
16. Heleen Ransijn, June 20, 2003
17. Barbara Smedema, June 21, 2003
18. Fredrik Ivarsson, June 23, 2003
19. Susan van der Hijden, June 24, 2003
20. Stellan Vinthagen, June 24, 2003
21. Hasse Leander, June 27, 2003
22. Chris Cole, July 3, 2003
23. Father Martin Newell, July 4, 2003
24. John Schuchardt, July 22, 2003
25. Martin Holladay, July 23, 2003
26. Peter DeMott, July 23, 2003
27. John Heid, July 24, 2003

28. Ciaron O'Reilly, July 27, 2003
29. Bruce Friedrich, July 30, 2003
30. Ellen Grady, July 31, 2003
31. Claire Grady, August 12, 2003
32. Anonymous interview, August 8, 2003
33. Krista van Velzen, August 15, 2003
34. Anonymous interview, August 22, 2003
35. Rowan Tilly, October 17, 2003

Appendix C

United States

1980, September 9	Plowshares Eight, General Electric Nuclear Missile Re-Entry Division (PA)
1980, December 13	Plowshares Number Two, General Dynamics Electric Boat shipyard (CT)
1982, July 4	Trident Nein, General Dynamics Electric Boat shipyard (CT)
1982, November 14	Plowshares Number Four, General Dynamics Electric Boat shipyard (CT)
1983, July 14	AVCO Plowshares, AVCO Systems Division (MA)
1983, November 24	Griffiss Plowshares, Griffiss Air Force Base (NY)
1984, April 22	Pershing Plowshares, Martin Marietta (FL)
1984, August 10	Sperry Software Pair, Sperry Corporation (MN)
1984, October 1	Trident II Plowshares, EB Quonset Point facility (RI)
1984, November 12	Silo Pruning Hooks, Whiteman Air Force Base (MO)

1985, February 19	Minuteman II Plowshares, Whiteman Air Force Base (MO)
1985, April 18	Trident II Pruning Hooks, EB Quonset Point facility (RI)
1985, May 28	Michigan ELF Disarmament, ELF communication system transmitter site (MI)
1985, July 16	Pantex Disarmament, Amarillo, TX
1985, August 14	Wisconsin ELF Disarmament, ELF communication system transmitter site (WI)
1985, September 27	Martin Marietta MX Witness, Martin Marietta (CO)
1986, March 28	Silo Plowshares, Whiteman Air Force Base (MO)
1987, January 6	Epiphany Plowshares, Willow Grove Naval Air Station (PA)
1987, April 17	Paupers Plowshares, Naval Air Development Center (PA)
1987, June 2	White Rose Disarmament, Vandenberg Air Force Base (CA)
1987, August 5	Transfiguration Plowshares (West), Whiteman Air Force Base (MO)
1987, August 6	Transfiguration Plowshares (East), South Weymouth Naval Air Station (MA)
1987, August 16	Harmonic Disarmament for Life, ELF communication system transmitter site (WI)
1988, April 3	Nuclear Navy Plowshares, Norfolk Naval Station (VA)
1988, June 26	Kairos Plowshares, General Dynamics Electric Boat shipyard (CT)
1988, August 1	Kairos Plowshares Two, EB Quonset Point facility (RI)

Chronological List of Plowshares Actions

1988, September 20	Credo Plowshares, Air Force Association arms bazaar (Washington DC)
1989, September 4	Thames River Plowshares, Naval Underwater Systems Center (NC)
1990, April 3	Doves of Peace Disarmament, Physics International Laboratory (CA)
1991, January 1	Anzus Plowshares, Griffiss Air Force Base (NY)
1991, March 31	Aegis Plowshares, Bath Iron Works (ME)
1992, April 17	Good Friday Plowshares Missile Silo Witness, Whiteman Air Force Base (MO)
1992, May 10	Harriet Tubman–Sarah Connor Brigade Disarmament, space systems complex at Rockwell International (CA)
1993, April 9	Good News Plowshares, Newport News Shipbuilding (VA)
1993, December 7	Pax Christi–Spirit of Life Plowshares, Seymour Johnson Air Force Base (NC)
1994, April 1	Good Friday–April Fool's Day Plowshares, Grand Forks missile field (ND)
1995, August 7	Jubilee Plowshares West, Lockheed-Martin Corporation (CA)
1995, August 7	Jubilee Plowshares East, Newport News Shipbuilding (VA)
1996, July 27	Weep for the Children Plowshares, Naval Submarine Base (CT)
1997, February 12	Prince of Peace Plowshares, Bath Iron Works (ME)
1996, April 22	Laurentian Shield Trident ELF Disarmament, ELF communication system transmitter site (WI)
1998, May 17	Gods of Metal Plowshares, Andrews Air Force Base (Washington DC)

1998, August 6	Minuteman III Plowshares, Greeley missile field (CO)
1999, December 19	Plowshares vs. Depleted Uranium, Warfield Air National Guard Base (MD)
2000, June 24	Silence Trident Plowshares, ELF communication system site (WI)
2000, September 9	Sacred Earth and Space Plowshares, Petersen Air Force Base (CO)
2002, October 6	Sacred Earth and Space Plowshares II, missile silo field (CO)
2003, March 25	Riverside Plowshares, Navy "Fleet Week" (NY)
2006, June 20	Weapon of Mass Destruction Here Plowshares, missile silo field (ND)

West Germany

| 1983, December 4 | Plowshares Number Seven, U.S. Army base, Schwäbisch-Gmünd |
| 1986, December 12 | Pershing to Plowshares, U.S. Army base, Schwäbisch-Gmünd |

Australia

1987, December 28	Australian Plowshares Action, Sydney Harbor
1991, August 17	Darwin Plowshares, Darwin Royal Australian Air Force base
1998, August 9	Jabiluka Plowshares, Jabiluka uranium mine

The Netherlands

1989, January 1	NF-5B Plowshares, Woensdrecht Air Base
1989, February 9	Dutch Plowshares Two, Dutch military base
1989, March 24	Dutch Plowshares Three, Dutch military base

Chronological List of Plowshares Actions

1989, July 16	Dutch Plowshares Four, Valkenburg Air Base
2003, February 9	NATO Plowshares, Volkel NATO Air Base
2005, August 10	Dutch Plowshares Six, Woensdrecht Air Base

Sweden

1988, April 20	Choose Life, Uddevalla harbor
1989, February 16	Stop the Weapons Exports, Kristinehamn railroad yard
1990, March 20	Plowshares Eskilstuna, FFV-Ordinance weapons factory
1991, March 1	Arms Factory Plowshares, FFV-Ordinance weapons factory
1992, January 8	Soldier Disarms Rifle
1993, June 22	JAS into Plowshares, Saab airplane factory
1994, January 27	Anarchist Plowshares, Såtenäs F7 Swedish military base
1996, October 24	Disarmament for Peace, export warehouse near Gothenburg
1997, April 19	Choose Life Disarmament Action, Bofors arms factory
1998, August 14	Corpus Christi Plowshares, Faslane Naval Base (Great Britain)
1998, September 13	Bread Not Bombs Plowshares, VSEL Barrow (Great Britain)

Great Britain

Orthodox Plowshares

1990, March 21	Upper Heyford Plowshares, Upper Heyford U.S. Air Force Base

1993, January 6	BAe Plowshares, British Aerospace weapons factory
1996, January 29	Seeds of Hope Plowshares, British Aerospace site
2000, November 3	Jubilee 2000, Wittering Air Force Base

Trident Plowshares Maximum Disarmament Actions

1998, November 23	HMS Vengeance Disarmament Action, Barrow shipyard
1999, February 1	Aldermaston Women Trash Trident, Barrow shipyard
1999, June 8	Trident Three Disarmament Action, Loch Goil
2001, April 26	HMS Vanguard Disarmament, Faslane submarine base
2003, March 11	RAF Leuchars Plowshares, Royal Air Force Leuchars Base

Irish Republic

| 2003, January 29 | Shannon Plowshares, Shannon Airport |
| 2003, February 3 | Pit Stop Plowshares, Shannon Airport |

Bibliography

Aditjondro, George. 2000. "Ninjas, Nanggalas, Monuments, and Massad Manuals: An Anthropology of Indonesian State Terror in East Timor," pp. 158–188 in Jeffrey Sluka (ed.), *Death Squad: The Anthropology of State Terror*. Philadelphia: University of Pennsylvania Press.

Aho, James. 1994. *This Thing of Darkness: A Sociology of the Enemy*. Seattle: University of Washington Press.

Aldridge, Robert C. 1983. *First Strike! The Pentagon's Strategy for Nuclear War*. Boston: South End Press.

Allen, Nathalie J. and John P. Meyer. 1990. "The Measurement and Antecedents of Affective, Continuance, and Normative Commitment to Organization." *Journal of Occupational Psychology* 63: 1–18.

Balz, Dan. 1991. "Protester Disrupts Service at Church Attended by Bush." *The Washington Post*, February 18, p. A27.

Banaszak, Lee Ann. 1996. *Why Movements Succeed or Fail: Opportunity, Culture, and the Struggle for Woman Suffrage*. Princeton, NJ: Princeton University Press.

Barkan, Steven E., Steven F. Cohn, and William H. Whitaker. 1993. "Commitment Across the Miles: Ideological and Microstructural Sources of Membership Support in a National Antihunger Organization." *Social Problems* 40: 362–373.

———. 1995. "Beyond Recruitment: Predictors of Differential Participation in a National Antihunger Organization." *Sociological Forum* 10: 113–134.

Berger, Peter. 1969. *A Rumor of Angels*. Garden City, NY: Doubleday.

Berrigan, Daniel. 1984. "The Box within a Box: A Tale of Chastened Expectations," p. 58 in Dedria Bryfonski (ed.), *Contemporary Authors: Autobiography Series, Volume 1*. Detroit: Gale Research Co.

———. 1987a. *To Dwell in Peace: An Autobiography*. San Francisco: Harper and Row.

———. 1987b. "Swords into Plowshares," pp. 54–65 in Arthur Laffin and Anne Montgomery (eds.), *Swords into Plowshares: Nonviolent Direct Action for Disarmament*. San Francisco: Harper and Row.

Berrigan, Frida. 2004. "Frida Berrigan Speaks at Greenham Common at the Unveiling of a Monument Celebrating the Life of Philip Berrigan." www.jonahhouse.org/frida1004.htm

Berrigan, Frida and Kate Berrigan. 2003. "Fearless, and Full of Hope: In Prison and Out, Philip Berrigan Lived for Freedom." *Sojourners* 32(2) March–April: 30–32.

Berrigan, Philip. 1971. *Prison Journals of a Priest Revolutionary*. New York: Ballantine Books.

———— 1984. "The November Elections—To Vote or Else…" *Year One*, Vol. X, No. 3, July.

———— 1996. *Fighting the Lamb's War: Skirmishes with the American Empire*. Monroe, ME: Common Courage Press.

———— 1997. "How to Spend Time in Jail, A Useful Guide." *Church World: Maine's Catholic Weekly* 68 (9): August 7.

Berrigan, Philip and Elizabeth McAlister. 1989. *The Time's Discipline: The Beatitudes and Nuclear Resistance*. Baltimore: Fortkamp Publishing.

Billings, Dwight. 1990. "Religion as Opposition: A Gramscian Analysis." *American Journal of Sociology* 96: 1–31.

Blumer, Herbert. 1969. "Social Movements," pp. 8–29 in Barry McLaughlin (ed.), *Studies in Social Movements: A Social Psychological Perspective*. New York: Free Press.

Bob, Clifford. 2005. *The Marketing of Rebellion: Insurgents, Media, and International Activism*. New York: Cambridge University Press.

Bob, Clifford and Sharon Erickson Nepstad. 2007. "Kill a Leader, Murder a Movement? The Impact of Assassination on Social Movements." *American Behavioral Scientist* 50 (10): 1370–1394.

Bourdieu, Pierre. 1991. *Language and Symbolic Power*. Cambridge, MA: Harvard University Press.

Boutwell, Jeffrey. 1983. "Politics and the Peace Movement in West Germany." *International Security* 7 (4): 72–92.

Brennan, Claire. 1984. "Griffiss 7 Strategy Allowed." *The Post-Standard*, May 31, p. 8.

Carman, Diane. 2003. "Nuns' Faith Finds Chink in U.S. Armor." *Denver Post*, April 6, p. B-01.

Castelli, Jim. 1984. *The Bishops and the Bomb: Waging Peace in the Nuclear Age*. Garden City, NY: Doubleday.

Chabot, Sean. 2000. "Transnational Diffusion and the African-American Reinvention of the Gandhian Repertoire." *Mobilization* 6: 201–216.

Chatfield, Charles. 1996. "The Catholic Worker in the United States Peace Tradition," pp. 1–13 in Anne Klejment and Nancy Roberts (eds.), *American Catholic Pacifism: The Influence of Dorothy Day and the Catholic Worker Movement*. Westport, CT: Praeger.

Colaianni, James. 1968. *The Catholic Left: The Crisis of Radicalism within the Church*. Philadelphia: Chilton Book Company.

Cooney, Robert and Helen Michalowski. 1987. *The Power of the People: Active Nonviolence in the United States*. Philadelphia: New Society Publishers.

Cornell, Tom. 1990 [1968]. "Nonviolent Napalm in Catonsville," pp. 203–208 in Angie O'Gorman (ed.), *The Universe Bends Toward Justice*. Philadelphia: New Society Publishers.

Bibliography

Coser, Lewis. 1956. *The Functions of Social Conflict*. New York: The Free Press.

Coy, Patrick and Timothy Hedeen. 2005. "A Stage Model of Social Movement Co-optation: Community Mediation in the United States." *The Sociological Quarterly* 46(3): 405–438.

Cress, Daniel, J. Miller McPherson, and Thomas Rotolo. 1997. "Competition and Commitment in Voluntary Memberships: The Paradox of Persistence and Participation." *Sociological Perspectives* 40: 61–79.

Cullman, Oscar. 1963. *The State and the New Testament*. London: SCM Press.

Day, Dorothy. 1952. *The Long Loneliness*. San Francisco: Harper & Row.

_____ 1968. "Tribute." *Catholic Worker Newsletter* (New York), p. 2.

Dear, John. 1994. *The Sacrament of Civil Disobedience*. Baltimore: Fortkamp Publishing.

_____ 1996. *Apostle of Peace: Essays in Honor of Daniel Berrigan*. Maryknoll, NY: Orbis Books.

_____ 2001. *Living Peace: A Spirituality of Contemplation and Action*. New York: Doubleday.

DeBoer, Connie. 1985. "The Polls, the European Peace Movement and the Deployment of Nuclear Missiles." *Public Opinion Quarterly* 49 (1): 119–132.

della Porta, Donatella. 1992. *Social Movements and Violence: Participation in Underground Organizations*. Greenwich, CT: JAI-Press.

Douglass, James. 1968. *The Nonviolent Cross: A Theology of Revolution and Peace*. Toronto: The Macmillan Company.

Downton, James and Paul Wehr. 1997. *The Persistent Activist: How Peace Commitment Develops and Survives*. Boulder: Westview Press.

Duneier, Mitchell. 1999. *Sidewalk*. New York: Farrar, Straus & Giroux.

Dunn, David H. 1997. *The Politics of Threat: Minuteman Vulnerability in American National Security Policy*. New York: St. Martin's Press.

Edwards, Bob and Sam Marullo. 1995. "Organizational Mortality in Declining Social Movements: The Demise of Peace Movement Organizations in the End of the Cold War Era." *American Sociological Review* 60: 908–927.

Epstein, Barbara. 1991. *Political Protest and Cultural Revolution: Nonviolent Direct Action in the 1970s and 1980s*. Berkeley: University of California Press.

Evans, Sarah M. and Harry C. Boyte. 1992. *Free Spaces*. Chicago: University of Chicago Press.

Festinger, Leon, Henry W. Riecken, and Stanley Schachter. 1956. *When Prophecy Fails*. Minneapolis: University of Minnesota Press.

Flacks, Richard and J. Whalen. 1989. *Beyond the Barricades*. Philadelphia: Temple University Press.

Forest, Jim. 1991. *Living with Wisdom: A Life of Thomas Merton*. Maryknoll, NY: Orbis Books.

_____ 1997. *Love Is the Measure: A Biography of Dorothy Day*. Maryknoll, NY: Orbis Books.

Fox, Richard. 1989. *Gandhian Utopia: Experiments with Culture*. Boston: Beacon Press.

Francisco, Ronald A. 2004. "After the Massacre: Mobilization in the Wake of Harsh Repression." *Mobilization* 9 (2): 107–126.

Freeman, Jo. 1983. *Social Movements of the Sixties and Seventies.* New York: Longman.

Gamson, William. 1975. *The Strategy of Social Protest.* Homewood, IL: Dorsey.

Gitlin, Todd. 1987. *The Sixties.* New York: Bantam.

Goodwin, Jeff, James Jasper, and Francesca Polletta (eds.). 2001. *Passionate Politics: Emotions and Social Movements.* Chicago: University of Chicago Press.

Greeley, Andrew. 1971. "L'Affair Berrigan." *The New York Times,* February 19, p. A37.

Hancock, Stephen. 1996. "Ploughshares Activists Find Unity in their Vulnerability, Despite Trans-Atlantic Tension." *Peace News,* August/September, p. 6.

Herngren, Per. 1993. *Path of Resistance: The Practice of Civil Disobedience.* Philadelphia: New Society Publishers.

Hertzke, Allen. 1988. *Representing God in Washington: The Role of Religious Lobbies in the American Polity.* Knoxville: University of Tennessee Press.

Jasper, James. 1997. *The Art of Moral Protest: Culture, Biography, and Creativity in Social Movements.* Chicago: University of Chicago Press.

_____ 1998. "The Emotions of Protest: Affective and Reactive Emotions in and around Social Movements." *Sociological Forum* 13: 397–424.

_____ 2004. "A Strategic Approach to Collective Action: Looking for Agency in Social Movement Choices." *Mobilization* 9 (1): 1–16.

Jenkins, J. Craig and Craig M. Eckert. 1986. "Channeling Black Insurgency: Elite Patronage and Professional Development of the Black Movement." *American Sociological Review* 51: 812–829.

Kanter, Rosabeth Moss. 1968. "Commitment and Social Organization: A Study of Commitment Mechanisms in Utopian Communities." *American Sociological Review* 33: 499–517.

Kellerman, Bill. 1987. "The Cleansing of the Temple: Jesus and Symbolic Action," pp. 245–261 in Jim Wallis (ed.), *The Rise of Christian Conscience.* San Francisco: Harper & Row.

King, Martin Luther, Jr. 1964. *Why We Can't Wait.* New York: Mentor Books.

Klandermans, Bert and Dirk Oegema. 1987. "Potentials, Networks, Motivations, and Barriers."*American Sociological Review* 52: 519–531.

Klandermans, Bert. 1989. "Introduction: Leadership in Decision-Making." *International Social Movement Research* 2: 215–224.

_____ 1997. *The Social Psychology of Protest.* Cambridge, MA: Blackwell Publishers.

Klejment, Anne. 1988. "War Resistance and Property Destruction: The Catonsville Nine Draft Board Raid and Catholic Worker Pacifism," pp. 272–309 in Patrick Coy (ed.), *A Revolution of the Heart: Essays on the Catholic Worker.* Philadelphia: Temple University Press.

_____ 1996. "The Radical Origins of Catholic Pacifism: Dorothy Day and the Lyrical Left During World War I," pp. 15–32 in Anne Klejment and Nancy L. Roberts (eds.), *American Catholic Pacifism: The Influence of Dorothy Day and the Catholic Worker Movement.* Westport, CT: Praeger.

Klejment, Anne and Nancy L. Roberts. 1996. "The Catholic Worker and the Vietnam War," pp. 153–169 in Anne Klejment and Nancy L. Roberts (eds.), *American Catholic Pacifism: The Influence of Dorothy Day and the Catholic Worker Movement.* Westport, CT: Praeger.

Bibliography

Laffin, Arthur. 2003. *Swords Into Plowshares: A Chronology of Plowshares Disarmament Actions, 1980–2003*. Marion, SD: Rose Hill Books.

Laffin, Arthur and Anne Montgomery 1987. *Swords into Plowshares: Nonviolent Direct Action for Disarmament*. San Francisco: Harper & Row.

———. 1987. "The Nuclear Challenge," pp. 3–24 in Arthur Laffin and Anne Montgomery (eds.), *Swords into Plowshares: Nonviolent Direct Action for Disarmament*. San Francisco: Harper and Row.

Leander, Hasse. 1997. "The Ploughshares Movement in Sweden and the U.S.: A Comparison." *The Daily Hammer: Newsletter of the Ploughshares Support Network*, No. 14 (Winter): 10–12.

Lewis, Daniel. 2002. "Philip Berrigan, Former Priest and Peace Advocate in the Vietnam War Era, Dies at 79." *The New York Times*, December 8, p. A36.

Lichterman, Paul. 1996. *The Search for Political Community: American Activists Reinventing Commitment*. Cambridge: University of Cambridge Press.

Lifton, Robert Jay. 1968. *Death in Life: Survivors of Hiroshima*. New York: Random House.

Lifton, Robert Jay and Richard Falk. 1982. *Indefensible Weapons: The Political and Psychological Case against Nuclear Weapons*. New York: Basic Books.

Lo, Clarence Y. 1982. "Countermovements and Conservative Movements in the Contemporary U.S." *American Review of Sociology* 8: 107–134.

Lofland, John. 1996. *Social Movement Organizations: Guide to Research on Insurgent Realities*. New York: Aldine De Gruyter.

Lynd, Staughton and Alice Lynd. 1995. *Nonviolence in America: A Documentary History*. Maryknoll, NY: Orbis Books.

Mandelbaum, Michael. 1983. *The Nuclear Future*. Ithaca: Cornell University Press.

——— 1984. "The Anti-nuclear Weapons Movements." *PS* 17(1): 24–32.

Mansbridge, Jane. *Beyond Adversary Democracy*. 1983. Chicago: University of Chicago Press.

Marullo, Sam. 1992. "Political, Institutional, and Bureaucratic Fuel for the Arms Race." *Sociological Forum* 7(1): 29–54.

Marx, Gary. 1979. "External Efforts to Damage or Facilitate Movements: Some Patterns, Explanations, Outcomes, and Complications," pp. 94–125 in Mayer Zald and John D. McCarthy (eds.), *The Dynamics of Social Movements: Resource Mobilization, Social Control, and Tactics*. Cambridge, MA: Winthrop.

McAdam, Doug. 1982. *Political Process and the Development of Black Insurgency, 1930–1970*. Chicago: University of Chicago Press.

——— 1983. "Tactical Innovation and the Pace of Insurgency." *American Sociological Review* 48: 735–754.

———. 1986. "Recruitment to High-Risk/Cost Activism: The Case of Freedom Summer." *American Journal of Sociology* 92 (1): 64–90.

——— 1988. *Freedom Summer*. New York: Oxford University Press.

McAdam, Doug and Dieter Rucht. 1993. "The Cross-National Diffusion of Movement Ideas." *The Annals of the American Academy of Political and Social Science* 529: 56–74.

McCarthy, Coleman. 2002. "After a Life of Resistance, He Died Sane: For Phil Berrigan, Being Faithful Counted More Than Being Successful." *National Catholic Reporter*, December 27, Vol. 39 (9): 18.

McCarthy, John and Mayer Zald. 1977. "Resource Mobilization and Social Movements: A Partial Theory." *American Journal of Sociology* 82: 1212–1241.

McCrae, Frances B. and Gerald E. Markle. 1989. *Minutes to Midnight: Nuclear Weapons Protest in America*. Newbury Park, CA: Sage Publications.

McKenna, Margaret. 1996. "The Angel of Recidivism," pp. 92–96 in John Dear (ed.), *Apostle of Peace: Essays in Honor of Daniel Berrigan*. Maryknoll, NY: Orbis Books.

McNeal, Patricia. 1992. *Harder than War: Catholic Peacemaking in Twentieth-Century America*. New Brunswick: Rutgers University Press.

McNichols, William Hart. 2003. *"Holy Prophet Phil Berrigan."* Available online at http://puffin.creighton.edu/jesuit/andre/berrigan.html.

Meconis, Charles A. 1979. *With Clumsy Grace: The American Catholic Left, 1961–1975*. New York: Seabury Press.

Melman, Seymour. 1985. *The Permanent War Economy*. New York: Simon and Schuster.

Meyer, David S. 1990. *A Winter of Discontent: The Nuclear Freeze and American Politics*. New York: Praeger.

_____ 1993a. "Institutionalizing Dissent: The United States Structure of Political Opportunity and the End of the Nuclear Freeze Movement." *Sociological Forum* 8 (2): 157–179.

_____ 1993b. "Protest Cycles and Political Process: American Peace Movements in the Nuclear Age." *Political Research Quarterly* 46 (3): 451–479.

Meyer, David S. and Suzanne Staggenborg. 1996. "Movements, Countermovements, and the Structure of Political Opportunity." *American Journal of Sociology* 101(6): 1628–1660.

Meyer, John P. and Nathalie Allen. 1991. "A Three Component Conceptualization of Organizational Commitment." *Human Resource Management Review* 1: 61–89.

Meyer, John P., Nathalie Allen, and Ian R. Gellatly. 1993. "Affective and Continuance Commitment to the Organization: Evaluation of Measures and Analysis of Concurrent and Time-lagged Relations." *Journal of Applied Psychology* 75: 710–720.

Michels, Robert. 1966 [1962]. *Political Parties*. New York: Free Press.

Minkoff, Debra. 1999. "Bending with the Wind: Strategic Change and Adaptation by Women's and Racial Minority Organizations." *American Journal of Sociology* 104(6): 1666–1703.

Montgomery, Anne. 1987. "Divine Obedience," pp. 25–31 in Arthur Laffin and Anne Montgomery (eds.), *Swords Into Plowshares: Nonviolent Direct Action for Disarmament*. San Francisco: Harper & Row.

Mottl, Tahi L. 1980. "The Analysis of Countermovements." *Social Problems* 27(5): 620–634.

Mueller, Harald and Thomas Risse-Kappen. 1987. "Origins of Estrangement: The Peace Movement and the Changed Image of America in West Germany." *International Security* 12(1): 52–88.

Bibliography

Murray, Harry. 1990. *Do Not Neglect Hospitality: The Catholic Worker and the Homeless.* Philadelphia: Temple University Press.

Musto, Ronald G. 1986. *The Catholic Peace Tradition.* Maryknoll, NY: Orbis Books.

Myers, Ched. 1987. "By What Authority? The Bible and Civil Disobedience," pp. 237–248 in Jim Wallis (ed.) *The Rise of Christian Conscience.* San Francisco: Harper & Row.

_____ 1988. *Binding the Strong Man: A Political Reading of Mark's Story of Jesus.* Maryknoll, NY: Orbis Books.

Nepstad, Sharon Erickson. 2004a. "Persistent Resistance: Commitment and Community in the Plowshares Movement." *Social Problems* 51(1): 43–60.

_____ 2004b. *Convictions of the Soul: Religion, Culture, and Agency in the Central America Solidarity Movement.* New York: Oxford University Press.

_____ 2004c. "Disciples and Dissenters: Tactical Choice and Consequence in the Plowshares Movement." *Research in Social Movements, Conflict, and Change* 25: 139–160.

Nepstad, Sharon Erickson and Clifford Bob. 2006. "When Do Leaders Matter? Hypotheses on Leadership Dynamics in Social Movements." *Mobilization* 11(1): 1–22.

Nepstad, Sharon Erickson and Christian S. Smith. 1999. "Rethinking Recruitment to High-Risk/Cost Activism: The Case of Nicaragua Exchange." *Mobilization* 4 (1): 25–40.

Nielsen, Joyce M. 1990. *Feminist Research Methods: Exemplary Readings in the Social Sciences.* Boulder: Westview Press.

Oberschall, Anthony. 1978. "The Decline of the 1960s Social Movements." *Research in Social Movements, Conflict, and Change* 1: 257–289.

O'Gorman, Angie and Patrick G. Goy. 1988. "Houses of Hospitality: A Pilgrimage into Nonviolence," pp. 239–271 in Patrick Coy (ed.), *A Revolution of the Heart: Essays on the Catholic Worker.* Philadelphia: Temple University Press.

O'Neill, Patrick. 2002. "Dominican Nuns Face Federal Charges." *National Catholic Reporter*, November 8, Vol. 39 (3): 6–7.

O'Reilly, Ciaron. 1996. "For Swords into Plowshares, the Hammer Has to Fall!" *Mutual Aid: Newsletter of the West End Catholic Worker*, Issue 43: 3.

_____ 2001. *Remembering, Forgetting: A Journey of Resistance to the War in East Timor.* Sydney, Australia: Otford Press.

Pagnucco, Ronald. 1996. "A Comparison of the Political Behavior of Faith-Based and Secular Peace Groups," pp. 205–222 in Christian Smith (ed.), *Disruptive Religion: The Force of Faith in Social Movement Activism.* New York: Routledge.

Pihl, Anna-Carina. 1996. "Daughters of Lilith." *The Daily Hammer: Newsletter of the Ploughshares Support Network*, March: 10–11.

Piven, Francis Fox, and Richard Cloward. 1977. *Poor People's Movements: Why They Succeed, How They Fail.* New York: Pantheon.

Polletta, Francesca. 2002. *Freedom Is an Endless Meeting: Democracy in American Social Movements.* Chicago: University of Chicago Press.

Polner, Murray, and Jim O'Grady. 1997. *Disarmed and Dangerous: The Radical Lives and Times of Daniel and Philip Berrigan.* New York: Basic Books.

Reinharz, Shulamit. 1992. *Feminist Methods in Social Research*. New York: Oxford University Press.

Roberts, Nancy L. 1984. *Dorothy Day and the Catholic Worker*. Albany: State University of New York Press.

Rochon, Thomas R. 1988. *Mobilizing for Peace: The Antinuclear Movements in Western Europe*. Princeton: Princeton University Press.

Rochon, Thomas R. and David S. Meyer. 1997. *Coalitions and Political Movements: The Lessons of the Nuclear Freeze*. Boulder: Lynne Reinner Publishers.

Rothman, Jack. 1974. *Planning and Organizing for Social Change*. New York: Columbia University Press.

Rupp, Leila and Verta Taylor. 1990. *Survival in the Doldrums: The American Women's Rights Movement, 1945 to the 1960s*. Columbus: Ohio State University Press.

Rush, Molly. 1987. "Faith, Hope, and a Nonviolent Campaign," pp. 104–109 in Arthur Laffin and Anne Montgomery (eds.), *Swords Into Plowshares: Nonviolent Direct Action for Disarmament*. San Francisco: Harper & Row.

Ruzza, Carlo. 1990. "Strategies in the Italian Peace Movement." *Research in Social Movements, Conflicts and Change* 12: 111–138.

Schaeffer-Duffy, Claire. 2002. "The Life of an Inside Agitator." *National Catholic Reporter*, December 20, 39 (8): 17–18.

Shannon, William H. (ed). 1985. "Letter to Jim Forest, February 21, 1966," pp. 294-297 in *The Hidden Ground of Love: The Letters of Thomas Merton on Religious Experience and Social Concerns*. New York: Farrar, Straus & Giroux.

Sharp, Gene. 1990. *The Role of Power in Nonviolent Action*. Cambridge, MA: The Albert Einstein Institute.

Simmel, Georg. 1950. "The Triad," pp. 145–169 in Kurt H. Wolff (ed.), *The Sociology of Georg Simmel*. New York: Free Press.

Snow, David A. 2004. "Social Movements as Challenges to Authority: Resistance to an Emerging Conceptual Hegemony." *Research in Social Movements, Conflicts and Change* 25: 3–25.

Snow, David A. and Robert D. Benford. 1988. "Ideology, Frame Resonance and Participant Mobilization." *International Social Movement Research* 1: 197–217.

———— 1995. "Alternative Types of Cross-National Diffusion in the Social Movement Arena," pp. 23–39 in Donatella della Porta, Hanspeter Kriesi, and Dieter Rucht (eds.), *Social Movements in a Globalizing World*. London: Macmillan.

Snow, David, A. Burke Rochford Jr., Steven K. Worden, and Robert D. Benford. 1986. "Frame Alignment Processes, Micromobilization, and Movement Participation." *American Sociological Review* 51: 464–481.

Snow, David A., Louis Zurcher, and Sheldon Ekland-Olson. 1980. "Social Networks and Social Movements: A Microstructural Approach to Differential Recruitment." *American Sociological Review* 45: 787–801.

Staggenborg, Suzanne. 1988. "Stability and Innovation in the Women's Movement: A Comparison of Two Movement Organizations." *Social Problems* 36: 75–92.

Strang, David and John H. Meyer. 1993. "Institutional Conditions for Diffusion." *Theory and Society* 22: 487–511.

Bibliography

Stringfellow, William and Anthony Towne. 1971. *Suspect Tenderness: The Ethics of the Berrigan Witness*. New York: Holt, Rinehart and Winston.

Swanbrow, Diane. 1997. "Study of Worldwide Rates of Religiosity, Church Attendance." University of Michigan press release available at http://www.umich.edu/~newsinfo/Releases/1997.

Tarrow, Sidney. 1993. "Cycles of Collective Action: Between Moments of Madness and the Repertoire of Contention." *Social Science History* 17(2): 281–308.

———— 1994. *Power in Movements: Social Movements, Collective Action and Politics*. New York: Cambridge University Press.

Taylor, Verta. 1989. "Social Movement Continuity: The Women's Movement in Abeyance." *American Sociological Review* 54: 761–775.

Taylor, Verta and Nancy Whittier. 1992. "Collective Identity in Social Movement Communities: Lesbian Feminist Mobilization," pp. 104–129 in Aldon Morris and Carol McClurg Mueller (eds.), *Frontiers in Social Movement Theory*. New Haven, CT: Yale University Press.

Ter Kuile, Frits. 1996. "In Memoriam Kees Koening." *The Daily Hammer: Newsletter of the Ploughshares Support Network*, October 1996, Vol. 13: 13.

Tilly, Charles. 1978. *From Mobilization to Revolution*. Reading, MA: Addison-Wesley.

———— 1993. *European Revolutions, 1492–1992*. Oxford: Blackwell.

Useem, Bert and Mayer N. Zald. 1980. "From Pressure Group to Social Movement: Organizational Dilemmas of the Effort to Promote Nuclear Power." *Social Problems* 30 (2): 149.

Weber, Max. 1946. "The Sociology of Charismatic Authority," pp. 245–252 in Hans Gerth and C. Wright Mills (eds.), *From Max Weber*. New York: Oxford University Press.

Weber, Max. 1964. *The Theory of Social and Economic Organization*. New York: Free Press.

Wehr, Paul. 1986. "Nuclear Pacifism as Collective Action." *Journal of Peace Research* 22: 103–113.

Weinstein, Jeremy M. 2006. *Inside Rebellion: The Politics of Insurgent Violence*. New York: Cambridge University Press.

Wilcox, Fred. 2001. *Disciples and Dissidents: Prison Writings of the Prince of Peace Plowshares*. Athol, MA: Haleys.

Wink, Walter. 1987. *Violence and Nonviolence in South Africa: Jesus' Third Way*. Philadelphia: New Society Publishers.

Wittner, Lawrence S. 1984. *Rebels Against War: The American Peace Movement, 1933–1983*. Philadelphia: Temple University Press.

———— 1993. *One World or None: A History of the World Disarmament Movement Through 1953*. Stanford: Stanford University Press.

———— 1997. *Resisting the Bomb: A History of the World Disarmament Movement, 1954–1970*. Stanford: Stanford University Press.

———— 2003. *Toward Nuclear Abolition: A History of the World Nuclear Disarmament Movement, 1971 to the Present*. Stanford: Stanford University Press.

Wood, Elisabeth Jean. 2003. *Insurgent Collective Action and Civil War in El Salvador*. New York: Cambridge University Press.

Wood, Richard L. 2002. *Faith in Action: Religion, Race, and Democratic Organizing in America*. Chicago: University of Chicago Press.

Yoder, John Howard. 1992. *Nevertheless: Varieties of Religious Pacifism*. Scottsdale, PA: Herald Press.

Zald, Mayer N. and Roberta Ash. 1966. "Social Movement Organizations: Growth, Decay, and Change." *Social Forces* 44 (3): 327–241.

Zaroulis, Nancy and Gerald Sullivan. 1984. *Who Spoke Up? American Protest against the War in Vietnam, 1963–1975*. Garden City, NY: Doubleday.

Zelter, Angie. 2001. *Trident on Trial: The Case for People's Disarmament*. Edinburgh: Luath Press Limited.

Zinn, Howard. 2003. "A Holy Outlaw." *The Progressive* 67 (2): 14–15.

Zwerman, Gilda and Patricia Steinhoff. 2005. "When Activists Ask for Trouble: State–Dissident Interactions and the New Left Cycle of Resistance in the United States and Japan," pp. 85–107 in Christian Davenport, Hank Johnston, and Carol Mueller (eds.), *Repression and Mobilization*. Minneapolis: University of Minnesota Press.

Index

Made in the USA
Middletown, DE
31 January 2016